Far Eastern Literatures in the 20th Century

A Guide

Based on the ENCYCLOPEDIA OF WORLD LITERATURE IN THE 20TH CENTURY, Revised Edition, Leonard S. Klein, General Editor

Ungar · New York

1986
The Ungar Publishing Company
370 Lexington Avenue, New York, N.Y. 10017

Based on *Encyclopedia of World Literature in the 20th
Century*, Revised Edition, copyright © 1981, 1982, 1983,
1984 by Frederick Ungar Publishing Co., Inc.

Printed in the United States of America

Library of Congress Cataloging-in-Publication Data

Far Eastern literatures in the 20th century.

"Based on the Encyclopedia of world literature in
the 20th century, revised edition, Leonard S. Klein,
general editor."
 Bibliography: p.
 Includes index.
 1. East Asian literature–20th century–Dictionaries.
2. East Asian literature–20th century–Bio-
bibliography. 3. Asia, Southeastern–Literatures–
20th century–Dictionaries. 4. Asia, Southeastern–
Literatures–20th century–Bio–bibliography
I. Klein, Leonard S. II. Encyclopedia of world
literature in the 20th century (Rev. ed.)
PL493.F37   1986   895′.03   86-16036

ISBN 0-8044-6352-2 (pbk.)

Contents

Preface

This guide is based on the five-volume *Encyclopedia of World Literature in the 20th Century*, revised edition, published by Ungar 1981–84. With the exception of a few minor revisions and corrections, the articles herein are reproduced exactly as they appeared in the original work, and no attempt has been made to update them. The purpose of the present volume, rather, is to provide a handy compilation of articles about the literatures of the Far East that contain information available nowhere else in such a compact form.

Coverage encompasses the nations of East and Southeast Asia as well as the three major countries of the Pacific Islands (Fiji, Western Samoa, and Papua New Guinea). The article on Chinese literature covers writing in both the People's Republic and Taiwan.

Articles are arranged alphabetically by country, and where applicable, national surveys are followed by articles about major writers of that country. An index to author articles is provided at the back of the book.

The reader should note that the order of authors' names has not been westernized; that is, names are given as they are in the native country. For example, with Japanese names, the family name is given first, as Abe Kōbō rather than Kōbō Abe.

RITA STEIN
Editorial Supervisor
EDITH FRIEDLANDER
Project Coordinator

Abbreviations for Periodicals

AAS	Asian and African Studies
ASch	The American Scholar
ASPACQ	Asian Pacific Quarterly of Cultural and Social Affairs
ChinaQ	China Quarterly
ChinL	Chinese Literature
ChiR	Chicago Review
CNLR	CNL/Quarterly World Report
ConL	Contemporary Literature
HJAS	Harvard Journal of Asiatic Studies
HSL	University of Hartford Studies in Literature
HudR	Hudson Review
JATJ	Journal of the Association of Teachers of Japanese
JBRS	Journal of the Burma Research Society
JCLTA	Journal of the Chinese Language Teachers Association
JJS	Journal of Japanese Studies
JOL	Journal of Oriental Literature
JSSB	Journal of the Siam Society (Bangkok)
JTamS	Journal of Tamil Studies
LE&W	Literature East and West
LitR	Literary Review
MD	Modern Drama
MN	Monumenta Nipponica
NYTMag	New York Times Magazine
PQM	Pacific Quarterly (Moana)
PSM	Philippine Studies (Manila)
RELC	RELC Journal
SEACS	South East Asian Cultural Studies
SoRA	Southern Review (Adelaide, Australia)
TkR	Tamkang Review
WLT	World Literature Today
WLWE	World Literature Written in English
YCGL	Yearbook of Comparative and General Literature

BURMESE LITERATURE

In classical Burmese literature imaginative works, including drama, were written in verse, while prose was used for historical chronicles, didactic works and, by the late 18th c., for translations of the *jataka*, the richly varied stories of the previous lives of the Buddha that were the main source of inspiration for Burmese art and literature until the beginning of the 20th c. The natural development from a poetic court literature to popular prose fiction that would have followed soon after the establishment of Burmese-owned printing presses in the 1870s was delayed by the arrival of English as the language of government (and thus of social and educational advancement).

The earliest form of popular printed literature, from 1875 onward, was short verse plays, complete with songs; the first novel, *Maung Yin Maung Ma Me Ma* (Maung Yin Maung and Ma Me Ma), by James Hla Gyaw (1886–1920), a government translator, did not appear until 1904. The author was inspired by the memorable escape episode in *The Count of Monte Cristo* to write this totally nontraditional work—a love and adventure story—in Burmese. Other novels soon followed but, true to the tradition of prose writing, tended to contain much useful knowledge, ornate language, and short sermons, as well as poems and songs. The most famous early novel, *Shwei-pyi-zo* (1914; ruler of the golden land), by U Lat (1866–1921), has all these features together with the earliest portrayal of disillusion with the West caused by young men educated abroad returning home and rejecting traditional Burmese Buddhist values.

The development of the true modern novel, followed by the short story, is closely linked to the emergence of weekly literary magazines. Among their regular contributors were two writers who were largely responsible for abandoning traditional palace tales and introducing modern stories about contemporary people to the reading public: P. Mo-nin (1883–1940) and Shwei U-daung (1899–1973). The former, the father of simple modern Burmese prose, was a journalist and novelist who encouraged Burmans to think for themselves and to break with tradition; the latter, through a great number of masterly adaptations and translations, familiarized the Burmese reader with many of the favorite works of Western literature. Shwei U-daung's autobiography, *Bawa tathet-ta hmattan-hnin atwei-ahkaw-mya* (1962; notes and thoughts of a lifetime), is a major document in the history of Burmese literature.

During the 1920s, at the same time that short stories and novels, often inspired by Victorian fiction, were spreading new attitudes toward personal and family relationships, a new feeling of national consciousness, of pride in their traditional Buddhist culture, was awakening in the country. This feeling was strengthened by the first historical novels, about two great kings of Burma—*Nat-shin-naung* (1919; Nat-shin-naung) and *Tabin-shwei-hti* (1925; Tabin-shwei-hti) by U Maung Gyi (1879–1949)—and more especially by the brilliant satirical verses of the great patriot and writer Thahkin Ko-daw Hmaing (q.v.). No less a patriot in her own way was Burma's first important woman writer, Dagon Hkin Hkin Lei (1904–1981), granddaughter of a minister from the Mandalay court. During the 1920s and 1930s she wrote stories and novels; one in particular shows the hard life of the ordinary peasant: *Mein-ma bawa* (1931; a woman's life); this was followed by stirring historical novels such as *Shwei-sun-nyo* (1933; Shwei-sun-nyo) and *Sa-hso-daw* (1935; court poet).

The 1930s brought demands for independence from Britain, concern for the status of the Burmese language, and a new interest in the style and content of literature—especially evident in the works of the "Testing the Age" group. One member was U Sein Tin (1899–1942), who wrote of small-town and village life exactly as he experienced it working as a district officer in *Hkit-san pon-byin* (1934, 1938; experimental tales), a type of semifictional sketch copied by many writers then and after the war, notably Maung Htin (b. 1909), in *Ko Daung* (1946; Ko Daung) and *Myo-ok pon-byin* (1976; tales of a township officer); and Man Tin (b. 1915), in *Ko Hpo-lon* (1956; Ko Hpo-lon) and *Myo-baing Maung Pyon Cho* (1968; Township Officer Maung Pyon Cho). Zaw-gyi (pseud. of U Thein Han, b. 1908), a "Testing the Age" writer and Burma's leading literary historian and critic, experimented with translations of drama, short stories, and new freer verse forms; his cycle of poems *Bei-da lan* (1963; the hyacinth's way) is an outstanding work that traces a person's journey through life.

Major novels written between 1930 and 1945, reflecting the growing desire for independence, had a strong ideological content: characters more often stood for causes, plots were allegories showing the oppressed rising against the oppressor. Representative are the works of Maha Hswei

(1900–1953), such as *Do mei mei* (1934; our mother) and *Thabon-gyi* (1934; the rebel). Authors wrote of the particular Burmese condition, not of the larger human predicament.

Little could be published between 1942 and 1946, but as soon as the war was over writing and publishing burst forth in many forms, seeking new sources of inspiration in Soviet as well as English and American literature. Numerous literary magazines were started—vital channels for the country's literary lifeblood, since they carry all first printings of novels and short stories. The two most important have been *Shu-mawa* and *Mya-wadi* (the latter government-controlled since 1964).

Naturally, many authors wrote of their wartime experiences, such as Min Shin (b. 1929), in a collection of stories *Tahka-don-ga do yebaw* (1963; our comrade once). In addition, a dominant theme now became Burma's age-long struggle for independent nationhood: Min Kyaw's (b. 1933) *Pagan-tha* (1963; son of Pagan) is set at a critical moment in history when the Mongol hordes threatened the capital in the 13th c.; *Myan-ma-tha* (1966; son of Burma) by Yan-gon Ba Hswei (b. 1925) describes resistance to the British colonization. In contrast to earlier historical novels, the hero is a peasant, not a king.

An important development in serious fiction after the war was the increase in closely observed, realistic portrayals of all aspects of life and of all classes of people. A model of this genre was Maung Htin's *NgaBa* (1947; NgaBa), a moving account of the appalling sufferings of a simple peasant during the Japanese occupation. Aung Lin (b. 1928) often shows us the poor peasant struggling to make a living in the town, for example as a sidecar peddler in the company of bus drivers and prostitutes in *Pyit-daing htaung* (1958; never say die), while the independent-minded woman writer Hkin Hnin Yu (b. 1925), takes pagoda slaves—still social outcasts in Burma—as the subject of *Hmyaw-lin-lo-hpyin mahson-hnaing-de* (1958; hope never ends). Among many works describing the lives of prisoners, those of Lu-du U Hla (b. 1910) are memorable, especially *A-lon kaung-gya-ye-la* (1961; are you all all right).

Many writers felt that, having been at the forefront of the fight for independence, they should now lead the struggle to establish a new, equitable socialist society. Especially after the military regime enunciated the "Burmese Way to Socialism" policy in 1962, authors were under great pressure to produce works of Socialist Realism, preferably showing workers and peasants coping with and overcoming their hard lot. Maung Tha-ya (b. 1931), popular author of many sophisticated novels about the urban elite, showed that he was versatile enough to respond to this summons by working as, and then writing a very perceptive work about, a Rangoon taxi driver, *Mat-tat yat-lo lan-hma ngo* (1969; stood in the road and wept).

However, only when this detailed, often critical observation is combined with successful character drawing, as for example in the prize-winning novel *Mon-ywei mahu* (1955; not out of hate) by the leading woman writer, Gya-ne-gyaw Ma Ma Lei (b. 1917), do we see modern Burmese fiction at its best. This novel shows the suffering of an intelligent young woman of traditional upbringing who falls in love with and marries a Westernized Burman who has lost all sympathy and understanding for the things she cherishes. Perhaps the most influential writer and novelist of the last thirty years is Thein Hpei Myint (q.v.), whose works, such as *Ashei-ga nei-wun htwet-thi-pama* (1958; as surely as the sun rises in the east), set against the background of the nationalist movement, successfully combine well-drawn characters, a strong plot, and love interest with immediate relevance to issues facing Burmese society.

Although theatrical shows are immensely popular, written drama does not flourish in Burma today. Poetry, on the other hand, is everyone's pastime and pleasure. Established favorites are the poets Nu Yin (b. 1916), Tin Mo (b. 1939), and Daung Nwe Hswei (b. 1931). But by far the most widely written and widely read genre is the short story (about a thousand are produced each year), and in this field it is the humorous, mocking, utterly honest Thaw-da Hswei (q.v.) who more than any other speaks for and to his fellow citizens.

Uncertainty about what works will be approved for publication after compulsory review by the government's Press Scrutiny Committee has led, in the 1970s, to a decline in the quality of original works and a proliferation of adapted thrillers, romances, and comic books, a state of affairs deplored by serious writers.

BIBLIOGRAPHY: On Pe, "Modern Burmese Literature," in *Perspective of Burma, Atlantic Monthly Supplement* (1958), 56–60; Minn Latt, "Mainstreams in Burmese Literature," *New Orient-Bimonthly*, 2, 6 (1961), 172–75; 3, 6 (1962), 172–76; Bernot, D., "Quelques tendances actuelles de la littérature birmane," *Revue de l'École Nationale des Langues Orientales*, 1 (1964), 159–78; Hla Pe, "The Rise of Popular Literature in Burma," *JBRS*, 51, 2 (1968), 125–44; Bernot, D., "Littérature birmane contemporaine," in Lafont, P. B., and Lombard, D., eds., *Littératures contemporaines de l'Asie du Sud-est* (1974), pp. 9–17;

Allott, A. J., "Prose Writing and Publishing in Burma," in Tham Seong Chee, ed., *Literature and Society in Southeast Asia* (1981), pp. 1–35

ANNA J. ALLOTT

THAHKIN KO-DAW HMAING

(pseud. of U Lun; other pseuds.: Maung Lun, Mit-sata Maung Hmaing) Burmese poet, dramatist, and novelist, b. 23 March 1876, Wale; d. 27 July 1964, Rangoon

T. K. H. was sent at an early age to Mandalay for a monastic education but returned in 1895 to his native Lower Burma to work on newspapers. Writing under the pseudonym of Maung Lun, he had by 1910 reached a wide audience through numerous traditional stage plays in verse on themes drawn from Burmese history and legend. Few survive, as he did not want to become known by such unserious works.

In 1911 T. K. H. became interested in politics through working on the newly established newspaper *Thu-ri-ya;* from then on he regularly wrote articles and poems commenting on contemporary events for this paper and other publications, such as the magazine *Dagon,* of which he later became editor. A master of Burmese classical literature, he wrote a great many works in verse (or in mixed verse-prose style), brilliantly presenting satires in the form of learned religious commentaries (*tika* in the Pali language) on worldly subjects, such as the series called *Hkwei ti-ka* (1925–27: commentary on dogs), in which he reproves Burmese politicians for wasting their efforts against the British in futile squabbling.

For his single novel, *Mit-sata Maung Hmaing hma-daw-bon wut-htu* (1921; the epistles of Mr. Maung Hmaing), he used a pen name which made fun of those Burmese who aped their British masters by using "Mr." in front of their names. Maung Hmaing was the name of a notorious rascal in an early Burmese novel, *Maung Hmaing wut-htu* (1904; the story of Maung Hmaing) by U Kyi (1848–1908). T. K. H. became known by his regular pseudonym in 1934, when he joined the Do-bama party (a group of young Burmese nationalists who called themselves "Thahkin," or "master").

T. K. H. is considered to be unequaled in the *lei-gyo-gyi,* a traditional poetic form to which he gave striking new content with great popular appeal, and through which he was an inspiration to the younger generation of Burmese nationalists. He fostered their interest in history, aroused their pride in their language and culture, urged them to take positive action such as student strikes—as in *Bwaing-kauk ti-ka* (1927; boycott commentary)—but also mocked those who were mere political opportunists. After World War II he wrote less, devoting his energies to persuading his fellow citizens to live in peace and unity in independent but politically divided Burma.

The allusive and highly memorable style of his poems made them very popular with his fellow countrymen while at the same time preserving them from British government censorship. A man of many skills—a true Buddhist and a staunch patriot; poet and playwright; historian and teacher; pioneer writer and satirist—T. K. H. is the single most revered literary figure in modern Burma.

SELECTED FURTHER WORKS: *Bo ti-ka* (1920); *Myauk ti-ka* (1923); *Galon-byan di-pani ti-ka* (1930); *Thahkin ti-ka* (1934)

BIBLIOGRAPHY: Tin Htway, U., "The Role of Literature in Nation Building," *JBRS*, 55, Parts 1–2 (1972), 19–46

ANNA J. ALLOTT

THAW-DA HSWEI

(pseud. of U Kyin Hswei) Burmese short-story writer, humorist, and satirist, b. 26 May 1919, Kyo-bin village, Paung-de township

The eldest son of a well-to-do paddy farmer in Lower Burma, T. H. finished secondary school and was studying English when war broke out. He worked as a pony-cart driver, then tried trading, lost money, lived an irregular life, and finally turned to writing, with a very funny story, "Baran-di tapalin" (1947; a bottle of brandy) in the newly established magazine *Shumawa*. Encouraged by the success of his story, T. H. began writing regularly, first humorous stories, then, in the 1950s, realistic accounts of urban and country life.

In his earliest stories T. H. was rarely able to resist a laugh, a pun, or a vulgar joke; but he soon turned to satire, presenting sometimes quite unflattering portraits of his fellow writers, more often powerful condemnations of human stupidity, greed, and cruelty. Thus, in the collection *Bawa hto hto* (1961; many lives), based on his wartime experience of running a tea shop, he shocks the reader with the life story of a young prostitute whom he had befriended. This story, "Lu lu-gyin kaik-sa-nei-gya-ba-thi" (man preys on man), describes without a trace of sentimentality, how heartlessly local menfolk look forward to the death of the exhausted young prostitute, as her funeral will be the excuse for seven days of gambling and feasting.

T. H.'s full and varied life style provides rich material for his many-sided talent as a storyteller. He can vividly evoke a typical Burmese scene by the brief description of sights, sounds, and smells; he can conjure up the inhabitants of both town and countryside by means of a few lines of dialogue or a brief account of an incident. Two prize-winning collections, *Thadawa-do-i than-thaya* (1964; all creatures that on earth do dwell) and *I law-ka myei mahi-we* (1970; life on this earth), depict many of the less pleasant realities of country life such as theft of animals and brigandage.

In a country in which the writer's role is, by tradition and by present government policy, a didactic one, T. H. is unusual in refusing to offer himself as a model. On the contrary, many of his most popular stories are honest accounts of his own sins, written with such self-mockery and humor that all criticism is disarmed. In the collection *Pyei myan-ma pya-yok-mya* (1962; what life is like in Burma) he turned his satire against the cruelty of antigovernment insurgents who have been active since Burma's independence was declared in 1948.

In Burma T. H. is particularly liked for his sincerity and forthrightness. Recent stories either deal with basic moral dilemmas or are episodes from his own life, since present political conditions have made it difficult even for such well-established authors as T. H. to write of life exactly as it is.

SELECTED FURTHER WORKS: *Lu-bon hkan-wa* (1966); *Lawka lu-pyei* (1968); *Kyun-daw bawa-zat-kyaung* (1972 ff.)

BIBLIOGRAPHY: Khin Myo Chit, "Thaw-dar-swe," *The Guardian Magazine,* Oct. 1957, 19–20; Allott, A. J., "The Short Story in Burma, with Special Reference to Its Social and Political Significance," in Davidson, J. H. C. S., and Cordell, H., eds., *The Short Story in South East Asia* (1982), pp. 101–39

ANNA J. ALLOTT

THEIN HPEI MYINT
Burmese novelist, short-story writer, essayist, and journalist, b. 10 July 1914, Bu-dalin; d. 15 Jan. 1978, Rangoon

Son of a minor government official, T. H. M. began writing fiction while a student at the University of Rangoon. He took up journalism while studying law in Calcutta, where he came in touch with Bengali Communists and made a lifelong commitment both to writing with a social purpose and to left-wing politics.

His first novel, *Tet hpon-gyi* (1937; the modern monk), created a sensation because of its portrayal of certain Buddhist monks as corrupt and sexually immoral. Angry monks demanded that the work be banned. In 1938 he helped found the Nagani (Red Dragon) Book Club, whose first title was T. H. M.'s biography of the revered nationalist writer, Thahkin Ko-daw Hmaing (q.v.), entitled *Hsaya Lun ahtok-pat-ti* (1938; biography of U Lun).

His prewar experiences with the nationalist movement as a student, his extensive travels inside and outside Burma, especially after the war, his expulsion from the Burmese Communist Party, and his involvement in political and social matters have been used by him as material for several major novels and thirty or so important short stories; he has also chronicled his experiences in numerous memoirs and travelogues and in an autobiography, *Kyun-daw-i ahcit-u* (1974; literature, my first love).

Thabeik-hmauk kyaung-tha (1937; the student boycotter) gives a picture of the 1936 students' strike at Rangoon University; *Lanza paw-bi* (1949; the way out) covers the confused period of 1945–47; *Ashei-ga nei-wun htwet-thi-pama* (1958: as sure as the sun rising in the east) captures the excitement of the growing anti-British nationalist movement between 1936 and 1942. All three of these are novels, but they are based on events in T. H. M.'s own life. *Wut-htu-do baung-gyok* (1966; collected short stories) contains stories written between 1934 and 1966 on such themes as the poverty that leads to dishonesty and prostitution, the plight of refugees fleeing from insurgent attacks, and the corruption of politicians.

T. H. M. is one of the most widely read writers in Burma today and probably one of the most influential. He applied his versatile talents to a wide range of subjects and never hesitated to deal with controversial matters—venereal disease in *Tet-hkit nat-hso* (1938; evil spirits of modern times), alcoholism in *Thu-do lin-maya 34 hnit* (1978; married for thirty-four years)—or to criticize segments of the community that might have preferred to remain unchallenged, such as the *sangha* (Buddhist monkhood) and the government. He was never content to approach literature merely as a diversion; he rarely wrote humorously but nearly always sought to provoke and to convince, to inform and to influence his readers.

SELECTED FURTHER WORKS: *Ngaing-nganyei atwei-akyon-mya* (1956); *Sit-atwin hkayithe* (1966). FURTHER VOLUME IN ENGLISH: *Selected Short Stories* (1973)

BIBLIOGRAPHY: Milne, P. M., Introduction to T. H. M., *Selected Short Stories* (1973), pp. 1–19; Allott, A. J., "The Short Story in Burma, with Special Reference to Its Social and Political Significance," in Davidson, J. H. C. S., and Cordell, H., *The Short Story in South East Asia* (1982), pp. 101–39

ANNA J. ALLOTT

CAMBODIAN LITERATURE

During the period of the French Protectorate (1863–1953), Cambodian writers tended to treat well-known themes, using the traditional medium of verse and the "high" language, although employing some postclassical meters (the "seven-syllabled" and the "eight-syllabled"). Thus, the greatly esteemed Acar In (1859–1924) wrote a long poem describing Angkor: *Nireas Angkor* (1926; a visit to Angkor). Madame Sit (1881–1963) retold an Indian tale in verse: *Pimpeapileap* (written 1920, pub. 1942; the lament of Pimpea). Nu-Kan (1874–1950) rewrote a much-loved Cambodian story, *Teav ek* (1942; the one and only Teav).

Among prose works of the period were In's *Katilok* (1936; the way of the world), a collection of retold Buddhist moral tales; new versions of old folktales; translations of European novels; and articles, such as those by Bu-Po (dates n.a.) and Chhim-Sum (dates n.a.), on Buddhist or other cultural subjects.

A forerunner of the literature of the period after independence was the first modern Cambodian novel, a love story by Kim-Hak (b. 1905), *Tik Tonle Sap* (1939; the waters of the Tonle Sap). The significance of this work lay in the new style of writing (in plain and even colloquial prose) and in the subject matter (the present-day life of ordinary Cambodians instead of the exploits of gods and heroes).

After the gaining of independence in 1953, nationalist ideas soon penetrated the arts. Writers such as Leang Hap An (dates n.a.), director of the Buddhist Institute, wrote articles urging authors to help to raise the national literary standards. Ly Theam Teng (dates n.a.), in his *Aksarsastr Khmer* (1960; Cambodian literature), criticized some Cambodian authors for incorporating in their work undesirable Western ideas. However, the characters in the novels of the time—their background and their problems—were thoroughly Cambodian. Themes ranged from the arranged marriage in Im Chudet's (dates n.a.) *Bandol kon pa* (1956; Bandol, father's darling) to crime detection in Kang Bun Chhoeun's (dates n.a.) *Pecchakheat kramom* (1960; a young murderess). Adventure was provided by writers like Hel Sumphar (1921–1971) in *Chao bit muk* (1951; the masked bandit) or historical novelists such as R. Kovid (dates n.a.) in *Banteay Longvek* (1954; the citadel of Longvek). Social injustices were frequent themes. Suon Surin (dates n.a.) portrayed the struggle of a poor employee against his oppressive employers in *Preah atit thmey reah loe phen dey chas* (1961; the new sun rises over the old land), while Lang Peng Siek (dates n.a.) highlighted the corruption of officials in *Khyal kambot tbong* (1972; the hurricane).

Politics became an important element in novels by, for example, Bun-Chan Mol (dates n.a.), the author of *Kuk neayobay* (1971; political imprisonment). Autobiography is represented by Madame Sothivongs (dates n.a.) with *Veasna khnhom* (1959; my fate). Characteristic of the mood of the times was a pessimistic novel by Sot-Polin (dates n.a.), *Chivit it ney* (1965; the futility of life). Other well-known novels are *Sophat* (written 1938, pub. 1960; Sophat) by Rim-Kin (1911–1959), an artist, poet, and playwright; *Kolap Pailin* (written 1944, pub. 1959; the rose of Pailin) by Nhok-Them (b. 1903), who is also a successful translator of works from Pali, Thai and French; and *Phka srapon* (1965; the faded flower) by Nu Hach (b. 1916).

Much anonymous poetry, voicing new ideas about contemporary Cambodia, appeared in journals. Some poets' names are known, however. Makhali Phal (dates n.a.) wrote *Chamrieng santepheap* (c. 1953; song of peace) and Keng Vannsak (dates n.a.) published a collection of romantic poetry, *Chitt kramom* (c. 1955; a young girl's heart).

Two further genres emerged after 1953: the Western-style play (at first incorporating song, music, and dance) and the short story. Hang Thun Hak (dates n.a.) wrote many plays, among them one contrasting traditional and modern behavior entitled *Sambok it me-ba* (1965; nest without parents). Short stories, chiefly love stories, are to be found here and there in journals. Finally, postindependence publications have included many translations of Chinese novels.

The political upheavals of the 1970s, both from within and outside Cambodia, seem to have limited publication to propagandistic writing and to have stunted the development of imaginative literature and an audience for it.

BIBLIOGRAPHY: Bitard, P., "La littérature cambodgienne moderne," *France-Asie*, 114–15 (1955), 467–82; Whitaker, D. P., et al., "Literature and Scholarship," *Area Handbook for Cambodia* (1973), pp. 131–32; Lafont, P. B., "Introduction aux littératures contemporaines de la Péninsule Indochinoise," in Lafont, L. P., and Lombard, D., eds., *Littératures contemporaines de l'Asie du Sud-Est* (1974), pp. 3–7; Piat, M., "Contemporary Cambodian Literature," *JSSB*, 63, 2 (1975), 251–59

JUDITH M. JACOB

CHINESE LITERATURE

There are three periods in the development of 20th-c. Chinese literature, which shows a radical departure from the literature of the classical age. In the first period (1900–17), influenced by new-fangled Western ideas borrowed mainly from Japan, writers initiated a revolutionary movement that broke away from the past in thought and subject matter, although not in form and language. It paved the way for the rise in the second period (1917–49) of a nascent vernacular literature, which represented the mainstream of modern Chinese literature in opposition to traditional classical writings. This achievement would have been greater had it not been for the disruptions caused by the Sino-Japanese War (1937–45) and later the civil war between Nationalists and Communists. While literary activity continued unabated during these years, much of the war literature was ephemeral and mediocre. Meanwhile, in the guerrilla areas under Communist control literary works for mass propaganda flourished. The Communist conquest of mainland China further extended this movement and produced during the third period (1949–present) a nationwide proletarian literature characterized by inflexible Socialist Realism and stereotyped ideological content. Simultaneously, there was a resurgence of literary activity in Taiwan, where a new generation of writers brought to the West an awareness of Taiwanese literature and a wave of anti-Communist fiction.

First Period: 1900–17

Chinese literature in the first years of the c. was noted for its innovativeness, versatility, and productivity. Its representative author was Liang Ch'i-ch'ao (1873–1929), whose polemic discourses in lucid and effective prose exerted a great influence. Turning from political activity to journalistic writing after the failure of the Reform Movement (1898), he led the campaign for new fiction and poetry, and advocated the emancipation of prose from its classical restraints, so as to better introduce new Western knowledge and ideas. Other noteworthy writers were Chang Ping-lin (1868–1936), who later became China's foremost classical scholar; Tsou

Yung (1885–1905), author of the pamphlet, *Kê-ming chün* (1903; the revolutionary army), which led to his arrest and death in prison; and Ch'iu Chin (1878–1907), a woman revolutionary martyr, who left a slender volume of patriotic verses.

Three poets stood out for their multifarious accomplishments: Huang Tsun-hsien (1848–1905), Su Man-shu, Liu Ya-tzu (qq.v.). A widely traveled diplomat, Huang brought to Chinese poetry refreshingly new materials culled from experiences abroad; he also anticipated the movement in colloquial poetry in his dictum: "My hand writes words from my mouth." Cofounder of the Southern Society (Nan-shê), a large revolutionary literary organization, Liu Ya-tzu was a prolific poet who wrote on a wide variety of topics. As a revolutionist, he engaged in political activities that spanned the first half of the century and contributed significantly in his poems to the chronicling of contemporary historical events and figures. His friend Su Man-shu, a Sino-Japanese genius, gained fame for his poignantly emotional lyrics and sentimental love stories.

The bulk of Chinese fiction in this period, however, consisted of sociopolitical novels that served as powerful weapons for attack on the evils of Chinese society. Continuing an early tradition in satirical fiction, the novelists used their enormous creative energy to expose the bureaucratic corruptions of their time, while simultaneously advocating a new form of democratic government, revolution against the Manchu regime, and the emancipation of women. Among the hundreds of novels published in Shanghai, the newly prosperous treaty port, are *Kuan-ch'ang hsien-hsing chi* (1903; bureaucracy exposed) by Li Pao-chia (1876–1906); *Nieh-hai hua* (1905; a flower in an ocean of sins) by Tseng P'u (1872–1935); *Lao Ts'an yu-chi* (1907; *The Travels of Lao Ts'an*, 1952) by Liu E (1857–1909); and *Erh-shih nien mu-tu chih kuai hsien-chuang* (1906; *Bizarre Happenings Eyewitnessed over Two Decades*, 1975) by Wu Wo-yao (1866–1910). While different from each other in scope and treatment, these satirical novels presented realistic vignettes of decadent Chinese life and society at the turn of the century. By affirming the social functions of fiction, they raised its status as a form of serious literature. Unfortunately, satirical fiction soon gave way to erotic fiction of the so-called Mandarin Duck and Butterfly School, which featured the sensual life of the courtesans in Shanghai's red-light district. Much of this immense activity in fiction was shared by the translators, led by the classical scholar Lin Shu (1852–1924), who brought to China for the first time the wealth of Western fiction, totaling some 170 titles, including such English masters as Swift, Defoe, Scott, and particularly Dickens. Most of the translators wrote in the classical language and were quite free in their renditions.

One exception to the use of the classical language is the new drama, which had its origin abroad. Under the auspices of the Spring Willow Society (1907), Chinese students in Tokyo produced in a crude amateurish form stage plays performed in spoken vernacular Chinese, with naturalistic scenery and realistic social content. These plays were in sharp contrast to the traditional Peking opera, which stressed singing, dancing, and gesticulating. Later, these amateur actors returned to China and together with their followers initiated a new drama movement in Shanghai and other cities, but they met with little success. Their short-lived efforts served only as a prelude to the more sophisticated *hua-chü* (spoken drama) of the May Fourth (1919) era.

Second Period: 1917–49

The second and the major period of modern Chinese literature was heralded by the publication in 1917 of Hu Shih's (q.v.) "Wen-hsüeh kai-liang ch'u-i" (a modest proposal for literary reform) in *Hsin ch'ing-nien,* a leading scholarly magazine. In this article, Hu Shih, sometimes called the "Father of the Chinese Renaissance," advocated the creation of a new national literature based upon the living language of the people. His call to arms was supported by Ch'en Tu-hsiu (1879–1942), editor of *Hsin ch'ing-nien,* who later became one of the founders of the Chinese Communist Party. Ever since its inception, the literary movement, reinforced by the May Fourth political movement, was revolutionary in nature and youthful in spirit; it served as a rallying point in the endeavor of Chinese intellectuals to free themselves from the shackles of a feudal past. It made a profound impact on modern Chinese thought and contributed to the current Chinese outlook toward life and society.

The leading writer of this period—and, in fact, the greatest name in 20th-c. Chinese literature—was Lu Hsün (q.v.), whose short stories and essays have exerted a tremendous influence on the younger generation. In "Ah Q cheng-chuan" (1921; "The True Story of Ah Q," 1926) and elsewhere, Lu Hsün presented tales and characters of a backward traditional society about to disintegrate and collapse on the eve of a far-reaching but still transitional revolution. A born fighter, he was noted for his caustic satire and fearless exposure of the dark aspects of the old society, thus initiating the modern trend toward social criticism. In his last years, Lu Hsün became increasingly resentful of the repressive nationalist literary policy. To combat it, he organized the League of Left-Wing Writers (1930) with alleged Communist support. Acrimonious controversy with the rightist and bitter dissension in the leftist camp pursued Lu Hsün to his grave.

Of the numerous narrative writers of this epoch, the most outstanding were Mao Tun, Pa Chin, and Lao She (qq.v.). A founder of the Literary Research Association (1920), Mao Tun exemplified its creed of "literature for life's sake" in his stories and novels by presenting a realistic analysis of contemporary Chinese society. The characters who live in the pages of his social chronicles range from peasants in bankrupt rural villages—"Ch'un-ts'an" (1932; "Spring Silkworms," 1956), "Ch'iu-shou" (1932; "Autumn Harvest," 1956), "Ts'an-tung" (1932; "Winter Ruin," 1956)—to industrial workers and capitalists caught in the financial maelstrom of metropolitan Shanghai—*Tzu-yeh* (1933; *Midnight,* 1957). Pa Chin, one of the most prodigious writers, started his career as an anarchist and romanticist, fascinating his readers with a series of novels featuring the romantic love and revolutionary activities of his youthful heroes and heroines. A typical theme of his novels—such as *Chia* (1931; *The Family,* 1958)—is the conflict between old and young in a large patriarchal family, where the children either submit passively to their elders' bigotry and dogmatism, or rebel against them in a vehement struggle. Conscientious and skillful in the art of fiction writing, Lao She excelled in architectural plot, vivid characterization, and racy dialogue. All these qualities characterize his best-selling *Lo-t'o hsiang-tzu* (1938; *Rickshaw Boy,* 1945). A good-natured sense of humor, running through a number of his novels, enlivens the otherwise somber and sometimes sordid atmosphere in modern Chinese fiction. Mention must also be made of Ting Ling (q.v.), the only major Communist writer to have made a name in this period. Her socialist-inspired conscience dictated that she switch from her candid tales of women's uninhibited love, for which she became popular, to stories of peasant struggles against poverty, hunger, and natural calamities.

In poetry, Hu Shih's experiments in vernacular free verse, despite strong initial opposition, attracted a large following among contemporary writers. Kuo Mo-jo (q.v.), leader of the Creation Society (1921), first earned his reputation as a poet with a volume of boldly original poems, *Nü-shen* (1921; *Selected Poems from the Goddesses,* 1958). Although opposite to Hu Shih in literary temperament and political view, Kuo Mo-jo, the spokesman of leftist writers, is as gifted and versatile as his rightist counterpart. In his later years he turned from poetry to autobiographical stories, historical plays, literary criticism, revolutionary polemics, and studies of ancient Chinese society based on bone and bronze inscriptions.

In the wake of these pioneers three important groups emerged: the Crescent Society (1928), the Contemporary Age (1932), and the Chinese Poetry Association (1932). Under the leadership of Hsü Chih-mo and Wen I-to (qq.v.), the Crescent poets, who laid great stress on form and technique, attempted to introduce the beauty of music (rhyme and rhythm), painting (color), and architecture (form and structure) into poetry. Their efforts suffered a setback with the tragic deaths of their two leaders Hsü Chih-mo in an airplane accident and Wen I-to by assassination. The poets of the Contemporary Age group attempted to express subtle emotions and delicate situations through the use of colors and images in the manner of French symbolism. This aesthetic delight in sheer lyricism was opposed by members of the Chinese Poetry Association, which was an arm of the League of Left-Wing Writers. In their view, poetry should sing realistically of the prevailing mood of the new era, "an era of the people's resistance against feudalism and imperialism." Their adoption of colloquial language, popular tunes, and folk forms led to a new mass-oriented poetry, to which the Communist poets eventually turned.

Some of the major poets of modern China, such as Feng Chih (b. 1906), Pien Chih-lin (b. 1910), Tsang K'o-chia (b. 1905), and Ho Ch'i-fang (q.v.), started their poetic careers under the shadow of the Crescent Society. While each had his individual traits—the contemplative mood and mythic experience of Feng's sonnets; the articulate, urbane poems of Pien about the streets and people of Peking; the robust, rustic verses of Tsang, smelling of the soil of a wide-open country; the haunting romantic verses of Ho in his youthful dreams of love and beauty—they were all devoted to their craft and fastidious in their search for "words that will startle the readers." This concern for poetic style and diction was still apparent in their later poems, even though there was a drastic change in theme and content. Unlike them, Ai Ch'ing (q.v.) and T'ien Chien (b. 1916) broke away completely from lingering academic traditions and foreign influences to return to a colloquial style in their songs of peasants and soldiers. T'ien Chien especially quickened the pulses of the new age with his drumbeat poetry, which has only two to three words in each line.

Realistic social drama written in the vernacular, as mentioned earlier, was introduced from abroad even before the literary revolution; but it never secured a foothold on the popular stage until the advent in the early 1930s of a young playwright, Ts'ao Yü (q.v.), whose first play, *Lei-yü* (1934; *Thunder and Rain*, 1936), literally took the audience by storm. Previously, several notable attempts in staging vernacular plays had been made by Ou-yang Yü-ch'ien (1887–1962), a veteran of the Spring Willow Society; T'ien Han (1898–1968), leader of the South China Society; and Hung Shen (1894–1955), who had been a student in G. P. Barker's famous English 47 playwriting course at Harvard University. None of these efforts, however, had survived the competition of such popular entertainments as the Peking opera and American movies, with the result that the spoken drama was cultivated only by amateur groups and student dramatic organizations. Significantly, some of the better plays in their repertory were translations from the West, such as Ibsen's *A Doll's House,* Wilde's *Lady Windermere's Fan,* and Dumas's *La dame aux camélias.* The situation changed with the appearance, in rapid succession, of Ts'ao Yü's *Lei-yü, Jih-ch'u* (1936; *The Sunrise,* 1940), and *Yüan-yeh* (1937; *The Wilderness,* 1979), each a brilliant play that won immediate popular and critical acclaim. Whether it is the tragedy of an ill-fated rich industrialist family smitten by the past sins of its members, or a realistic drama of a group of upper-class social parasites dragging out their useless existence, or a melodrama of rural revenge full of sound and fury, they haunt the reader's mind with their universal human appeal, emotional conflict, and dramatic tension. While still in his mid-twenties, Ts'ao Yü became overnight the major dramatist of modern China.

During the Sino-Japanese War, most writers mentioned above fled to the unoccupied hinterland, where they rallied under the banner of the All-China Anti-Aggression Federation of Writers and Artists and contributed to the war effort through literary works of a propagandist nature. The paths some of them trod, however, were quite different. While Ch'en Tu-hsiu pined away in a nationalist cell, Hu Shih became the Chinese ambassador to the United States, Kuo Mo-jo held a nominal government position in Chungking, and Lao She busied himself with patriotic work for the All-China Anti-Aggression Federation. Among them, Kuo Mo-jo and Lao She were the most productive; others like Mao Tun, Pa Chin, and Ts'ao Yü made similar important contributions. The young poets mellowed; faced with the harsh realities of life, they now sang of the living drama of war and blood enacted before them. Some visited the Communist stronghold in Yenan, and others, like Ai Ch'ing and T'ien Chien, stayed on to work for the Communist cause. As the war progressed, more and more intellectuals were disappointed with the Nationalist government in Chungking and turned to look northwestward to Yenan, where a new breed of proletarian writers began to emerge on the literary scene. The raging civil war that followed the Japanese surrender did not change the attitude of the writers. Most of them chose to remain in China, rather than flee to Taiwan, after the Communist victory (1949), which ushered in the third and present period of modern Chinese literature.

Third Period: 1949–Present

Since 1949, Chinese literature on the mainland is as much a record of political campaigns and ideological battles as it is one of individual writers and their literary creations. The roots of this literature could be traced to guidelines promulgated by Mao Tse-tung in his "Tsai Yenan wen-i tso-t'an-hui shang ti chiang-hua" (1942; "Talks at the Yenan Forum on Literature and Art," 1956), which laid down for Communist writers certain requirements concerning the role and form of literature in a socialist society and which initiated a series of rectification campaigns that determined the future course of literary activities. The convening of the First National Conference of Writers and Artists (1949) in Peking resulted in the founding of the All-China Federation of Literary and Art Circles, with Kuo Mo-jo as chairman. The majority of older, established writers, however, soon ceased producing creative works, and over the ensuing three decades, their ranks were thinned by death and political purges; although many have resurfaced as a result of the recent anti-"gang of four" campaign, they are now well past their creative primes.

Mao's ideals in his Yenan talks were first realized by Chao Shu-li (q.v.), whose early short stories, such as "Li Yu-ts'ai pan-hua" (1943; "The Rhymes of Li Yu-tsai," 1950), and his novel of land reform, *Li-chia-chuang ti pien-ch'ien* (1950; *Changes in Li Village*, 1953), were models of proletarian literature embellished with folklore traditions. Land reform was central to two major works of this period, *Pao-feng tsou-yü* (1949; *The Hurricane*, 1955) by Chou Li-po (q.v.) and *T'ai-yang chao tsai Sang-kan-ho shang* (1949; *The Sun Shines over the Sangkan River*, 1954) by Ting Ling, which won a 1951 Stalin Prize for literature. Other novels written in this period sang the praises of the Party, the revolution, and the proletariat—the era of the exposé had passed. Among the most popular novels were *Pao-wei Yen-an* (1954; *Defend Yenan*, 1958) by Tu P'eng-ch'eng (b. 1921), *Hung-ch'i p'u* (1957; *Keep the Red Flag Flying*, 1961) by Liang Pin (b. 1914), *Ch'ing-ch'un chih ko* (1958; *The Song of*

Youth, 1964) by the woman writer Yang Mo (b. 1915), and a novel of PLA (People's Liberation Army) heroism, *Lin-hai hsüeh-yüan* (1962; *Tracks in the Snowy Forest,* 1962) by Ch'ü Po (b. 1923). Special mention must be made of the novels of Hao Jan (b. 1932), which stood virtually alone during the Cultural Revolution. The older poets— prominent among them were Ai Ch'ing, Ho Ch'i-fang, T'ien Chien, and Tsang K'o-chia—fared well in the early years of the regime. They were most active in the revolutionary struggle, creating poems in praise of the heroism of soldiers during the Korean War, of peasants involved in land reform, and of workers who were building a new China in the cities. All continued to write up until the Cultural Revolution, when their voices were silenced.

Perhaps the greatest change took place in drama, which had a direct appeal to the less well-educated masses. Initially, the most noteworthy revolutionary plays came from the pens of Lao She—*Lung-hsü kou* (1951; *Dragon Beard Ditch,* 1956) and *Ch'a-kuan* (1957; teahouse)—and Ts'ao Yü—*Ming-lang ti t'ien* (1956; bright skies) and *Tan-chien p'ien* (1962; gall and sword). Immensely popular was *Pai-mao nü* (1945; *The White-haired Girl,* 1953) by Ho Ching-chih (b. 1924) and Ting Yi (d. 1954). During the Cultural Revolution, model revolutionary Peking operas such as *Sha-chia pang* (1964; *Shachiapang,* 1972) and *Hung-teng chi* (1964; *The Red Lantern,* 1965) gained preeminence. Since then, the spoken drama has made a resurgence and is showing signs of surprising vitality.

Taiwanese Literature since 1949

Across the Taiwan Strait, following upon the exodus of the Nationalist government to the island in 1949, a new beginning in literary production ensued, but with predictably poor results. Patriotic propaganda was the order of the day in a period that witnessed the creation of stereotyped anti-Communist fiction, and poetry and essays that were either benignly lyrical or dripping with sentimentality. The literary situation improved in the late 1950s, and anti-Communist fiction reached its high point with the publication of Chang Ai-ling's (q.v.) *Yang-ko* (1954; *The Rice-Sprout Song,* 1955) and Chiang Kuei's (1908–1980) *Hsüan-feng* (1959; *The Whirlwind,* 1977). The founding of the journals *Wen-hsüeh chi-k'an* and *Hsien-tai wen-hsüeh* ushered in the modernist era. Heavily indebted to such Western masters as Joyce, Kafka, Fitzgerald, and others, a number of young authors, most notably Chu Hsi-ning (b. 1927), Pai Hsien-yung

(b. 1937), and Wang Wen-hsing (b. 1939), exerted a strong influence. Modern vernacular poetry developed around three societies: the Modernist School, under the leadership of Chi Hsien (b. 1913); the Blue Stars Society, whose most prominent member was Yü Kuang-chung (b. 1928); and the Epoch Society, where French surrealism was popular. The alien nature of much of the poetry produced by these poets did not gain wide acceptance for them, although they passed on a legacy of highly original imagery and a modern poetic idiom. Unlike prose fiction and poetry, the spoken drama never gained a foothold in Taiwan, although Peking opera has been exceedingly popular.

The mid-1960s witnessed a recrudescence of provincialism with the emergence of several native Taiwanese poets and novelists. For the first time in many decades the central subject in the works of a major segment of the writing community was the lives of the ordinary, predominantly rural Taiwanese. Under the leadership of Huang Ch'un-ming (b. 1939), Wang Chen-ho (b. 1940), and others, this regional school has only recently begun to give way to a more organized and nationalistic literature, which reflects Taiwan's current political situation. Other Taiwan authors came to the U.S. to pursue professional careers. One of them, Ch'en Jo-hsi (b. 1938), went to the People's Republic for several years and described her firsthand impressions and experiences of Chinese life during the Cultural Revolution in a series of novels and story collections, notably *Yin hsien-chang* (1976; *The Execution of Mayor Yin,* 1978), an outstanding example of dissent literature from Communist China.

BIBLIOGRAPHY: Hu Shih, *The Chinese Renaissance* (1934); Chow, Tse-tsung, *The May Fourth Movement* (1960); Hsia, C. T., *A History of Modern Chinese Fiction* (1961, 2nd ed. 1971); Birch, C., ed., *Chinese Communist Literature* (1963); Průšek, J., ed., *Studies in Modern Chinese Literature* (1964); Liu, Wu-chi, "The Modern Period, 1900–1950," supplement to Giles, H. A., *A History of Chinese Literature* (enlarged ed., 1967); Goldman, M., *Literary Dissent in Communist China* (1971); Lin, J., *Modern Chinese Poetry: An Introduction* (1972); Lee, L., *The Romantic Generation of Modern Chinese Writers* (1973); Huang, J., *Heroes and Villains in Communist China: The Contemporary Chinese Novel as a Reflection of Life* (1973); Hsu, K. Y., *The Chinese Literary Scene* (1975); Goldman, M., ed., *Modern Chinese Literature in the May Fourth Era* (1977); Faurot, J. L., ed., *Chinese Fiction from Taiwan: Critical Perspectives* (1980); Gálik, M., *The Genesis of Modern Chinese Literary Criticism* (1980); Průšek, J., *The Lyrical and the Epic: Studies of Modern Chinese Literature* (1980); Hsu, K. Y., ed., *Literature of the People's Republic of China* (1980)

LIU WU-CHI
HOWARD GOLDBLATT

Ai Ch'ing

(pseud. of Chiang Hai-ch'eng) Chinese poet, b. 17 February, 1910, Iwu, Chin-hua County, Chekiang Province

Owing to his involvement with the League of Leftist Artists, A., a landlord's son from a southern province recently returned from Paris, where he had been introduced to the works of such European masters as Rimbaud and Apollinaire, was arrested and detained in Shanghai's French Concession from 1932 to 1935. There he wrote his first poetry, later published as *Ta-yen-ho* (1936; great-dike river). The title poem, dedicated to his beloved wet nurse, portrays the tragic existence of an illiterate woman who took the name of her native village. From that point on, A. turned his back on his own class, dedicating his life and art to China's dispossessed masses; proclaiming that "the poet must speak the truth," he was quickly caught up in patriotic-revolutionary activities, gathering material from the ordinary people and from his adopted home in northern China.

A.'s poems are among the most straightforward written in his time and display striking images and a bold use of color. A. was unwavering in his insistence that poetry must be a utilitarian art form, the "spiritual and educational instrument of the masses"; he exhorted his colleagues to "persist in the revolution brought into poetry by Whitman, Verhaeren, and Mayakovsky. We must make poetry into something that adequately meets the needs of a new era, without hesitating to use whatever poetic form is most suitable for this purpose."

The first of three periods in his career, which coincided with his incarceration, is marked by heavily autobiographical free and unrhymed verse, generally cast in sentimental hues. The second period, the early war years of 1935–41, witnessed the creation of his most important and influential works. The artistic self-assurance of the poet was complemented by a growing patriotic ardor and an even deeper involvement with the people and the land. The most noteworthy poem of this period is "T'a szu tsai ti-erh tz'u" (1939; he died a second time), a twelve-part narrative about the death of a soldier. The successful contrast of gruesome imagery with scenic beauty and of human glory with human indifference, the changing moods, and the simplicity of language make this poem a representation not only of a poet's sensitivities, but of an era.

The third period, which began after A.'s arrival in the Communist stronghold of Yenan in 1941, saw the complete politicization of his art. Having accepted the tenets and goals of Communism, he used folk forms to attack fascism and praise the party and Chairman Mao. This was not so much a change in philosophy as one of emphasis and degree. Although his poems from this period are generally undistinguished, his individualism occasionally surfaced, placing him in opposition to party policy. Mildly censured in 1942 and condemned as a rightist in the mid-1950s, he disappeared from public view for more than two decades, but has been rehabilitated following the fall of the "gang of four." In 1980 he participated in a writers' workshop at the University of Iowa.

FURTHER WORKS: *Hsiang t'ai-yang* (1938); *Li-ming te t'ung-chih* (1939); *Shih lun* (1940); *Huo-pa* (1940); *K'uang-yeh* (1940); *Hsüeh li tsuan* (1945); *Hsien-kei hsiang-ts'un te shih* (1945); *Wu Man-yu* (1946); *Shih hsin min-chu chu-i te wen-hsüeh* (1947); *Tsou hsiang sheng-li* (1950); *Ai Ch'ing hsüan-chi* (1951); *Hsin wen-i lun-chi* (1952); *Pao-shih te hung-hsing* (1953); *Ai Ch'ing shih-hsüan* (1955); *Hei man* (1955); *Ch'un-t'ien* (1956); *Hai-chia shang* (1957)

BIBLIOGRAPHY: Goldman, M., *Literary Dissent in Communist China* (1967), passim; Boorman, H. L., and Howard, R. C., *Biographical Dictionary of Republican China* (1971), Vol. I, pp. 317–19; Lin, J. C., *Modern Chinese Poetry: An Introduction* (1972), pp. 172–88 and passim; Průšek, J., ed., *Dictionary of Oriental Literatures* (1974), Vol. I, pp. 1–2; Friend, R. C., "Return from Silence," *ChinL*, June 1979, pp. 42–51

HOWARD GOLDBLATT

CHANG Ai-ling

(Anglicized as Eileen Chang) Chinese novelist, short-story writer, and essayist, b. 1921, Shanghai?

Central to C.'s unusual childhood were the decline of her father's family, once prominent in the service of the last imperial dynasty, and traumatic episodes involving her father's separation from her Europeanized, cosmopolitan mother. After being tutored for a time, she received a grant to attend the University of Hong Kong, where her studies were ended by the Japanese attack and occupation of the British colony. Singlemindedly devoted to being a writer since childhood, C. returned to Shanghai to begin her career. In 1952 she went back to Hong Kong as a refugee from Communist China and then took up residence in the United States. C. has held positions at several universities in Great Britain and the United States, currently at the University of California at Berkeley.

C.'s earliest published stories were first collected as *Ch'uan-ch'i* (1944; romances) and later as *Chang Ai-ling tuan-p'ien hsiao-shuo chi* (1954; collected short stories of Chang Ai-ling). Fine, ironic studies of love and courtship set in Shanghai and Hong Kong, the stories offer skeptical portraits of Europeans, Eurasians and Chinese trapped by circumstance and self-delusion. Their sensuous imagery and their diction recall traditional Chinese literature, yet the style is controlled by symbolic technique and modern psychological vision. The most representative of these stories is "Chin-suo chi" ("The Golden Cangue," 1971).

The desolateness C. reveals at the core of her characters' experiences is accentuated in the first novel she wrote following her return to Hong Kong, *Yang-ko* (1954; *The Rice-sprout Song*, 1955). As a depiction of peasants balking and rioting at excessive Communist demands to aid the Korean War effort, the novel is a dissident's work. The thematic continuity with her earlier stories is evident, however: time and circumstance are triumphant over the characters' attempts to transcend them through appeals to love or revolt, whether those characters be Communist cadres or peasants.

Similarly, in C.'s second major novel, *Ch'ih-ti chih lien* (1954; *Naked Earth*, 1956), Communism appears as the vehicle for more permanent themes in C.'s writing. Insofar as Maoist thought is fiction and simplification of reality, its actual implementation requires that party cadres perpetrate a callous charade in order to survive and to enjoy shallow rewards as the new elite of society. As prisoners of this system, two disillusioned cadres paradoxically face their first true freedom of choice as prisoners of war in Korea. In seeking to evoke the complexity of her characters and their careers during the founding years of the People's Republic, the novel does not always maintain the degree of control over setting and imagery evident in C.'s best work.

C. has belonged to no school or major trend in modern Chinese literature, but she has had imitators. As a young writer she showed little of the concern for China's political fate that dominated the work of so many of her contemporaries, yet her treatment of love stands in marked contrast to that of other love literature of the time. Elements of the social protest in her later works correspond to the dissent of writers within China as well as outside, but her novels bear only superficial resemblance to the run of anti-Communist fiction in Chinese. To date, C.'s use of imagery, by turns compelling and subtle, remains unsurpassed.

FURTHER WORKS: *Liu-yen* (1944); *T'ai-t'ai wan-sui* (1948); *Shih-pa ch'un* (under pseud. Liang Ching, 1950); *Yuan-nü* (1968); *Pan-sheng yuan* (1960); *Hung-lou yen-meng* (1976); *Chang k'an* (1976). FURTHER VOLUME IN ENGLISH: *The Rouge of the North* (1967)

BIBLIOGRAPHY: Hsia, C. T., *A History of Modern Chinese Fiction*, 2nd ed., (1971), pp. 389–431; Cheng, S., "Themes and Techniques in Eileen C.'s Stories," *TkR*, 8 (1977), 169–200; Gunn, E., *Unwelcome Muse: Chinese Literature in Shanghai and Peking, 1937–45* (1980), pp. 200–231

EDWARD M. GUNN

CHAO Shu-li

Chinese novelist and short-story writer, b. 1906, Ch'in-shui County, Shansi Province; d. 23 Sept. 1970

The son of peasants, C. had his secondary school education cut short by his imprisonment for activities against the provincial warlord. After his release he worked in theater and journalism until, following the call of Mao Tse-tung in 1942 for a new literature to serve the population of northwest China, C. emerged as a writer of fiction. With the establishment of the People's Republic in 1949, C. chaired or served on various writers' organizations and edited several cultural periodicals, notably *Ch'ü-i*, devoted to folk-style oral and performing literature. In early 1967 he fell victim to the massive purges of writers and intellectuals during the Cultural Revolution and, according to later published accounts in the official press, died from maltreatment. In 1979 his reputation was restored, and some of his works were reissued.

With the stories "Hsiao Erh-hei chieh-hun" (1943; "Hsiao Erh-hei's Marriage," 1950) and "Li Yu-ts'ai pan-hua" (1943; "Rhymes of Li Yu-ts'ai," 1950) C. won recognition as being among the first and ablest interpreters of the new official prescriptions for literature. Breaking with the dominant trend to write fiction employing techniques learned from the West, C. addressed his peasant audience as one that largely needed to be read to, and consequently adopted the style common to popular storytellers, also making strong use of doggerel verse and colorful colloquialisms without resorting entirely to local dialect. These early stories of peasants overcoming superstitions, exploitive landlords, and corrupt authorities in matters of courtship and community affairs with the support of the Communist Party are also told with considerable humor.

A more serious tone dominates the novel *Li-chia-chuang ti pien-ch'ien* (1950; *Changes in Li Village,* 1953), which portrays developments in a village from the period of warlord control in 1928 to land reform in 1946. Generally valued for its superior depiction of Shansi and its suffering peasantry, the novel in its latter portion is unexceptional party propaganda.

C.'s major work, *San-li-wan* (1955; *San-li-wan Village,* 1957) returns to a lighter vein in telling of village tensions over construction of irrigation canals and the creation of an agricultural cooperative. Yet, here again, C. was unable to make convincing characters of the "politically correct" party cadres or do more than provide a simplistic resolution to the complexities of the situation he introduced in which a significant number of the peasants are skeptical of and opposed to the cooperative movement.

After this work C. was overshadowed by other writers. His greatest supporter was always Chou Yang, vice-minister of propaganda, and C.'s fall from grace shortly followed Chou's. One of C.'s strongest points as a writer was his droll description of "backward" peasants uncommitted to Communist Party policies, and his not unsympathetic attention to them figured in charges of his inadequacy as a writer. C.'s importance as a writer lies primarily in the style he cultivated in most of his fiction in response to the policies inaugurated by Mao Tse-tung.

FURTHER WORKS: *Ling ch'üan tung* (1959); *Hsia-hsiang chi* (1963). FURTHER VOLUME IN ENGLISH: *Rhymes of Li Yu-ts'ai and Other Stories* (1950)

BIBLIOGRAPHY: Chou Yang, "The Creative Works of C. S.," in C. S., *Rhymes of Li Yu-ts'ai, and Other Stories* (1950), pp. 7–30; Birch, C., ed., *Chinese Communist Literature* (1963), pp. 77–82, 197–99; Hsia, C. T., *A History of Modern Chinese Fiction,* 2nd ed. (1971), pp. 482–84, 491–94; Huang, J., *Heroes and Villains in Communist China* (1973), pp. 238–42, 284

EDWARD M. GUNN

CHOU Li-po
Chinese novelist and short-story writer, b. 9 Aug. 1908, I-yang County, Hunan Province; d. 25 Sept. 1979

The son of a village schoolteacher, C. was early drawn to leftist activism in Shanghai, for which he was imprisoned. In 1934, following his release, he joined the League of Leftist Writers as an ardent supporter of the Communist vice-minister of propaganda, Chou Yang, a native of his home county. C. published short stories and translations of Russian literature. In 1937 he followed Chou Yang to the Communist base at Yenan, taught at the Lu Hsün Academy of Arts, and participated extensively in the land-reform campaigns of the 1940s. After 1949 he was an editor of *Jen-min wen-hsüeh* magazine and traveled among workers and peasants to do research for his novels. In 1966, in the general purge of intellectuals (which included Chou Yang), C. was disgraced. In 1977 he was rehabilitated and his works were republished.

C.'s reputation rests almost entirely on two long novels of socialist reconstruction: *Pao-feng tsou-yü* (1949; *The Hurricane,* 1955) and *Shan-hsiang chü pien* (1958; *Great Changes in a Mountain Village,* 1961). Both novels are written in the Soviet-inspired style of Socialist Realism, using a realistic style to portray and idealize the implementation of Communist programs. *Pao-feng tsou-yü* was part of a crop of novels celebrating land reform and was awarded a third-place Stalin Prize for Literature in 1951. With scrupulous attention to the language and details of peasant life that he had observed closely, C.'s novel is perhaps the most dramatic portrayal of the tenacious work of party cadres in the late 1940s to involve the peasantry of a Hunan town in the trial and punishment of their landlords, to motivate them through land reform and property redistribution, and to instill in them socialist values and support for the Communist Party in its struggle with the Nationalists.

C.'s principal work, *Shan-hsiang chü pien,* is representative of the novels about the agricultural cooperative movement. The indebtedness of the novels to Soviet models is strong enough for aspects of it to be compared with Mikhail Sholokhov's *The Quiet Don.* While C. gives individuality to his party cadre characters, they are unimpressive figures, and the focus of the novel is on peasant reluctance to give up their newly won private ownership of land to proposed cooperatives. While the peasants' resistance verges on defiance, the novel abruptly and anticlimactically concludes with an inadequate statement on the founding of the cooperatives.

When they were published, C.'s novels were recommended to inexperienced party cadres as illustrations of issues they had to face. In the West they attracted attention for C.'s sympathetic and sometimes poignant description of peasants' unhappiness with Communist programs and his revelation of the harsh treatment the party meted out to its enemies. While C.'s actual loyalty to the party at the time was never questioned, the implication in his novels that peasants commonly lacked enthusiasm for Mao's policies of collectivization had run afoul of party politics by 1966, and he was condemned for distorting the view of the people.

FURTHER WORKS: *Chin-ch'a-chi pien-ch'ü yin-hsiang chi* (1938); *Su-lien cha-chi* (1953); *Ts'an chün* (1953); *T'ieh-shui pen-liu* (1955); *T'ieh-men li* (1957); *Chou Li-po hsüan-chi* (1959); *Wen-hsüeh ch'ien-lun* (1959); *Shan-hsiang chü pien hsü-p'ien Shou-huo* (1960); *Ho-ch'ang shang* (1960); *San-wen t'e-hsieh hsüan* (1963)

BIBLIOGRAPHY: Birch, C., ed., *Chinese Communist Literature* (1963), pp. 116–19, 199–203; Hsia, C. T., *A History of Modern Chinese Fiction*, 2nd ed. (1971), pp. 518–20; Huang, J., *Heroes and Villains in Communist China* (1973), pp. 183–85, 195–210, 242–43, 284

EDWARD M. GUNN

HO Ch'i-fang

Chinese poet, journalist, critic, and essayist, b. 1912, Wanhsien Szechwan Province; d. 24 July 1977, Peking

Destined to become one of the more influential cultural figures in the People's Republic of China, H. began his literary career as a holdout among his youthful peers who advocated increased social involvement. Born into a wealthy Szechwan family at a time when warlords and bandits were ravaging the country, he developed an intense abhorrence of war and a keen distrust of political authority. His taste in poetry, which tended toward romanticism, was nurtured during his studies at Peking University (1931–35), when he came under the influence of the work of French symbolist Paul Valéry. H.'s earliest poems were published in the literary quarterly *Wen-hsüeh chi-k'an* and subsequently included in a volume by him and two of his schoolmates, entitled *Han-yüan chi* (1936; the garden of Han). His first individual volume, a collection of essays entitled *Hua-meng lu* (1936; record of painted dreams), won the prestigious Ta Kung Pao literary award, not because of the themes of romantic love and the musings of a young artist but because of the poet's polished diction and vivid imagery. He then embarked on an often agonizing journey from noninvolvement and individualism to ardent patriotism and eventually to socialism. Falling under the influence of Romain Rolland, H. began to use poetry as a weapon of political struggle; in 1937 he traveled to Yenan, where he soon became a dedicated Marxist. Up until his death in 1977, just as the Cultural Revolution was ending, he remained an unwavering supporter of Mao's literary policy and, as such, an influential member of the cultural hierarchy.

Although primarily remembered as a poet, H. also made his mark as a journalist during the Sino-Japanese War (1937–45), when he spent much time traveling with and observing Communist troops. His philosophical convictions spawned a succession of polemical works, satirical essays, and propaganda pieces that placed him firmly among the upholders of Maoist literary theories.

Owing to his fine traditional training in Chinese literature, a keen eye for nature, and an early appreciation of Western romanticism, H. wrote highly refined poetry. A deft application of symbols and rich imagery characterized his verse, particularly that of his university days. Although it occasionally lapses into sentimentality, his early verse is appealing in its sparseness of language and the captured essence of natural beauty. Following his conversion to Marxism, H. published a volume of poems, *Yeh-ko* (1945; nocturnal songs), that focused on his new experiences among the soldiers and villagers and reflected his newly acquired outlook on the role of the writer. He soon renounced this attempt as too feeble, however, sensing that his poetic language was still mired in his intellectual, romantic past. Over the next decade he wrote no poetry, immersing himself instead in a study of the people of New China and of their folk songs. His reemergence in the mid-1950s was accompanied by active participation in public debates over literary orthodoxy and by a corpus of poems in praise of socialism.

FURTHER WORKS: *K'o-yi chi* (1938); *Huan-hsing jih-chi* (1939); *Yü-yen* (1945); *Hsing huo chi* (1945); *Wu Yü-chang t'ung-chih ko-ming ku-shih* (1949); *Hsing huo hsin-chi* (1949); *Kuan-yü hsien-shih chu-yi* (1950); *Hsi-yüan chi* (1952); *Kuan-yü hsieh-shih ho tu shu* (1956); *San-wen hsüan-chi* (1957); *Mei-yu p'i-p'ing chiu pu-neng ch'ien-chin* (1958); *Lun "Hung lou meng"* (1958); *Ch'ih-mu te hua* (1961); *Shih-ko hsin-chang*

(1962); *Wen-hsüeh yi-shu te ch'un-t'ien* (1964); *Huang-hun* (1970). FUR-
THER VOLUME IN ENGLISH: *Paths in Dreams: Selected Prose and Poetry
of H. C.* (1976)

BIBLIOGRAPHY: Goldman, M., *Literary Dissent in Communist China*
(1967), pp. xii, 30–32, and passim; Boorman, H. L., and Howard, R.
C., *Biographical Dictionary of Republican China* (1971), Vol. II, pp.
58–60; Průšek, J., *Dictionary of Oriental Literature* (1974), Vol. I, p.
49; Gálik, M., "Early Poems and Essays of H. C.," *AAS*, 15 (1979),
31–64

HOWARD GOLDBLATT

HSÜ Chih-mo
Chinese poet, diarist, essayist, and translator, b. 15 Jan. 1897, Hsia-shih,
Chekiang Province; d. 19 Nov. 1931, Tsinan, Shantung Province

In his own lifetime the fame of H. as a poet rested as much on his life,
which epitomized a fearless attack on conventions and a relentless pursuit of freedom, love, and beauty, as on his work. The son of a wealthy
banker, he first sought reform in China through a study of law and
politics at Peiyang University (later known as Peking University), of
banking and sociology at Clark University in Massachusetts (1918–19),
and of political science at Columbia University, where he obtained a
master's degree in 1920. As early as 1915 he had come under the strong
influence of the most liberal reformist thinker of his time, Liang Ch'i-
ch'ao (1873–1929). He left the U.S. for England, and it was at King's
College, Cambridge, that H. discovered his affinity with literature and
began to write poetry.

At this time he also discovered love. Before leaving China, H. had
been married to an educated, modern girl from a prominent family, and
the young bride had followed him to Cambridge. But H. carried on a
secret love affair with Lin Hui-yin, the seventeen-year-old daughter of a
friend. He clamored for a divorce which was granted in 1922, but
because of objections of family and friends, he did not marry Miss Lin.

For several years following his return to China in 1922, H. wrote
and taught; he was rocketed to national fame when he became the
interpreter for the Indian poet Rabindranath Tagore on his 1924 tour of
China. At about the same time, he became the center of a cause célèbre
by falling in love with yet another prominent woman, the wife of a

young Chinese military officer. To cure himself of this attachment and to allay gossip, H. took a trip through Europe in 1925; but he returned to Peking to insist upon his right to marry the woman he loved, which he did in 1926. These several episodes of his love life found curious parallels in the life of the English poet he admired most, Shelley; and they accomplished as much in shocking the traditional Chinese society and tearing down the old conventions as did his bold and lyrical treatment of his experience in his writings.

In 1925, the year his first volume of poetry, *Chih-mo ti shih* (poems of Chih-mo), was published, H. became the editor of the literary supplement of the newspaper *Ch'en pao*. For this magazine, a year later, he started the now famous poetry journal *Shih-k'an,* which ran for eleven issues. (It resumed publication in 1931 as an independent journal with the aid of Wen I-to [q.v.].) Also for the pages of *Ch'en pao,* to introduce Western-style plays to China, he started a drama section. Together with Wen I-to, H. became the founder in 1928 of the monthly *Hsin-yüeh,* or *Crescent.* In the manifesto of the new journal H. called for a union of music (rhythm), painting (color), and architecture (form and structure) as the sine qua non of *pai-hua* (vernacular) poetry. The *Crescent* poets countered the popularity of the Whitmanesque free verse by insisting upon the supremacy of form and the fusing of classical diction with colloquial speech. With unerring sensitivity to the rhythm of spoken Chinese, H. successfully experimented with metrics, producing a poetry that is simple, direct, and never bookish. One particularly famous poem, "Ai ti lin-kan" (love's inspiration), included in the posthumously published collection *Yün-yu* (1932; wandering in the clouds), a dramatic monologue of over four hundred unrhymed lines that effectively rely upon enjambment and the natural rhythm of vernacular speech, became a classic of the new poetry. His imagery is highly visual and often ethereal, again bespeaking a kinship with Shelley. While some of his early poems were mildly satiric, most of his works reflect the basic romantic attitude concerning the attainability of a dream or an ideal in an imperfect, transitory world. Some of the poems written during the last two years of his life, however, are imbued with a deep sense of despair. "Huo-ch'ê ch'in chu kuei" (night train)—included in *Yün-yu*—a poem in sixteen stanzas with two decasyllabic lines in each, and designed to appear in print like parallel railroad tracks, is H.'s most philosophical— and most pessimistic—work.

During the last years of his life H. held teaching posts at several universities in Shanghai, Nanking, and Peking. He was killed in a plane crash. Like Shelley, whose life was also cut short, H. seems for modern Chinese poetry the "beautiful angel" whose "luminous wings" symbolize a poet's constant search for order and cadence, for beauty and truth.

FURTHER WORKS: *Lo-yeh* (1926); *Fei-leng ts'ui ti i-yeh* (1927); *Pa-li ti lin-chua* (1928); *Tzu-p'ou wen-chi* (1928); *Pien-k'un Kang* (1928, with Lu Hsiao-man); *Meng-hu chi* (1929); *Lung-p'an hsiao-shuo chi* (1929); *Ch'iu* (1931); *Ai-mei hsiao-cha* (1947, with Lu Hsiao-man)

BIBLIOGRAPHY: Birch, C., "English and Chinese Meters in H. C.'s Poetry," *Asia Major,* New Series, 7 (1959), 258–93; Lin, J. C., *Modern Chinese Poetry: An Introduction* (1972), pp. 100–132; Lee, L. O., *The Romantic Generation of Modern Chinese Writers* (1973), pp. 124–74

IRVING YUCHENG LO

HU Shih

(birth-name: Hu Hung-hsing) Chinese poet, literary reformer, and scholar (writing in Chinese and English), b. 17 Dec. 1891, Shanghai; d. 24 Feb. 1962, Taipei, Taiwan

H. changed his name to mean "to fit into" after being inspired by T. H. Huxley's (1825–1895) *Evolution and Ethics.* He studied under the American philosopher John Dewey (1859–1952) at Columbia University, from which he received a doctorate in philosophy in 1917. He then taught at Peking University and other colleges. H. lectured extensively in Europe and the U.S.—he received numerous honorary degrees—and was the Chinese ambassador to the U.S. from 1938 to 1942. He returned to China in 1946 but came back to the U.S. in 1948 and worked as a librarian at Princeton University. During the 1950s he was condemned by the Communist Chinese government as a lackey of U.S. imperialism. In 1958 H. became president of the Academia Sinica in Taiwan.

In the field of literature, H. is better known for advocating reforms and for his scholarship in vernacular literature, than he is for his creative writing. A skeptic and critic of traditional Chinese mores, he wrote a story entitled "Chen-ju tao" (1906; the surrealist isle) in which Chinese superstitious practices were attacked. Another short story, "I-ko wen-t'i" (1919; a problem), and the play *Chung-shen ta-shih* (1919; marriage), a farce, were both quite superficial in dealing with social issues.

In his youth, H. called for the reform of the literary tradition. In essays like "Wen-hsüeh kai-liang ch'u-i" (1917; a modest proposal for literary reform), he declared basically that the *wen-yen* (literary written language) should be abolished and that the practical *pai-hua* (spoken language) should be adopted for all writing, and he published *Ch'ang shih chi* (1919; the experiment), a collection of poems written in the vernacular. The work itself was very immature, as H. admitted; nonetheless, its publication signified the quest and victory of the *pai-hua* literary movement over the time-honored *wen-yen* literary tradition.

H.'s contribution to the new literature movement also lies in his scholarship. His *Pai-hua wen-hsüeh shih* (1928; history of vernacular literature) proved the existence of a vernacular tradition in Chinese literature. Unfortunately, the book's contents ended prematurely with the 9th c. In addition, H. published numerous research studies that dealt with matters of the authorship and textual and historical significances, as well as the literary merits of almost all the well-known Chinese vernacular fictional works. Until very recently, for example, his research on *Dream of the Red Chamber*, which linked it to the family history of its author, Ts'ao Hsüeh-ch'in (1717–1764), dominated all studies on the novel. The fact that vernacular fiction is now respected in Chinese literature is due mainly to H.'s efforts.

H. also promoted the writing of *chuan-chi wen-hsüeh* (biographical literature), claiming that China has yet to produce an interesting and readable biography. He tried writing some himself, including one of his mother, and an autobiography.

As a believer in reforming China through "wholesale Westernization" and "wholehearted modernization," H. is admired and condemned for the destruction of the Chinese literary tradition and for his pro-Western outlook. Nevertheless, his importance in modern Chinese literature is undeniable: known as the "father of the literary revolution," H. was a pioneer in the dawning of a new era of literary expression in China.

FURTHER WORKS: *Chung-kuo che-hsüeh shih ta-kang, shang p'ien* (1919; *The Development of the Logical Method in Ancient China*, 1922); *China's Own Critics: A Selection of Essays* (1931); *The Chinese Renaissance* (1934); *H. S. yen-lun chi* (2 vols., 1953–55); *H. S. liu-hsüeh-jih-chi* (1959); *H. S. wen ts'un* (rev. ed., 1961)

BIBLIOGRAPHY: Forster, L., *The New Culture in China* (1936), pp. 221–34; Chow, T., *The May Fourth Movement* (1960), pp. 271–79; Shih, V.,

"A Talk with H. S.," *ChinaQ*, 10 (1962), 149–65; Grieder, J., *H. S. and the Chinese Renaissance: Liberalism in the Chinese Revolution, 1917–1937* (1970)

MARLON K. HOM

KUO Mo-jo

Chinese poet, dramatist, and essayist, b. 16 Nov. 1892, Tung-he, Ssu-ch'uan Province; d. 12 June 1978, Peking

K. was trained in medicine in Japan but never practiced it. Instead, he became interested in literature and cofounded the Creation Society, which advocated the concept of "art for art's sake" during the height of the new literature movement in the early 1920s. Soon thereafter K. fled to Japan, where he stayed for ten years to escape the purge of Communists. When he returned to China in 1937, he became a prominent scholar of ancient Chinese social history and was a key figure in the national defense literature movement of the 1930s. After 1949 he was active in the upper echelons of the government of the People's Republic and became president of the Chinese Academy of Science.

K.'s prominence in literature came after the publication of *Nü-shen* (1921; partial tr., *Selected Poems from the Goddesses*, 1958), a poetry collection full of impulsive outbursts echoing the feelings of reform-minded intellectuals in search of a new China. The language was uninhibited, and K. was particularly criticized for his frequent use of foreign words. He continued with his poetry writing, collected in *Hsing k'ung* (1923; starry sky), *P'ing* (1927; vase), *Hui-fu* (1928; recovery), *Chan sheng chi* (1938; battle cries), and other volumes, but none received the same acclaim as *Nü-shen*. Nevertheless, he remained consistent in his sloganlike outcries, especially on nationalism. After 1949 K. published more poems in collections such as *Hsin-hua chung* (1953; in praise of new China), *Ch'ang ch'un chi* (1959; forever spring), and *Tung feng chi* (1963; east wind). In most of these, K. glorified political causes. His poems of the 1970s were written in a more formal, classical style.

K.'s most celebrated dramatic work is *Ch'ü Yüan* (1942; *Ch'ü Yüan*, 1955). It is a creative reconstruction of the political defeat of China's first known poet-statesman, Ch'ü Yüan (c. 343–290 B.C.), whose loyalty led to his despair and self-destruction. K. utilized this historical play as propaganda for nationalism during the war with Japan. In *Ts'ai Wen-chi* (1956; Ts'ai Wen-chi), K. dramatized the return from the Huns to the

Chinese kingdom of Ts'ai Yen (c. A.D. 162–239), a famous Han poetess. By using Ts'ai's return to vindicate the villainous image of statesman Ts'ao Ts'ao (A.D. 155–220), K. was in line with the current political issue of redefining Ts'ao's role in Chinese history.

K. also wrote a few essays of literary criticism and some short stories, none of which were outstanding. He often wrote stories with a very strong tendency toward autobiography, and he sometimes just retold historical anecdotes.

A prolific writer, K. was the only one to survive the numerous political purges against writers because his versatility and flexibility enabled him to adapt easily to every new political tide. K.'s early poetry shows a lack of discipline, and his later poems lost the impulsive energy that was his earlier trademark. His plays and later poetry reveal how he followed the Maoist doctrine that creative writing should support political and revolutionary activities.

FURTHER WORKS: *M. shih chi* (1935); *M. hsüan chi* (1936); *K. M. wen chi* (1949); *M. wen chi* (1957); *M. shih tz'u hsüan* (1977)

BIBLIOGRAPHY: Moy, C., "K. M. and the Creation Society," *Papers on China* (Harvard), 4 (1950), 131–59; Schultz, W., "K. M. and the Romantic Aesthetic: 1918–1925," *JOL* 6, 2 (1955), 49–81; Průšek, J., *Three Sketches of Chinese Literature* (1969), pp. 99–140; Gálik, M., "Studies in Modern Chinese Literary Criticism: IV. The Proletarian Criticism of K. M.," *AAS*, 6 (1970), 145–60; Roy, D. T., *K. M.: The Early Years* (1971); Lee, L. O., "K. M.," *The Romantic Generation of Modern Chinese Writers* (1973), pp. 177–200

MARLON K. HOM

LAO SHE

(pseud. of Shu Ch'ing-ch'un) Chinese novelist, short-story writer, and dramatist, b. 3 Feb. 1899, Peking; d. 24 Aug. 1966, Peking

Fatherless since early childhood, L. S. worked his way through Peking Teachers' College. After graduation he managed to support himself and his mother through a series of teaching and administrative posts. In 1924 he went to London, where he taught Chinese at the School of Oriental and African Studies.

While in London, L. S. became a great admirer of Dickens, and in

1926 he wrote his first novel, *Lao Chang te che-hsüeh* (1928; the philosophy of Old Chang), in imitation of *Nicholas Nickleby*. It was an immediate success, for in addition to being written in the lively dialect of the Peking streets, this novel was the first to introduce humor into the New Literature movement (launched in 1918). In 1930, with his literary reputation already established, he returned to China, where he continued to teach and began to write short stories.

Renewed exposure to the harsh realities of Chinese society increasingly shifted the emphasis of L. S.'s works. *Mao ch'eng Chi* (1933; *Cat Country*, 1970), is one of the bitterest satires about Chinese society ever written. L. S. considered the novel a failure and soon turned his hand again to humor. The results were the eminently successful *Li-hun* (1933; *The Quest for Love of Lao Lee*, 1948) and *Niu T'ien-tz'u chuan* (1934; *Heavensent*, 1951), which was partly modeled on Fielding's *Tom Jones*.

Lo-t'o hsiang-tzu (1938; *Rickshaw*, 1979; also tr. as *Camel Xiangzi*, 1981) is his best novel. This tragic tale, in which he attempted to show the complete bankruptcy of individualism, traces, without sentimentality, the moral ruin of an honest Peking rickshaw puller brought about by a callous, cruel society. The first American translation of this work, *Rickshaw Boy*, became a best seller shortly after its publication in 1945. This version, however, in which the translator took the liberty of providing the story with a happy ending, was not acceptable to L. S. (He was later to disapprove of the same man's translation of *Li-hun* [*Divorce*, 1948], and commissioned a new translation of the same work, *The Quest for Love of Lao Li*.)

The outbreak of the second Sino-Japanese War (1937–45) radically altered L. S.'s writing. Essentially apolitical (he mistrusted all government officials), in 1938 he was elected head of the Chinese Writers' Anti-Aggression Association, a group formed to pull writers of all political persuasions together in the common cause of the war with Japan. L. S. became a patriotic propagandist and indulged his lifelong interest in popular forms of entertainment by writing ballads, plays, and short skits on wartime themes.

After the war, L. S. published a gigantic novel in three parts, *Ssu-shih t'ung-t'ang* (abridged tr., *The Yellow Storm*, 1951), which deals with life in Peking during the Japanese occupation of Manchuria. The first two parts, *Huang-huo* (bewilderment) and *T'ou-sheng* (ignominy), were published in 1946, while part three, *Chi-huang* (famine), was not published until 1950–51, when it appeared in serialized form. Like his wartime works, this trilogy seems dated because of its emphasis on brave patriots and sniveling collaborationists.

Between 1946 and 1949 L. S. lived in the U.S., having gone there at the invitation of the Department of State. While there, he completed a new novel that was translated and published in 1952 as *The Drum Singers;* the Chinese version of this novel has not yet appeared. When the People's Republic was established in 1949, he returned to China and held a number of important cultural posts. During these years he wrote many propagandistic works, the most successful of which was the play *Lung hsü-kou* (1951; *Dragon Beard Ditch*, 1956).

L. S. had a lifelong interest in the craft of writing. In his early collection of essays *Lao-niu p'o-ch'e* (1939; an old ox and worn-out cart) he explains how he wrote much of his best work. His essays after 1949, however, are less concerned with his own writing than with teaching the craft of writing to a new generation; the most noteworthy of these later essayistic works is *Ch'u-k-'ou ch'eng-chang* (1964; spoken so well it's ready to print).

In 1966, during the Cultural Revolution, L. S. was driven to suicide by the Red Guards. Since the fall of Chiang Ch'ing (guiding hand of the Cultural Revolution) in 1976, L. S. has been officially praised, his early works republished, and his persecutors blamed, although not brought to trial.

L. S. will probably be best remembered for the excellent novels and stories he wrote during the 1920s and 1930s. These works show a warm humanitarian humor, graceful handling of the Peking dialect, deep love for China, and sympathy for the underdog, all of which will assure L. S. international readers for a very long time to come.

FURTHER WORKS: *Chao Tzu-yüeh* (1927); *Erh Ma* (1929; *Ma and Son,* 1980); *Hsiao-p'o te sheng-jih* (1931); *Kan-chi* (1934); *Ying-hai-chi* (1935); *Ko-tsao-chi* (1936); *Chien-pei 'Pien* (1940); *Kuo-chia chih-shang* (1940, with Sung Chih-ti); *Huo-ch'e-chi* (1941); *Wen Po-shih* (1941); *Kuei-ch'-ü-lai hsi* (1943); *Ts'an-wu* (1943); *Mien-tzu wen-t'i* (1943); *Chung-lieh t'u* (1943); *Wang-chia Chen* (1943); *Chang Tzu-chung* (1943); *Ta-ti lung-she* (1943); *T'au-li ch'un-feng* (1943); *Shei nsien tao-le Ch'ung-ch'ing* (1943); *Huo-tsang* (1944); *Tung-hai pa-shan-chi* (1946); *Wei-shen-chi* (1947); *Fang Chen-chu* (1950); *Pieh mi-hsin* (1951); *Ch-un-hua ch'iu-shih* (1953); *Ho kung-jen t'ung-chih-men t'an hsieh-tso* (1954); *Wu-ming kao-ti yu-le ming* (1954); *Shih-wu kuan* (1956); *Hsi-wang Ch'ang-an* (1956); *Ch'a-kuan* (1957); *Fu-hsing-chi* (1958); *Hung Ta-yüan* (1958); *Ch'üan-chia fu* (1959); *Nü-tien-yüan* (1959); *Pao-ch'uan* (1961); *Ho Chu p'ei* (1962); *Shen-ch'üan* (1963). FURTHER VOLUME IN ENGLISH: *Two Writers and the Cultural Revolution: L. S. and Chen Jo-hsi* (1980)

BIBLIOGRAPHY: Slupski, Z., *The Evolution of a Modern Chinese Writer: An Analysis of L. S.'s Fiction, with Biographical and Bibliographical Appendices* (1966); Boorman, H. L., and Howard, R. C., eds., *Biographical Dictionary of Republican China* (1970), Vol. III, pp. 132–35; Hsia, C. T., *A History of Modern Chinese Fiction: 1917–1957* (1971), pp. 165–88, 366–75, 546–50; Vohra, R., *L. S. and the Chinese Revolution* (1974); Kao, G., ed., *Two Writers and the Cultural Revolution: L. S. and Chen Jo-hsi* (1980), pp. 5–34.

WILLIAM A. LYELL

LIU Ya-tzu

Chinese poet and historian, b. 28 May 1887, Wu-chiang, Kiangsu Province; d. 21 June 1958, Peking

Born of a landholding gentry-scholar family, L. early imbibed revolutionary ideas prevalent among Chinese youth at the turn of the century. In 1906, while in Shanghai, he joined Sun Yat-sen's China Alliance and wrote inflammatory essays and poems to advocate the overthrow of the Manchu regime. His major activity in this period was the founding (1909) of the Southern Society, which grew under his leadership into a large literary organization with over one thousand members. As a veteran Kuomintang member, he made occasional forays into the political arena in the 1910s and 1920s, but fared better as writer and scholar. He was director of the Gazetteer Bureau of the Shanghai Municipality (1932–37) and supervised the publication of a series of its yearbooks and historical studies. He withdrew from active life during the Sino-Japanese War, but political differences with the Kuomintang faction under Chiang Kai-shek led to L.'s dismissal from the party (1941) and to his subsequent support of the Communist cause. He was invited to Peking by Mao Tse-tung after the Communist victory in 1949 and held various offices in the new regime until his death nine years later.

L. left to posterity a large legacy of poetic works written in the classical style, in which he showed great skill and expertise, even though it was his contention that the future belonged to the new vernacular poetry of the May Fourth era (see Chinese Literature). For almost fifty years—from his first published poems (in *Kiangsu,* a Tokyo-based Chinese periodical) in 1903 to his last poems, written in 1951—he cultivated the poetic art with devotion and diligence. His verses contain fresh ideas and powerful, overflowing emotions that best express the aspirations and ideals of the Chinese revolution. He was also adept at extempore pieces compiled for his many friends on various occasions. Whether occasional or topical, his poems abound in historical and classical allusions that bear witness to his erudition.

L. was dedicated to the memories of his friends. He not only wrote essays and poems to them, but also collected and published their writings after their deaths. Among the works he edited were those of early revolutionary martyrs. L.'s great effort, however, was directed toward the collection of Su Man-shu's (q.v.) literary remains and biographical materials, which he published in five volumes: *Man-shu ch'üan-chi* (1928–31; Man-shu's complete works). Indefatigable in his research, L. succeeded in disentangling the confused threads of his friend's life in a series of new studies. The same interest led to his compilation of *Nan-shê chi-lüeh* (1940; a short account of the Southern Society). Its title notwithstanding, the book is a comprehensive record of the activities of the Southern Society (1909–24) with a complete listing of its members. In another volume, *Huai-chiu chi* (1947; essays in remembrance of old times and friends), L. wrote fondly on some of his friends as well as on topics of current and historical interest.

During the first years of his self-imposed seclusion in Japanese-occupied Shanghai (1937–40) L. started his most ambitious project, on the history of Southern Ming (covering two decades of the mid-17th c. during which the Ming loyalists rallied in south China against the conquering Manchus), which he continued when he moved to Hong Kong (1940–41). Although the work was disrupted by the Japanese occupation of the island after Pearl Harbor and L.'s subsequent flight to the Chinese hinterland, he was able to complete and publish several articles on the subject. The entire work, however, was left unfinished.

The life and thought of L., poet and scholar, was affected by the major political upheavals of his time. Impelled by an inborn patriotism and strong ideological conviction, he plunged, if only for short periods, into the maelstroms. Using his unique experiences reinforced by ardent feelings, he created a new type of revolutionary heroic verse unsurpassed by his contemporaries. Discarding the hackneyed, pedantic classical clichés, he rescued Chinese poetry from degeneration by infusing it with a vigorous spirit and strong individualism. Not an innovator, he was rather a master of age-old poetic conventions, which he artfully transformed into new modes and into a powerful vehicle for the communication of patriotic sentiments.

L.'s influence was widespread. He was beloved of younger writers, to whom he was especially considerate and helpful, and by whom he was acclaimed modern China's great poet.

FURTHER WORKS: *Ch'eng-fu chi* (1928); *L. Y. shih-tz'u hsüan* (1959)

BIBLIOGRAPHY: Boorman, H. L., ed., *Biographical Dictionary of Republican China* (1967), Vol. II, pp. 421–23; Liu Wu-chi, *Su Man-shu* (1972), pp. 68–82

LIU WU-CHI

LU HSÜN

(pseud. of Chou Shu-jen) Chinese short-story writer, essayist, critic, translator, and literary theorist, b. 25 Sept. 1881, Shaoshing, Chekiang Province; d. 19 Oct. 1936, Shanghai

Born into the gentry class, rapidly declining under the Ching (Manchu) dynasty, L. H. was brought up in the twilight of a vanishing way of life. He received a traditional education before he enrolled in new-style schools in Nanking. He was sent to Japan in 1902 on a government scholarship to study medicine, but in 1905 he abruptly terminated his medical studies and decided to devote his full energies to literary endeavors. He wanted to explore the Chinese national character through his writing. After a decade of constant failure following his return to China in 1909, he was finally catapulted to literary renown in 1918 with the short story "K'uang-jen jih-chi" (1918; "The Diary of a Madman," 1941), published in *Hsin ch'ing-nien*, the journal that initiated the intellectual revolution in China known as the New Culture Movement. The work has been called China's first modern story because of its use of the vernacular and its highly subjective, devastating critique of traditional culture.

Two collections of short stories followed: *Na han* (1923; *Call to Arms*, 1981) and *P'ang huang* (1926; *Wandering,* 1981)—published together in English as *The Complete Stories of Lu Xun* (1981). Between 1918 and 1936, the year he died, he also wrote sixteen volumes of essays, a collection each of personal reminiscences, prose poetry, and historical tales, some sixty classical-style poems, half a dozen volumes of scholarly research (mainly on Chinese fiction), and numerous translations of Russian, eastern European, and Japanese writers.

In 1928 L. H. settled in Shanghai, where he became the doyen of literati. Having witnessed the vicissitudes of the Chinese political situation, he turned increasingly leftist and was a founding member of the League of Left-Wing Writers in 1930. While sympathetic to the underground Chinese Communist Party, he was never a Party member. He eventually became embroiled in the internecine squabbles on the leftist front and died a tormented and alienated man. After his death, however, he was deified by Mao Tse-tung as China's greatest "writer, thinker, and revolutionist" and enjoyed a renown comparable to Mao's.

L. H.'s works have often been read as scathing critiques of Chinese society and culture. His sardonic, satirical essays have been seen as effective weapons with which he launched attacks on enemies of all hues. Privately, however, he was seized with periodic spells of spiritual nihilism and seemed unable to shake off the inner ghosts of his traditional past. Thus, some of his literary works, particularly his later fiction and prose poetry, reveal a subtle lyricism and a philosophical depth unparalled in modern Chinese literature.

L. H. is known in the West chiefly for his short stories, which have been translated into more than a dozen languages. In them he succeeded brilliantly in rendering a multifaceted portrait of Chinese people caught in all their tribulations. Aside from his first modern story, "K'uang-jen jih-chi," his most celebrated story, both in China and abroad, is "Ah Q cheng-chuan" (1921; "The True Story of Ah Q," 1926), a satirical "biography" of an ignorant village laborer who experiences, with an utter lack of self-awareness, a series of humiliations and finally dies a victim of the chaos of the Republican revolution of 1911. Comparable in cultural significance to Cervantes's Don Quixote, L. H.'s Ah Q stands as a personification of the negative traits of the Chinese national character.

Less allegorical and more realistic and moving are such well-known stories as "Kung I-chi" (1919; "Kung I-chi," 1932), "Ku-hsiang" (1921; "My Native Town," 1935), "Chu-fu" (1924; "The New Year Blessing," 1936), and "Fei-tsao" (1924; "The Cake of Soap," 1941), in all of which the hypocrisy and insensitivity of upper-class intellectuals are contrasted with the suffering of the lower-class people. Nonetheless, L. H.'s own profound ambivalence toward his countrymen and his sophistication as an artist infused his stories with layers of ambiguity in both characterization and narrative technique, which defy easy ideological analysis. In most of his stories there can be found a metaphysical level, centering on an alienated loner besieged and persecuted by an uncomprehending crowd. Thus, the "philosophical" messages of L. H.'s works are much less positive than they are perceived to be in the numerous eulogistic biographies, monographs, and articles that have poured out continually from his Chinese adulators. This introspective, almost tragic, side of L. H.'s works, ignored by his admirers in China, is notably present in his classical-style poetry, his prose poetry collection *Yeh-ts'ao* (1927; *Wild Grass*, 1974), and some of his early essays.

Despite these darker and apolitical aspects of L. H.'s art and psyche, his name has been constantly used in successive political campaigns by the Chinese Communists since 1949, including the Cultural Revolution, in which his reputation remained unscathed, although his numerous disciples, friends, and scholars were purged. L. H. is still modern China's most admired and respected writer.

FURTHER WORKS: *L. H. ch'uan-chi* (20 vols., 1938); *L. H. ch'uan-chi pu-i* (2 vols., 1946, 1952); *L. H. shu-chien* (2 vols., 1952). FURTHER VOLUMES IN ENGLISH: *Ah Q and Others* (1941); *Selected Works of L. H.* (4 vols., 1956–57); *Selected Stories of L. H.* (1960)

BIBLIOGRAPHY: Huang S., *L. H. and the New Culture Movement of Modern China* (1957); Hsia, C. T., *A History of Modern Chinese Fiction* (1961), pp. 28–54; Hsia, T. A., *The Gate of Darkness* (1968), pp. 101–62; Hanan, P. "The Technique of L. H.'s Fiction," *HJAS*, 34 (1974), 53–95; Lyell, W. A., *L. H.'s Vision of Reality* (1976); Lee, L. O., "Genesis of a Writer: Notes on Lu Xun's Educational Experience," Mills, H. C., "Lu Xun: Literature and Revolution—from Mara to Marx," Doleželová-Velingerová, M., "Lu Xun's 'Medicine,' " in Goldman, M., ed., *Modern Chinese Literature in the May Fourth Era* (1977), pp. 161–232; Semanov, V. I., *L. H. and His Predecessors* (1980)

LEO OU-FAN LEE

MAO TUN

(pseud. of Shen Yen-ping) Chinese novelist and short-story writer, b. 25 June 1896, Tung-hsiang, Chekiang Province; d. 27 March 1981, Peking

M. T. came from a small-town, middle-class family and was educated in the big cities. After graduation from the junior division of the National Peking University, he worked in the editorial office of the Commercial Press, one of the large publishing houses in Shanghai. In 1921 he became editor of the company's *Hsiao-shuo yüeh-pao*, a monthly that published fiction. He was also one of the founding members, in 1920, of the Literary Research Association. With the support of the Association members, *Hsiao-shuo yüeh-pao* soon became a leading literary periodical of the time (1921–32); many important works of modern Chinese fiction, including those of M. T. himself, were published in it.

M. T.'s most popular novels are the trilogy *Shih* (1930; eclipse)—consisting of *Huan-mieh* (disillusion), *Tung-yao* (vacillation), and *Chui-ch'iu* (pursuit)—which depicts in successive stages the tensions and struggles of young Chinese intellectuals prior to Nationalist victory in China; *Hung* (1930; rainbow), detailing the adventures of an innocent and intelligent girl thrust into the maelstrom of life in a complex society; and *Tzu-yeh* (1933; *Midnight*, 1957), his best-known novel, about the filth and corruption of the business and industrial communities in metropolitan Shanghai. He also published several story collections, which include "Ch'un ts'an" (1932; "Spring Silkworms," 1956) and "Lin-chia p'u-tzu" (1932; "The Shop of the Lin Family," 1956). Both stories narrate with sympathy and pathos the sufferings respectively of peasants and small-townsfolk.

During the Sino-Japanese War (1937–45) M. T. joined the exodus of Chinese intellectuals to the southwest interior. His important works of this period are the novels *Fu-shih* (1941; corrosion) and *Shuang-yeh hung szu erh-yüeh hua* (1943; frosted leaves as red as flowers in February), and the play *Ch'ing-ming ch'ien hou* (1945; before and after the spring festival).

M. T. shared the modern Chinese writers' interest in politics, which was often inseparable from literature. Although he was not a member of the Communist Party early in his career, he had pronounced leftist tendencies and associated with authors who were ardent in their denunciation of the Nationalist government. After the founding of the People's Republic in 1949, he rose high in the literary hierarchy of the new regime and was elected chairman of the All-China Federation of Literary Workers (later called the Chinese Writers' Union). For sixteen years (1949–65) he was Minister of Culture in the Communist government. Beginning in 1951, he also served as editor of *Chinese Literature,* an official literary organ of Communist China, published in several languages for foreign readers. But he did little creative writing beyond revising and reissuing his earlier works in the ten-volume *M. T. wen-chi* (1958–61; M. T.'s collected works). He survived the purges of the intellectuals during the Cultural Revolution, but the most productive period of his life as a writer was long past.

A faithful chronicler of his time, M. T. recorded in a realistic manner the men and events of modern Chinese society, focusing on its ugliness and evils and on class distinctions that separate the rich from the poor.

He analyzed with meticulous care the disruptive social and political forces that plunged the country into chaos in the most critical years prior to the socialist revolution that ushered in the Communist regime. After the establishment of the People's Republic, his political activities and administrative duties all but superseded his role as the most accomplished and versatile author of modern China.

FURTHER WORKS: *Yeh ch'iang-wei* (1929); *San-jen hsing* (1931); *Lu* (1932); *Hua hsia-tzu* (1934); *M. T. tuan-p'ien hsiao-shuo chi* (1934); *Su-hsieh yü sui-pi* (1935); *Yin-hsiang kan-hsiang hui-i* (1936); *To-chiao kuan hsi* (1936); *Ti-i chiai-tuan ti ku-shih* (1945); *Wei-ch'ü* (1945); *Su-lien chien-wen lu* (1947). FURTHER VOLUME IN ENGLISH: *Spring Silkworms, and Other Stories* (1956)

BIBLIOGRAPHY: Liu Wu-chi, "The Modern Period, 1900–1950," supplement to Giles, H. A., *A History of Chinese Literature,* enlarged ed. (1967), pp. 490–92; Hsia, C. T., *A History of Modern Chinese Fiction* (1971), pp. 140–64, 350–59; Berninghausen, J., "The Central Contradiction in Mao Dun's Earliest Fiction," and Chen, Y., "Mao Dun and the Use of Political Allegory in Fiction: A Case Study of His 'Autumn in Kuling,' " in Goldman, M., ed., *Modern Chinese Literature in the May Fourth Era* (1977), pp. 233–59, 261–80; Gálik, M., *The Genesis of Modern Chinese Literary Criticism* (1980), pp. 191–213; Průšek, J., "M. T. and Yü Ta-fu," in Lee, O., ed., *The Lyric and the Epic: Studies of Modern Chinese Literature* (1980), pp. 121–77

LIU WU-CHI

PA CHIN

(pseud. of Li Fei-kan) Chinese novelist, b. 25 Nov. 1904, Chengtu

One of the most popular writers of 20th-c. China, P. C. experienced the social turmoil that accompanied the birth of modern China and produced a generation of youth committed to revolution. Despite his upper-class family background he was a self-professed anarchist and found political inspiration in the writings of Pyotr Kropotkin (1842–1921) and of Emma Goldman (1869–1940), with whom he corresponded. His literary influences came from Russian fiction (he later translated works by Gorky, Turgenev, and Tolstoy). After returning from France, where he lived from

1927 to 1929, he turned to social and political novels, which he produced prolifically during the 1930s and 1940s. After the Communist victory in 1949 he remained on the mainland; he was made a vice-chairman of the National Committee of the All China Federation of Literary and Art Circles and was given other assignments by the government. He was, however, persecuted during the Cultural Revolution in the late 1960s. Since his recent rehabilitation he has been twice nominated for the Nobel Prize in literature, and in 1981 was elected acting chairman of the Chinese Writers' Association. He was awarded the Dante International Prize by the Italian government in 1982.

P. C.'s first novel, *Mieh-wang* (1929; destruction), is noted more for its social message than for its literary excellence. The main character, Tu Ta-hsin ("Tu Big Heart"), hates the existing government so much that he plots its overthrow. Eventually he commits suicide after failing to assassinate a garrison commander. *Hsin sheng* (1931; new life), another political novel about revolution, is distinguished by its portrayal of a Chinese "dangling man," Li Leng. A masochistic sufferer, despairing and alienated, Li finally finds himself in the anarchists' cause and dies for it.

P. C.'s most acclaimed work is the *Chi-liu* (turbulent stream) trilogy, comprising *Chia* (1931; *The Family,* 1958), *Ch'un* (1937; spring), and *Ch'iu* (1939; autumn). It traces the fortunes of the Kao family during the early 20th c., when old and new values clashed, and it treats comprehensively such related themes as frustrated young love, the low status of women, concubinage, enmity between parents and children, and harsh treatment of the young. Of the three novels in the trilogy, *Chia* is the most widely known and is considered one of his finest works. All three, however, were extremely popular with the readers of the 1930s and 1940s, who easily identified with the characters.

During the Sino-Japanese War (1937–45) P. C. at first supported the war effort by writing about the activities of patriots in the trilogy *Huo* (1938–43; fire). Despite the lack of exciting battles or moving love scenes, the trilogy is memorable for P. C.'s concentration on the emotions of patriotic men and women whose idealism and fiery zeal are symbolized by the title itself.

P. C.'s loss of enthusiasm for the war can be seen in *Hsiao-jen, hsiao-shih* (1947; little people, little events), a collection of short stories written during the war in which he stripped the war of its glamour and described the "little people" exactly as they were. His pessimism about China grew as the war dragged on and was further reflected in *Ti-ssu ping-shih* (1945; ward number four), a novelette about the inhumane conditions in a substandard hospital in the interior.

P. C.'s harshest attack on the war and the Nationalist government, however, was in *Han yeh* (1947; *Cold Nights,* 1978), regarded, along with *Chia,* as one of his two masterpieces. Set in Chungking at the end of World War II, *Han yeh* portrays the strained and deteriorating relationships among a mother, a son, and a daughter-in-law, against a background of the social weariness and ennui that pervaded China in the 1940s. In addition to the realistic presentation of the grim realities in wartime Chungking, *Han yeh* is notable in its exploration of human motives and behavior.

Because of the Communist Party's rigid control of literature, P. C. wrote little after 1949. His visits to Korea in the early 1950s, however, led to his writing about the Chinese who fought there in *Ying-hsiung ti ku-shih* (1954; *Living Among Heroes,* 1954). Adopting a cautious attitude toward the government, he revised many of his pre-1949 works, excising references to anarchism and changing some endings.

During the height of the Cultural Revolution in the late 1960s P. C. was silenced. When he resumed writing in the late 1970s he produced more than sixty essays on a variety of topics and translated two volumes of Alexandr Herzen's (1812–1870) memoirs. Most recently he has been working on a novel about an elderly intellectual couple during the Cultural Revolution.

In his heyday P. C. was regarded as a counselor to the young. He probed the dynamics of social institutions during a time of radical change, and through the medium of fiction he eloquently communicated his vision of China's character. With the passing of time, many of the issues he wrestled with will lose their immediacy, and his works will be judged more on purely aesthetic grounds—and found to be of high artistic quality.

FURTHER WORKS: *Ssu-ch'ü-ti t'ai-yang* (1930); *Ai-ch'ing-ti san-pu-ch'u* (3 vols., 1931–33); *Hai ti meng* (1932); *Li-na* (1934); *Ch'i yüan* (1945); *P. C. wen-chi* (14 vols., 1959–62)

BIBLIOGRAPHY: Chen, T., "P. C. the Novelist," *ChinL,* No. 6 (1963), 84–92; Lang, O., *P. C. and His Writings* (1967); Hsia, C. T., *A History of Modern Chinese Fiction* (1971), pp. 237–56, 375–88; Mao, N. K., "P. C.'s Journey in Sentiment: From Hope to Despair," *JCLTA,* 11 (1976), 131–37; Mao, N. K., *P. C.* (1978)

NATHAN K. MAO
WINSTON YANG

SU Man-shu

(born Su Chien; also known as Su Yüan-ying and Su Hsüan-ying) Chinese poet and novelist, b. 1884, Yokohama, Japan; d. 2 May 1918, Shanghai

Son of a Cantonese merchant in Yokohama and a Japanese mother, S. was five years old when he was taken to Chung-shan in southern Kwangtung province to live with his father's clan. There he received a traditional Chinese education. At fourteen he went back to Japan to study in Yokohama and Tokyo. He participated in a movement of Chinese students to overthrow the Manchu government in China. In 1903 he went to Shanghai for teaching and newspaper work. In 1904, while on a trip to Kwangtung, he became a Buddhist monk, taking the name Man-shu. He spent the remaining fourteen years of his life writing, teaching, and traveling. He shuttled between Shanghai and Tokyo, visited Thailand, Ceylon, and Java, but never stayed long in any one place. In China he made friends with prominent men of letters, particularly members of a revolutionary literary society known as Nan-shê, and with leaders of the Nationalist Party. Disillusionment with political events in the country after the 1911 revolution and failing health made him pessimistic and melancholic during the last years of his life.

S. wrote extensively on a variety of topics, ranging from Sanskrit grammar to the flora of the Western hemisphere. He prepared a Chinese-English dictionary as well as the geographical terms and itinerary charts for the travelogues of two Buddhist pilgrims. He also compiled three anthologies of English translations of Chinese poems and essays. A fine painter, his landscapes were treasured by friends and other contemporaries.

As a poet, S. specialized in the *chüeh-chu*—a four-line lyric with five or seven words to the line. His poems, although written in traditional Chinese forms, are delicate, refreshing, and spontaneous. They show the sensitivity of a young poet in love with women and nature, all presented with consummate skill. Especially original and exquisite are his descriptions of rural scenery in Japan: the ice flag atop a thatched store signaling a nearby market: himself with straw sandals and a broken alms bowl, walking across bridges where cherry blossoms bloom. Buddhist attitudes also influence the mood and tone of his poetry.

The best-known of S.'s works, *Tuan-hung ling-yen chi* (1912; *The Lone Swan,* 1924), is a seemingly autobiographical narrative. It describes the tender love affair between Su San-lang—a Chinese youth of Japanese origin, who has become a Buddhist monk—and his Japanese cousin.

Torn by the conflict between his affection for her and his vow of celibacy, San-lang assumes a heroic stature at the end when, casting aside his doubts and timorous desires, he resolutely renounces his mundane attachments and decides to roam like a "lone swan" in this floating world. The delineation of delicate and yet poignant emotions, the novelty of a Sino-Japanese love affair, and the theme of the conflict between love and religion made the novel an instant success.

S.'s other literary works include the collection of miscellaneous writings *Yen-tzu-han sui-pi* (1913; random notes from a swallow's mausoleum). Although written in traditional style, these notes differ from their prototypes in content and substance. Their interest lies in the author's knowledge of Western languages and literatures, his familiarity with Sanskrit and with India, and his experiences in Japan and southeast Asia.

A "Sino-Japanese genius," S. bridged the cultural gap between China and Japan and contributed to the development of East-West literary relations, as well as to Chinese knowledge of Western literature through his translations of Hugo's *Les misérables* and poetry by Byron, Shelley, and others. His works were immensely popular and influential from the 1920s to the 1940s; his melancholy, romantic mood fascinated the young people of that period. S.'s writing occupies a prominent place in the literature of 20th-c. China.

FURTHER WORKS: *Wen-hsüeh yin-yüan* (1908); *Ch'ao-yin* (1911); *Han-Ying san-mei chi* (1914); *S. M. ch'üan-chi* (5 vols., 1928–31); *S. M. ta-shih chi-nien chi* (1943)

BIBLIOGRAPHY: McAleavy, H., *S. M.: A Sino-Japanese Genius* (1960); Liu Wu-chi, *S. M.* (1970); Lee, L., *The Romantic Generation of Modern Chinese Writers* (1973), pp. 58–78

LIU WU-CHI

TING LING

(pseud. of Chiang Ping-chih) Chinese novelist and short-story writer, b. 1904?, Li-ling, Hunan Province*

Born into a small-town landowning family, T. L. lived with her widowed mother until adolescence, when she left home for Shanghai, where she

*Ting Ling died 4 March 1986, Peking.

was exposed to new, revolutionary ideas. In 1930 she became a member of the League of Leftist Writers, headed by Lu Hsün (q.v.). Two years later she joined the Chinese Communist Party. She was arrested and imprisoned from 1933 to 1936. During the Sino-Japanese War (1937–45) she went to Yenan and was active in the Communist literary circle. When the Communists came to power in 1949, she was the leading writer of the new regime. Her international fame and her high position in the Communist literary hierarchy, however, did not prevent her from being purged as a revisionist in 1957. She disappeared from the Chinese literary scene until her reemergence in 1979.

T. L.'s early stories and novels (1927–30) are noted for their bold depictions of youthful love and the conflict between body and mind. The short story "So-fei nü-shih ti jih-chi" (1928; "The Diary of Miss Sophia," 1974) is an outcry of the agonizing soul of a "new woman" fighting for emancipation from the rigid traditional conventions governing relationships between the sexes in China. Its frank revelation of the protagonist's passionate sexuality startled the Chinese literary world of that time. The conflict between love and revolution is the theme of the novels *Wei Hu* (1930; Wei Hu) and *I-chiu san-ling nien ch'un Shang-hai* (1930; Shanghai, spring 1930), in both of which the young protagonist sacrifices love for the revolutionary cause.

The novella *Shui* (1931; *The Flood*, 1936), first published in *Pei-tou*, a literary organ of the League of Leftist Writers edited by T. L. herself, marks the beginning of her second phase (1931–36), the main goal of which was to present the life of the peasant masses. *Shui* is a powerful story of the struggle during a devastating flood of a group of destitute villagers, who later turn into a revolutionary force "fiercer than the flood." The work has no outstanding individual characters but portrays the masses as a composite protagonist. Since T. L. had no actual experience and contact with the peasants, however, her descriptions and characterizations are superficial, and she was criticized for her brand of romantic revolutionism.

This failure in her early attempt at Socialist Realism T. L. remedied in *T'ai-yang chao tsai Sang-kan-ho shang* (1948; *The Sun Shines over the Sangkan River*, 1954), the major novel of her third period (1937–57). Living among the peasants in Communist-controlled areas in north China, T. L. personally witnessed and actively participated in land-reform work in 1946 and 1947. The novel, which won the Stalin Prize, is a realistic presentation of the class struggle between peasants and landlords in a farming village, the breaking up of the feudal landowning system in Chinese society on the eve of the Communist victory, and the vital role of the Party cadres in land reform. Here again the protagonists are groups of peasants and Party workers. For its successful creation of new heroic images, for its fidelity to life, and for its artistry, the novel has been hailed by Communist critics as an "epic of our great land reform." It has been translated into thirteen languages.

In addition to fiction, T. L. wrote numerous essays, war reports, biographical sketches, and plays. In the critical essay "Life and Creative Writing" (1957), published in the Peking English-language periodical *Chinese Literature,* she urges writers to "go out to experience life" and, in keeping with the Party directive, to live among the masses and establish friendly relations with them.

The "correctness" of her ideology notwithstanding, T. L., once dubbed the "woman warrior of New China," eventually incurred the displeasure of Party authorities by her independent spirit and, perhaps, by her arrogance. For more than twenty years she was thrown into the limbo of ignominy until she was rehabilitated in early 1979. The announcement that she was working on a selected-works volume and a sequel to *T'ai-yang chao tsai Sang-kan-ho shang* perhaps signals a relaxation of government control over literature, although to date she has published nothing more of significance.

FURTHER WORKS: *Tsai heh-an chung* (1928); *Tzu-sha jih-chi* (1929); *I-ko nü-hsing* (1930); *Yeh-hui* (1933); *Mu-ch'in* (1933); *I-wai chi* (1936); *I-k'o wei-ch'u-t'ang ti chiang-tang* (1939); *T'uan-chü* (1940); *Wo tsai Hsia-ts'un ti shih-hou* (1946; *When I Was in Sha Chuan, and Other Stories,* 1946); *Yao-kung* (1949); *T. L. wen-chi* (1949); *K'ua-tao hsin ti shih-tai lai* (1951); *T. L. hsüan-chi* (1952); *Yen-an chi* (1954); *T. L. tuan-p'ien hsiao-shuo* (1954); *T. L. ming-chu hsüan* (1965)

BIBLIOGRAPHY: Feng Hsüeh-feng, Introduction to *The Sun Shines over the Sangkan River* (1954), pp. 335–46; Hsia, C. T., *A History of Modern Chinese Fiction* (1971), pp. 262–72, 484–92; Nieh, H., *Shen Ts'ung-wen* (1972), pp. 46–64; Feuerwerker, Y. M., "The Changing Relationship between Literature and Life: Aspects of the Writer's Role in Ding Ling," in Goldman, M., ed., *Modern Chinese Literature in the May Fourth Era* (1977), pp. 281–307; Feuerwerker, Y. M., *Ding Ling's Fiction: Ideology and Narrative in Modern Chinese Literature* (1982)

LIU WU-CHI

TS'AO Yü

(pseud. of Wan Chia-pao) Chinese dramatist, b. 26 Oct. 1910, Tientsin

Son of a well-to-do military official, T. obtained an early initiation in Western-style spoken drama while in high school, cultivating a special interest in Ibsen, Galsworthy, and Molière. After entering Tsinghua University in Peking in 1930, he expanded his technical and literary knowledge by studying the works of Gorky, Chekhov, Shaw, O'Neill, Euripides, Aeschylus, and others. Upon graduation, T. taught English at various colleges throughout China, and after the Sino-Japanese War (1937–45) worked as a scriptwriter for films. Since the beginning of the Communist regime in 1949, T. has given active support to the Party's literary policies, holding several key posts in the state bureaucracy. He is at present head of the Peking People's Art Theater.

T.'s plays reflect a continuing struggle to find the means for regenerating the Chinese spirit in the midst of war and national modernization. His first three plays—*Lei-yü* (1934; *Thunder and Rain,* 1936; later tr., *Thunderstorm,* 1958); *Jih-ch'u* (1936; *The Sunrise,* 1940), and *Yüan-yeh* (1937; *The Wilderness,* 1979)—which are often considered a trilogy, demonstrate the beginning of a philosophical ripening for T., combining Western and Chinese thought. In *Lei-yü* he uses Hellenic fate—what T. has called "cosmic cruelty"—and the Aristotelian form of tragedy to examine frustrated love, adultery, and revenge in an oppressively traditional middle-class Chinese family. In *Jih-ch'u,* a story of men and women prostituting themselves to a corrupt system for the sake of false freedom and short-term gain, T. hints at a Taoistic truth: man is subject to the disinterested dynamics of a Godless universe, with which he must harmonize or else perish. Finally, in *Yüan-yeh,* which tells of an escaped convict taking revenge on the landlord clan that ruined his family, T. recapitulates and blends the themes of *Lei-yü* and *Jih-ch'u* into a Promethean protagonist *manqué.* By adding an expressionism that T. borrowed from O'Neill's *The Emperor Jones,* T. created a notable cross-cultural fusion of ideas and forms.

If the trilogy represented a period of philosophical growth for T. and highlighted the inequities of Chinese society in the Republican era, the remainder of T.'s plays before 1949 turned more to the objective changes that must occur for China to regain its strength.

For example, *Pei-ching jen* (1941; Peking man), which is perhaps literarily the most sophisticated of T.'s works, presents a moving profile of a declining gentry family in Peking, the members of which are forced to decide how they should each reconcile the demands of tradition with those of modernity. And in T.'s last pre-Communist play, *Ch'iao* (1946; bridge), idealistic industrial engineers, in their conflict with self-seeking government officials after the war, show in concrete terms the need not only for a new spirit of sacrifice and national pride but also for innovative management techniques and a commitment to change. Although flawed artistically, *Ch'iao*, in its social-political message, is possibly the most mature of T.'s dramas.

T.'s plays after 1949, like those of other hopeful Republican playwrights who sided with the Communists, suffer artistically from Maoist literary strictures. One exception, perhaps, is *Tan chien p'ien* (1961; gall and sword), a historical play based on the traditional tale of Kou-chien, king of Yüeh (5th c. B.C.), avenging his defeat by Fu-ch'a, king of Wu, after many years of patient preparation. Although a play intended to illustrate the politically correct theme that a weak, oppressed nation such as China can eventually prevail over its imperialist overlords, T.'s skill in characterization and plot design makes this work extraordinary among usually mediocre Communist dramas.

There is little question that T.'s early plays place him among the best playwrights that China has produced in the 20th c. His talent for combining complex philosophical visions from both China and the West has made him a remarkable contributor to world literature. At the same time, by dramatizing the ideal of spiritual renascence in China, he was able to objectify his own people's dreams for fulfillment during a time of momentous national change.

FURTHER WORKS: *Hei tzu erh-shih-pa* (written 1938, with Sung Chih-ti, pub. 1945); *Cheng tsai hsiang* (1940); *Shui-pien* (1940); *Chia* (1942); *Yen-yang t'ien* (1948); *Ming-lang ti t'ien* (1954; *Bright Skies*, 1960); *Ying ch'un chi* (1958); *Wang Chao-chün* (1978)

BIBLIOGRAPHY: Ch'en, D. Y., "The Trilogy of T. Y. and Western Drama," in Frenz, H., ed., *Asia and the Humanities* (1959), pp. 26–37; Ch'en, D. Y., "*The Hairy Ape* and *The Peking Man:* Two Types of Primitivism in Modern Society," YCGL, 15 (1966), 214–20; Ch'en, D. Y., "The Chinese Adaptation of Eugene O'Neill's *The Emperor Jones,*" MD, 9 (1967), 431–39; Lau, J. S. M., *T. Y., the Reluctant Disciple of Chekhov and O'Neill: A Study in Literary Influence* (1970); Hu, J. Y. H., *T. Y.* (1972); Rand, C. C., Introduction to T. Y., *The Wilderness* (1979), pp. vi–l

CHRISTOPHER C. RAND

WEN I-to

Chinese poet, scholar, and critic, b. 24 Nov. 1899, Hsi-shui, Hupeh Province; d. 15 July 1946, Kunming, Yunan Province

Born into a traditional scholar's family, W. nonetheless received a modern, Western-style education at the Tsing Hua School in Peking (1913–21). There he came under the spell of English romantic poetry, especially the works of John Keats, his spiritual mentor. During the May Fourth (1919) Movement, he played only a minor role in the student attacks on China's feudal past and demands for the use of the vernacular language as a medium for serious literature.

In 1922 W. came to study in the U.S., where he remained for three years, enrolling first at the Art Institute of Chicago and later at Colorado College. After returning to China, W. taught Western literature at the Wusung Political Academy near Shanghai and at the Central University in Nanking. From 1928 to 1937 he taught Chinese literature at several universities, including his alma mater, Tsing Hua. For three years (1926–29) he was closely associated with Hsü Chih-mo (q.v.), with whom he founded the Crescent Moon Society, which published an influential monthly literary magazine. This society, which included Hu Shih (q.v.) and Liang Shih-ch'iu (b. 1901), served to check the growth of realism among writers; it fiercely championed the supremacy of form and technique for writing *pai-hua*, or vernacular, poetry.

Although W. published only two slim volumes of poetry during his life—*Hung-chu* (1923; *Red Candle,* 1972) and *Szu-shui* (1928; dead water)—he had an enormous influence on modern Chinese poetry. The first volume consists mostly of poems on nature and reflections on art, literature, and life. They are characterized by rich symbolism, by W.'s heavy reliance on synesthesia, and by his unrelenting concern with form through his invention of a predominantly ten-syllable, end-stopped verse line. The influence of classical Chinese poets such as Wang Wei (701–761), Li Po (701–762), and Li Shang-yin (813?–858) is strongly evident in W.'s verse.

Szu-shui offers a greater variety of stanzaic patterns, as well as a shift of emphasis in the subject matter. As indicated in the title poem, the poems in this volume focus on the uglier aspects of life and attest to the poet's frustration over the fate of a disunited China. Subjects include the tragedy of student demonstrations, the gloom of a war-torn village, death, and the sense of the futility of intellectuals.

Finding the Crescent Society's commitment to pure beauty unsatisfying, W. turned to the study of classical Chinese literature and published many volumes of critical studies, which are still held in high repute. Among them are annotated chronologies of Tu Fu (712–770) and Ts'en Shen (715–770); several commentaries on two classics of Chinese poetry, the *Shih ching* (book of songs), the earliest anthology of Chinese poetry, compiled by Confucius, and the *Ch'u tz'u* (song of Ch'u), the second oldest anthology in Chinese, originally ascribed to Ch'ü Yuan (d. 278 B.C.); two anthologies of early Chinese verse; a compendium of T'ang poetry; and an anthology of modern Chinese verse.

W. was always open to the appreciation of new forms of poetry. As late as 1943, in the famous essay "Shih-tai te ku-shou" ("The Drummer of the Age," 1947), he hailed the poetry of T'ien Chien (b. 1914), whose declamatory verse, usually in short staccato lines, was inspired by the poetry of Vladimir Mayakovsky. Although this poetry is very different from the poetry of Keats, whom W. so much admired, the drum, W. points out, is a more fitting expression of a war-torn China than the delicate sound of a lute, which belonged to another era.

Although up to the last moment of his life W. dedicated his energy and talents to his twin passions for beauty and truth, he never retreated into a poet's ivory tower or denied the responsibility of an artist in society. The 1938 long trek during the Sino-Japanese War, in which he walked more than a thousand miles from Changsha to Kunming with colleagues and students who were being evacuated from coastal cities; the plight of refugees and conscripted soldiers he saw on the road; and the general living conditions during the Sino-Japanese War rekindled in him a sense of political mission. In 1945 he joined the Democratic League, then a third force trying to negotiate between the Kuomintang, dominated by Chiang Kai-shek, and the Chinese Communist Party, led by Mao Tse-tung. W. refused to flee Kunming when a prominent member of the Democratic League was assassinated; instead he stayed and, at the memorial service on 15 July 1946, delivered a ringing speech denouncing political killings. A few hours later, in front of his house, W. himself was felled by the bullets of assassins.

FURTHER WORKS: *W. I. ch'üan-chi* (4 vols., 1948)

BIBLIOGRAPHY: Lin, J. C., ed., *Modern Chinese Poetry: An Introduction* (1972), pp. 75–100; Hsü, K., *W. I.* (1980)

IRVING YUCHENG LO

INDONESIAN LITERATURE

In 1928 the Second Congress of Indonesian Youth proclaimed Malay, which had been for centuries the lingua franca of the region, the language of the Indonesian nationalist movement. The language, since known as Indonesian (*Bahasa Indonesia*), is today the republic's official language and the principal vehicle for innovative literary expression.

The history of modern Indonesian literature must be viewed against the traditional literatures in regional languages. Many traditional theatrical genres remain vigorous. Djakartan *lenong* drama and Javanese *ludrug* are predominantly urban and contemporary in character, while Balinese *gong* drama, Javanese *ketoprak*, Sundanese *gending karesmen,* and Minangkabau *randai* present performances modernized to varying degrees of mainly historical stories.

Attempts at writing modern literature have been made in most of Indonesia's major regional languages, with Javanese and Sundanese exhibiting the greatest fecundity. Writing in these languages differs in some fundamental respects from that in Indonesian. Literature in Indonesian is governed by the values of the urban middle class, is influenced by foreign literatures, appears in expensive, hard-to-get books, and is written in a language most people do not use in their homes and do not learn until they go to school. By contrast, literature in the regional languages tends to deal more with life in rural areas or provincial towns, is stylistically more lively and linguistically more accessible to readers for whom the language concerned is their mother tongue. Regional literatures make more unself-conscious reference to the corpus of symbols, allusions, and literary conventions peculiar to certain regions and already familiar to readers there. Regional literature appears predominantly in magazines, which makes it cheaper and easier to obtain.

In Indonesian

Fiction

Fiction in Indonesian began toward the end of the 19th c. Three main streams contributed to its genesis: popular tales (*penglipur lara*) and narrative verse (*syair*) in Malay, Chinese romances of love and the martial arts, and melodramatic romances in Dutch. Early novels were predominantly romantic melodramas spiced with sensational crimes and supernatural occurrences, but soon a more serious strain of social criticism and nationalist sentiment appeared.

In 1908 the Netherlands Indies government established a state commission for reading matter in vernacular languages, later known as the Balai Pustaka publishing house. In the 1920s and 1930s Balai Pustaka encouraged the writing of fiction, but its editors carefully vetted manuscripts for what they regarded as politically or morally contentious content and insisted on a somewhat pedantic style.

Despite alterations at the insistence of Balai Pustaka, *Salah asuhan* (1928; a wrong upbringing) by nationalist activist Abdoel Moeis (1898–1959) remains the outstanding achievement of early Indonesian fiction. Racism and the question of cultural identity are the themes pursued with fluent passion in this narrative of a Dutch-educated Indonesian whose admiration for European society renders him contemptuous of his own people. The interaction of Indonesian and European value systems is, in fact, a consistent theme in preindependence novels.

In *Layar terkembang* (1936; sails unfurled), Sutan Takdir Alisjahbana (q.v.) contrasts two sisters, one independent, earnest, and an activist in the women's welfare movement, the other carefree, dreamy, and feminine in the traditional fashion. Takdir criticizes what he sees as the debilitating tendency of Indonesians to glorify the achievements and institutions of the past. *Belenggu* (1940; shackles) by Armijn Pane (1908–1970) also juxtaposes two women, one Western-educated and busily involved in social welfare work, the other a self-sacrificing prostitute who excels in the domestic arts and in singing traditional songs.

Possibly the most original and brilliantly executed work of preindependence fiction is *Sukreni, gadis Bali* (1936; Sukreni, virgin of Bali) by Anak Agung Pandji Tisna (1908–1978). Utilizing the symbols and conventions of traditional Balinese theater, Pandji Tisna portrays the destructive effect of contemporary commercial ethics on Balinese society. The fragility of traditional values is also the theme of *Atheis* (1949; *Atheis,* 1972) by Achdiat Karta Mihardja (q.v.), in which a young man from rural west Java finds that his mystically tinged Islamic faith crumbles before the materialism, Marxism, and atheism of urban radicals.

The Japanese occupation (1942–45) and Indonesia's armed struggle for independence from the Netherlands (1945–49) swept away the romanticism and dilettante nationalism of the contributors to the elite literary journal *Pujangga baru*. Disillusionment and a note of tough realism became evident in the fiction of the late 1940s and 1950s. The short-story writer Idrus (1921–1979), together with the novelist and short-story writer Pramoedya Ananta Toer (q.v.), wrought a revolution in prose style, replacing prewar formality and archness with an expressive but terse and colloquial style.

For both Idrus and Pramoedya, the Japanese occupation and the revolutionary war provided both the setting for their major works and the touchstone against which the characters in these works are tried. Idrus's influential early stories, laced with cynicism and sardonic humor, are collected in *Dari Ave Maria ke jalan lain ke Roma* (1948; from Ave Maria to another road to Rome). Pramoedya's novels are unmatched for their somber exploration of man's alienation and disillusion in the midst of war. *Keluarga gerilya* (1950; guerrilla family) depicts a family that, like Indonesian society, is split geographically and in political allegiance by the revolutionary war. *Bukan pasar malam* (1951; *It's Not an All Night Fair,* 1973) explores the essential loneliness of the human condition, catching the mood of dislocation and dispiritedness that marked the immediate postrevolutionary period.

While the revolutionary war and nationalism remained prominent themes in the fiction of the 1950s, writers increasingly turned their attention to the young republic's burden of social ills. The kaleidoscopic *Senja di Jakarta* (pub. 1964; *Twilight in Jakarta,* 1963) by Mochtar Lubis (b. 1922) is a mosaic of images contrasting Djakarta's corrupt rich with its helpless poor. Achdiat's collection of short stories *Keretakan dan ketegangan* (1956; fissures and tensions) turns a jaundiced eye on the country's hypocritical politicians and nouveaux riches.

From the late 1950s to the mid-1960s literary life was dominated by the conflict between leftist insistence on the social and political utility of art, and liberal insistence on the possibility of divorce between art and organized politics. Before the October 1, 1965, incident (a power grab in which right-wing forces emerged victorious), leftist pressure forced many liberal writers into silence, but after 1965 the tables were turned. A number of writers with leftist sympathies disappeared or were imprisoned and their works banned.

Curiously, the ideological conflict of the 1960s left popular fiction largely untouched. Fueled by newly created mass literacy and accompanied by a decline in the authority of elite literary magazines, popular publishing boomed in the late 1960s and throughout the 1970s. A leading figure in this boom was Motinggo Boesye (b. 1937), whose many novels combine a highly readable narrative style with mild sexual titillation and satirical observation of the urban middle class. Fiction by women writers swelled in quantity and quality. *Pada sebuah kapal* (1973; on a ship) by Nh. Dini (b. 1936) chronicles with rare sensitivity a young woman's disengagement from allegiance to traditional social and marital roles. The question of national identity, hitherto an almost inevitable element in fiction, virtually disappeared in the works of younger writers but remained prominent in those of the older generation. Sutan Takdir Alisjahbana's *Kalah dan menang* (1978; defeat and victory) explores Indonesia's cultural options against the background of Japan's wartime occupation, rejecting fascism and the authoritarianism of tradition for liberal values adopted from Western Europe. In a short novel, *Sri Sumarah* (1975; Sri Sumarah), Umar Kayam (b. 1932) vividly and sympathetically conveys the spirit of traditional Javanese culture and affirms its continuing relevance in the emerging national culture. Alienation attendant upon cultural deracination and urban life styles brought the appearance of absurdist fiction. *Ziarah* (1969; *The Pilgrim*, 1975) by Iwan Simatupang (1928–1970) is a Kafkaesque study of the encounter between the anarchic artist and the social reality of Indonesia.

Following his release from prison in 1979 Pramoedya Ananta Toer published *Bumi manusia* (1980; man's earth), a novel of epic proportions that traces in its central figure the first stirrings of a distinctly modern Indonesian consciousness in the early years of this century. Despite, or perhaps because of, its enthusiastic popular reception, the book was banned by the government in mid-1981.

Poetry

Distinctly innovative poetry began to appear in Indonesia in the 1910s. The European sonnet form was especially popular, but the influence of traditional verse forms remained strong. The poetry of the 1920s and 1930s was marked by an intense and largely reflective romanticism.

Arguably Indonesia's greatest modern poet, and certainly the most prominent figure in preindependence poetry, was Amir Hamzah (1911–1946), whose work is collected in two small volumes, *Nyanyi sunyi* (1937; songs of silence) and *Buah rindu* (1941; fruits of longing). Amir's best poetry expresses the agony of doubt about his Islamic faith.

The iconoclastic verse of Chairil Anwar (q.v.) released Indonesian poetry from the bonds of traditional forms and literary language, exerting a profound influence on postindependence poetry. His works convey a powerful, vitalistic individualism.

Sitor Situmorang (b. 1923) was strongly influenced by Chairil. A sojourn in Europe inspired his early work, represented most notably in the collection *Surat kertas hijau* (1953; a letter on green paper), which reveals an unquiet personality burdened with moral doubts and guilt, nostalgic for the Indonesian homeland. Like Pramoedya Ananta Toer and a number of other writers, Sitor became attracted to socialism in the late 1950s, and his poetry changed markedly. His *Zaman baru* (1961; new era) records the impact upon him of a visit to China. The anguished subjectivism of his earlier work disappeared, to be replaced with unequivocal praise of socialist ideals and achievements.

Zaman baru typifies the unadorned, politically committed verse of the 1960s. After the demise of the Indonesian Communist Party in 1965, the spare and strident poetry of protest against exploitation of workers and peasants gave way to equally strident protests against the illiberalism, economic bungling, and rhetorical humbug of the preceding years. Much poetry of the 1960s and 1970s was strikingly public in character, and no poet more dominated the public scene in the 1970s than the charismatic Rendra (b. 1935). His collections *Blues untuk Bonnie* (1971; *Indonesian Poet in New York*, 1971) and *Pamflet penyair* (1978; *State of Emergency*, 1980) are preeminently declamatory. They contain hard-hitting, sometimes crudely worded attacks on misuse of authority and the degradation of the poor at the hands of the rich.

Drama

Most plays of the 1920s and 1930s were ponderous historical dramas or allegories of nationalist struggle and colonial oppression. The Japanese occupation produced an upsurge of interest in more realistic dramas of everyday life, but neither these plays nor those of the prewar period are today of any more than academic interest.

Utuy Tatang Sontani (1920–1979) was the first Indonesian dramatist to gain wide recognition. His early plays, most notably *Bunga rumah makan* (1948; ornament of the restaurant) and *Awal dan Mira* (1952; Awal and Mira), are concerned with the possible avenues for dignified living open to ordinary individuals in the midst of a society obsessed with false and empty values. After aligning himself with the political left Utuy wrote *Si Sapar* (1964; Sapar) and *Si Kampeng* (1964; Kampeng), two short plays that treat class differences and exploitation, employing a style in which caricature is of paramount importance.

Drama in the 1970s was dominated, on the one hand, by the immensely popular satirical plays of Rendra, and, on the other, by the absurdist works of Arifin C. Noer (b. 1941) and Putu Wijaya (b. 1944). Rendra's *Kisah perjuangan suku Naga* (1975; *The Struggle of the Naga Tribe*, 1979) is a brilliantly funny condemnation of the Indonesian elite's economic and cultural dependence on foreigners. The play is thoroughly modern, but it draws upon the conventions of the traditional Javanese shadow play, thereby emphasizing in its form the theme of cultural autonomy that lies at its heart. Arifin C. Noer's *Kapai-kapai* (1970; *Moths*, 1974) is a crazy pastiche of episodes, sometimes macabre and mystical, dramatizing one man's suffering and his escape into unreality.

In Javanese

Fiction in Javanese (the language of central and east Java) is characterized by three somewhat overlapping streams. The *priyayi* (aristocratic and official class) stream is dedicated largely to the defense of aristocratic values and status in the face of social mobility and creeping egalitarianism. It is indebted to the belletristic writing of the Javanese courts and emphasizes refinement, etiquette, mystical knowledge, and mastery of formal Javanese. *Rangsang Tuban* (1913; song of Tuban) by Padmasusastra (1843–1926) is an early masterpiece of this type. Ostensibly a historical novel, it in fact gives complex expression to *kabatinan*, the characteristically Javanese form of mysticism. *Serat Riyanta* (1920; Riyanto's story) by Sulardi (1888–19??), often called the first true novel in Javanese, utilizes the conventional love romance to express aristocratic ideals. In *Ngulandara* (1936; wanderlust), Margana Djajaatmadja (dates n.a.) affirms the superiority of the *priyayi* by fashioning a contemporary transmutation of the traditional Panji romance of courtly love, while *Anteping tekad* (1975; unshakable determination) by Ag. Suharti (b. 1920) defends the *priyayi* ethic in a non-Javanese, postindependence context.

The second stream of writing, the popular, seems to be preoccupied with forging a sense of security and identity in the newly emergent lower middle class. Written, since its rise in the 1930s, at the informal level of Javanese, popular fiction has been much indebted to popular novels in Indonesian, especially those by Chinese-Indonesian authors. Popular theater, too, has been influential in this stream. The novel *Sala peteng* (1938; darkness in Solo) by Mt. Suphardi (b. 1913) has a plot strikingly similar to those of Javanese *ludrug* stage melodramas. The theme of unwitting incest, common in popular Javanese fiction, suggests that *Sala peteng* and similar novels are appealing for the preservation of the traditional family unit in the midst of fragmenting social change. The prolific giants of the postindependence romance were Any Asmara (b. 1913) and Widi Widajat (b. 1928), both of whose works are highly formulaic and strongly influenced by the conventions of oral narrative and popular theater.

Writers in the third, or "modernist," stream have sought to develop a prose style at once expressively literary yet close to colloquial usage. Unlike *priyayi* and popular writers, they evince strong interest in individualized characterization and taut structure. The romantic but frequently somber short stories of St. (Sulistyoutami) Iesmaniasita (b. 1933), in her collections *Kidung wengi ing gunung gamping* (1958; nocturne in the limestone hills) and *Kalimput ing pedhut* (1976; veiled in mist), are noteworthy for their vivid portraits of village and urban middle-class women. *Lara lapane kaum republik* (1967; agony and sacrifice in the republican cause) by Suparto Brata (b. 1932) is a down-to-earth and wryly humorous story of the revolution. Sudharma K. D. (1934–1980) and Esmiet (b. 1938) address the problem of economic development in the Javanese cultural context. Esmiet's *Tunggaktunggak jati* (1977; trunks of teak) examines the impact upon a rural community of the alliance between an unscrupulous Chinese businessman and corrupt community leaders.

Innovative poetry in Javanese has developed vigorously since Indonesia's independence. It has been dominated by St. Iesmaniasita and by Muryalelana (b. 1932), whose verse is mostly inward-looking. Modern stage drama has not developed significantly in Javanese, but the radio plays of Soemardjono (b. 1925), some of which are adaptations from European sources and others romances of his own creation, gained a huge following in the 1960s and 1970s.

In Sundanese

Preindependence fiction in Sundanese (the language of inland west Java) is almost synonymous with the name of Mohamad Ambri (1892–1936). His interest in rural life, particularly rural religious practices, is the common thread of his novels. *Ngawadalkeun nyawa* (1932; self-sacrifice) gives an absorbing portrait of life in a rural Islamic academy (*pesantren*), while *Munjung* (1932; homage) demonstrates how Sundanese villagers make sense of cash-based commerce by relating it to the demonic figures of the spirit world.

Mohamad Ambri's prose style has exercised an enormous influence on later writers. Some of his novels consist almost entirely of dialogue, in colloquial, unadorned, yet remarkably expressive language. Among postindependence writers indebted to him is Ki Umbara (pseud. of Wirdja Ranulaksana, b. 1914), whose collection of short stories *Diwadalkeun ka siluman* (1965; sacrificed to demons) explores some of the darker corners of Sundanese folk religion. By contrast, the novel *Manehna* (1965; she) by Sjarif Amin (pseud. of Mohamad Koerdie, b. 1907) is a lyrical, sometimes painfully nostalgic evocation of the Sundanese world of the author's youth.

Haji Hasan Mustapa (1852–1930) wrote poetry in traditional forms, but brought to his work a new spirit of individualism and innovation. Like Mohamad Ambri, he did not hesitate to make creative use of colloquial Sundanese, raising the poetic forms of folk narrative and children's songs to a new level of seriousness. Only in the 1950s did Sundanese poetry directly face contemporary society and achieve release from traditional verse forms. In the work of Sajudi (dates n.a.) Sundanese poetry found a powerful voice. In his collection *Lalaki di tegal pati* (1963; a man on the field of battle) he pays tribute to the heroic spirit of old Sunda, but also writes lyrically of love, patriotism, and the sufferings of the weak in postindependence Indonesian society. Allusions to the Sundanese past and a prominent note of romanticism are evident too in the works of Surachman R. M. (b. 1936) and the prolific Wahyu Wibisana (b. 1935). Wayhu Wibisana, together with Utuy Tatang Sontani and short-story writer Rachmatullah Ading Affandie (usually abbreviated R. A. F., b. 1929), have gained some recognition as playwrights, but by and large modern stage drama in Sundanese has been infertile.

In Minangkabau and Balinese

Of the other regional literatures, west Sumatran Minangkabau and Balinese writing have displayed promising stirrings of innovation. The traditional Minangkabau *kaba*—a romantic narrative in rhythmic prose—has been transformed by a few writers into a popular comic genre making satirical comment on contemporary life. Innovative verse has flourished in the lyrics of popular songs.

In the Balinese language two novels have appeared: *Nemu karma* (1931; punished by fate) by Wayan Gobiah (dates n.a.) and *Mlancaran ka Sasak* (1939; rev. ed. 1978; journey to Lombok) by Gde Srawana (dates n.a.). Both are romances, the former marked by the theme of karmatic retribution, the latter remarkable for its humor and its lively, earthy style. Stimulated by government and privately sponsored competitions, Balinese writers turned their attention to the short story in the late 1960s and 1970s. The stories in the collection *Katemu ring Tampaksiring* (1975; meeting at Tampaksiring) by Made Sanggra (b. 1926) examine the fate of the poor in Bali, but also touch on the persistence of traumatic memories in those who experienced the revolutionary war. In the anthology of poetry *Ganda sari* (1973; scent and blossoms) Made Sanggra and Nyoman Manda (b. 1938) display an idealistic but almost prosaic interest in the impact of economic development on Balinese society.

In Chinese-Indonesian

Chinese have lived in Indonesia from earliest historical times. In the second half of the 19th c. migration from China swelled, and many of the descendants of these migrants adopted the languages and cultures of their new home while still maintaining a distinctly Chinese identity. In the first half of the 20th c. the Chinese dialect of Indonesian became the vehicle for a lively literature.

Toward the end of the 19th c. Chinese-Indonesian writers adopted the traditional Malay *syair* verse form, using it for narratives of contemporary events and for romantic stories. An early and accomplished exponent of the *syair* was Lie Kim-hok (1853–1912), whose *Sair cerita Siti Akbari* (1884; the story of Siti Akbari), a legendary romance set in India, became the most admired work of the genre. Lie Kim-hok's many detective stories also played a key role in establishing the viability of prose fiction in this dialect. The finest Chinese-Indonesian novelist was Liem King-hoo (dates n.a.); in *Berjuang* (1934; struggle) and *Masyarakat* (1939; community) he analyzes the character and social role of Indonesia's Chinese, urging them to search for a humane, socialistic alternative to capitalism.

Indonesia's independence brought the death of the Chinese-Indonesian dialect as a literary language, but the spirit of Chinese-Indonesian literature lived on in the immensely popular works of Asmaraman Sukowati (previously Kho Ping Hoo, b. 1926) and Marga T. (previously Tjoa Liang Tjoe, b. 1943). Marga's *Gema sebuah hati* (1976; echoes in a heart) is a romantic and melodramatic novel depicting the lives of Chinese-Indonesian students caught in the conflicting loyalties and political turmoil of Djakarta in 1965.

In Dutch

Although Dutch was for hundreds of years the upper-echelon language of administration and commerce in Indonesia, indigenous Indonesians did not find it a congenial vehicle for literary expression. Among the few exceptions was Kartini (1879–1904), whose eloquent letters of protest against colonial paternalism and the feudal oppression of women were collected and published posthumously in *Door duisternis tot licht* (1911; *Letters of a Javanese Princess*, 1921). The most substantial work of fiction in Dutch by an Indonesian author is the novel *Buiten het gareel* (1940; out of harness) by Suwarsih Djojopuspito (1912–1978). It is a sensitive portrayal of day-to-day strains in the marriage and work of an educated woman.

Romance, interest in Oriental exotica, and, most recently, intense nostalgia for the colonial past are the hallmarks of the Indies novel by Dutch writers. A few outstanding works, however, echo the impassioned brilliance of Multatuli's (pseud. of Eduard Douwes Dekker, 1820–1887) *Max Havelaar* (1860; *Max Havelaar*, 1868; new trs., 1927, 1967) and capture the essence of Dutch colonial society with its special Indies character and its ambivalent attitude toward its Indonesian subjects. One such work is the novel *De stille kracht* (1900; *The Hidden Force*, 1922) by Louis Couperus (1863–1923), which superbly catches the superciliousness of Dutch officialdom in confrontation with the incomprehensible yet tangible power of Javanese culture. The works of Madelon Hermina Székely-Lulofs (a.k.a. Madelon Lulofs, 1899–1958), among them the popular *Rubber* (1931; *Rubber*, 1933) and *Koelie* (1932; *Coolie*, 1936), attack colonialism, especially as it manifested itself in the exploitative plantation enterprises of North Sumatra. The novel of nostalgia is raised to high art in the works of Maria Dermoût (1888–1962). Her *De tienduizend dingen* (1956; *The Ten Thousand Things*, 1958) is a justly praised evocation of colonial society in a remote corner of eastern Indonesia. The pithy short stories of Vincent Mahieu (a.k.a. Tjalie Robinson, pseuds. of Jan Boon, 1911–1974) are collected in *Tjies* (1954; pea rifle) and *Tjoek* (1960; constriction). Using dialect and the imagery of hunting and boxing, they conjure up the tough world of the Indonesian Eurasian.

The poet Notosoeroto (1888–1951), a Javanese, and Getrudes Johannes Resink (b. 1911), a Eurasian, were influenced by the neoromanticism of late-19th-c. European verse. But Notosoeroto's collection *Wayang-liederen* (1931; songs of the shadow play) and Resink's *Kreeft en steenbok* (1963; Cancer and Capricorn) both reveal an outlook profoundly colored by Javanese mysticism.

BIBLIOGRAPHY: Raffel, B., *The Development of Modern Indonesian Poetry* (1967); Nieuwenhuys, R., *Oost-Indische Spiegel* (1973); Aveling, H., *A Thematic History of Indonesian Poetry: 1920–1974* (1974); Balfas, M., "Modern Indonesian Literature in Brief," in Spuler, B., ed., *Handbuch der Orientalistik,* Vol. 3, Part 1 (1976), pp. 41–116; Freidus, A. J., *Sumatran Contributions to the Development of Indonesian Literature, 1920–1942* (1977); Johns, A. H., *Cultural Options and the Role of Tradition: A Collection of Essays on Modern Indonesian and Malaysian Literature* (1979); Ras, J. J., *Javanese Literature since Independence* (1979); Teeuw, A., *Modern Indonesian Literature* (2 vols., 1979)

GEORGE QUINN

ACHDIAT Karta Mihardja

Indonesian novelist, short-story writer, and dramatist, b. 6 March 1911, near Garut, Java

The marked diversity of A.'s writing reflects his social and educational background. Brought up in a rural, strongly conservative Islamic environment, he studied a variant of the Nakshbandi stream of Islamic mysticism. His formal schooling led him through a Dutch-language high school to the study of Western philosophy at the University of Indonesia. He became attracted to socialism, traveled widely overseas, and in later life taught Indonesian literature for ten years (1961–71) at the Australian National University.

A.'s reputation was immediately and firmly established with the publication of his first novel, *Atheis* (1949; *Atheis,* 1972). It deals with the failure of the mystically tinged Islam of rural Java to react resiliently to the impact of values espoused by Indonesia's new, Western-influenced urban intelligentsia. The pious and naïve young protagonist of the novel finds his Islamic faith a painfully inadequate foil to the materialism, atheism, socialism, and license of his acquaintances in the city of Bandung.

The same theme is taken up, though less poignantly, in the short story "Sensasi di puncak nyiur" (1956; "Sensations at the Top of a Coconut Tree," 1961), which appeared in the collection of short stories and short plays *Keretakan dan ketegangan* (1956; fissures and tensions). Exasperated by poverty and domestic tensions, a destitute slum dweller seeks a solution to his troubles in the traditional religious practice of meditation and ascetic withdrawal from society. With farcical and sometimes sardonic humor, A. points to the ineffectualness and incongruity of this practice in the context of contemporary society.

Keretakan dan ketegangan offers critical, sharply drawn, and often witty portraits of Indonesia's politicians and nouveaux riches. Especially memorable is the portrait in "Kisah Martini" (Martini's story) of an immature and irresponsible politician who is better able to talk to animals than to people and who cultivates women for sexual consumption in the same way he fattens pets for merciless consumption at his table.

In several short stories A. shows how the innocent victims of violence and immorality have to live with the traumatic effects of what they have experienced long after the immediate cause of their suffering has disappeared. The long-term, polluting effect of immorality is depicted as a physical presence in the lives of its victims, a kind of stain ultimately demanding its own, often violent, excision. In the vivid and grimly violent story "Belitan nasib" (a twist of fate) a villager murders the man who rapes his wife, but only later exorcises the evil effect of the rape from within himself by murdering his wife and newborn baby.

In the collection of short stories and vignettes *Kesan dan kenangan* (1961; impressions and images) A. draws upon his experiences overseas to present a patchwork view of Western society seen through Indonesian eyes. This is also a prominent ingredient in his second novel, *Debu cinta bertebaran* (1973; the scattered dust of love), which portrays the lives of expatriate Indonesians in the Australian city of Sydney on the eve of Indonesia's 1965 political upheaval.

A. has not been a prolific writer, yet the diversity of his small output makes it difficult to categorize his work. His writing is colored by fatalism and pessimism, but relieved by humor and a tentative faith in the power of love. His passionately felt novel *Atheis* deservedly stands as a major landmark in modern Indonesian literature, admired for its innovative structure, vivid characterization, and occasionally stiff but generally brilliant style. After *Keretakan dan ketegangan,* however, his work seems to suffer from a tendency to be more concerned with the perceived exotica of the West and with the unexpected twist to a story than with a satisfying exploration of themes. This later superficiality is exemplified in the revisions made in some short stories, including "Kisah Martini" and "Belitan nasib," which unquestionably diminish their power.

FURTHER WORKS: *Bentrokan dalam asmara* (1952); *Belitan nasib* (1975); *Pak Dullah in extremis* (1977); *Pembunuh dan anjing hitam* (1977); *Sensasi di puncak nyiur* (1978)

BIBLIOGRAPHY: Teeuw, A., *Modern Indonesian Literature* (1967), passim; Aveling, H., "Religion and Blasphemy in Modern Indonesian Literature," *Twentieth Century*, March 1970, 217–24; Johns, A. H., *Cultural Options and the Role of Tradition* (1979), pp. 1–18, 30–64

GEORGE QUINN

CHAIRIL Anwar

Indonesian poet, b. 26 July 1922, Medan, Sumatra; d. 28 April 1949, Djakarta

C. began to write as an adolescent, before he came to Djakarta in 1940. He had had six years of elementary school and the first two years of a Dutch-language middle school; he had no other education and nothing is known about his parents; nor did he ever have any stable means of support, other than what he could get from his writing. He was married and had a daughter. None of his early poetry survives (he says he destroyed it himself, but C. is not too much to be trusted); even some of the later poetry seems to have been fairly casually lost, or destroyed, along with a collection of short stories. He published only in periodicals during his lifetime, although there are several posthumous books.

C. lived wildly, even carelessly, but he wrote with infinite care, and with a rare ability to absorb and transform a host of influences. His use of the Indonesian language was both magical and as close to totally new as is possible: many Indonesian writers confessed that, until his work appeared, they had had no idea what Indonesian was capable of as a literary instrument. The sources of his poetry's tremendous power are his glowing, sometimes savage use of language, his divergence from traditional Indonesian themes and attitudes, his immensely fertile use of such Western writers as Rilke, T. S. Eliot, Emily Dickinson, and, of course, Edgar du Perron (1899–1940) and other modern Dutch writers; all of Indonesian writing, poetry and prose alike, was in a sense pushed bodily into the 20th c. by C. It is more than justified that the "Generation of '45" is interchangeably referred to as the "Generation of C. A."

Some of his driving power, and also one of his main themes, an obsessive concern with sex, can be seen in "Lagu biasa" (1949; "An Ordinary Song," 1962), while his wry humor, his active involvement with political and patriotic issues, as well as his ability to work the Indonesian language to its limits can be seen especially in "Persetujuan dengan bung Karno" (1948; "Agreement with Friend Soekarno," 1962).

And the soaring idealism of his affirmations is nowhere better displayed than in the final line of his most famous and most beloved poem, "Aku" (1943; "Me," 1970), a searing individualist challenge to Indonesia's communal ethic: "I want to live another thousand years."

Despite the slimness of his output—fewer than seventy poems, a handful of essays and radio addresses, and some fragmentary translations—C.'s position in Indonesian literature is and will forever be something like that of Pushkin in Russian letters. He may descend into shrillness now and then, he may posture and push drama to the point of melodrama, and he may (as he certainly did) occasionally plagiarize, but at his fierce best he is easily comparable to, say, Federico García Lorca and to Constantine Cavafy. Even his weakest verse rings; his poetry echoes and reechoes in the minds of Indonesians, making him an important social force as well as an artistic icon.

FURTHER WORKS: *Deru tjampur debu* (1949); *Kerikil tadjam, dan Jang terampas dan Jang Putus* (1951); *Tiga menguak Takdir* (1950, with Rivai Apin and Asrul Sani); *C. A., Pelopor Angkatan 45* (1956). FURTHER VOLUME IN ENGLISH: *The Complete Poetry and Prose of C.A.* (1970)

BIBLIOGRAPHY: Raffel, B., "C. A.—Indonesian Poet," *LitR*, 10 (1967), 133–57; Raffel, B., *The Development of Modern Indonesian Poetry* (1967), pp. 80–110; Aveling, H., *A Thematic History of Indonesian Poetry: 1920–1974* (1974), pp. 28–44; Johns, A. H., *Cultural Options and the Role of Tradition: A Collection of Essays on Modern Indonesian and Malaysian Literature* (1979), pp. 65–81; Teeuw, A., *Modern Indonesian Literature*, rev. ed. (1979), Vol. I, pp. 145–59

BURTON RAFFEL

PRAMOEDYA Ananta Toer

Indonesian short-story writer, novelist, essayist, and critic, b. 6 Feb. 1925, Blora, Java

The works of P., generally recognized as the master prose writer of his country, have fundamentally been shaped by his painful experiences under Dutch colonialism, Japan's occupation of Indonesia during World War II, the subsequent armed revolutionary struggle against the returning Dutch, and the many disappointments of postindependence society. The son of an embittered nationalist schoolteacher who ruined the family by obsessive gambling, P. never completed high school. As an adolescent during the Japanese occupation he worked as a stenographer; and when the revolution broke out, he joined the Indonesian armed forces. Between 1950 and 1958 he published a stream of fine novels, novellas, and short stories. After 1958 he steadily moved politically to the left and largely abandoned fiction for critical essays and historical studies.

In the wake of the October 1, 1965, coup, P. was imprisoned without trial by the ascendant military regime and was not freed until the end of 1979. In 1973 he was given access to a typewriter and began writing down a series of historical novels originally narrated orally to his fellow prisoners. In 1980 *Bumi manusia* (*This Earth of Mankind,* 1982) and *Anak semua bangsa* (child of all nations), the first two volumes of a tetralogy on the dawn of Indonesia's struggle against colonial capitalism, were published to great critical and popular acclaim. The military authorities responded to this success by banning both books and ordering thousands of copies seized and publicly burned. Typescripts of the last two volumes, *Jejak langkah* (steps forward) and *Rumah kaca* (house of glass) have been smuggled out of the country and are scheduled for publication abroad.

Initially, P.'s fame rested on three novels composed largely while he was imprisoned by the returning Dutch colonial government after the war. *Perburuan* (1950; *The Fugitive,* 1975) is a haunting description of the homeward flight of a military rebel against the Japanese, written in terms deliberately evocative of traditional Javanese legend. *Keluarga gerilya* (1950; guerrilla family), his best-known novel, depicts the agonizing destruction of a Javanese family during the national revolution. The father, a soldier in the colonial army, is killed by his own sons, who have joined the revolutionaries. Two of the sons die in battle, while the eldest is executed by the Dutch and their mother goes mad with grief. *Mereka yang dilumpuhkan* (1951; the paralyzed) depicts the strange assortment of P.'s fellow prisoners. While all three texts show P.'s narrative virtuosity, they are still couched in a semirealist style which he later abandoned for a more surrealistic one. Their prestige derived partly from their direct portrayal of grand historical themes—war and revolution—and partly on the idea, derived from Western critics of that era, that the novel was the test and confirmation of any great writer's achievement.

The passage of time, however, has shown that P.'s greatness lies, like that of another modern Asian master, the Chinese Lu Hsün, in his short stories. Most of the tales in *Subuh* (1950; dawn) and *Percikan revolusi* (1950; sparks of revolution) are set during the revolution. *Cerita dari*

Blora (1952; tales of Blora) deals with provincial Javanese society in the late colonial period, as well as with the Japanese occupation and the revolution. *Cerita dari Jakarta* (1957; tales of Djakarta) depicts an extraordinary range of postrevolutionary catastrophes in Indonesia's capital. While the key figures in these tales—maimed veterans, child-brides, failed writers, tubercular maids, careerist politicians, deracinated nouveaux riches, and so forth—are recognizable products of the breakdown of feudal Javanese society and of Indonesia's tumultuous modern political history, the peculiar power of the tales derives not from "realism," but from P.'s mature style.

Characteristic of this style is the infusion of the Indonesian language with eerily transformed images from classical Javanese culture and the use of Indonesian to describe the lower depths of Javanese-speaking communities. A polylingual living in a polylingual society, P. essentially writes "between languages," playing languages and cultures off against one another. It is characteristic that some of his best later stories are really about the marginality of the writer in Indonesian society and the problematic nature of writing itself.

The two novels published after P.'s fourteen-year imprisonment differ markedly from his earlier work. They are vast canvases of all strata of colonial society at the turn of the century. But this social and cultural complexity is conveyed in a plain, fast-paced narrative style in striking contrast to the polyphonic allusiveness of his great short stories. P. has said that he deliberately adopted some of the conventions of contemporary popular literature in order to reach the younger generation of Indonesian readers.

FURTHER WORKS: *Kranji dan Bekasi jatuh* (1947); *Bukan pasar malam* (1951; *It's Not an All Night Fair,* 1973); *Gulat di Jakarta* (1953); *Korupsi* (1954); *Midah—simanis bergigi emas* (1954); *Ditepi Kali Bekasi* (1957); *Suatu peristiwa di Banten Selatan* (1958); *Hoa Kiau di Indonesia* (1960); *Panggil aku Kartini saja* (1962). FURTHER VOLUME IN ENGLISH: *A Heap of Ashes* (1975)

BIBLIOGRAPHY: Johns, A. H., "P. A. T.—The Writer as Outsider: An Indonesian Example," *Meanjin,* 22 (1963), 354–63; Johns, A. J., "Genesis of a Modern Indonesian Literature," in McVey, R., ed., *Indonesia* (1963), pp. 410–37; Teeuw, A., "Silence at Life's Noon," *Papers of the Michigan Academy of Sciences, Arts and Letters,* 49 (1964), 245–50; Teeuw, A., *Modern Indonesian Literature* (1967), pp. 163–80; Siegel,

J., "P.'s 'Things Vanished,' with a Commentary," *Glyph*, 1 (1977), 67–100

BENEDICT R. O'G. ANDERSON

TAKDIR Alisjahbana, Sutan

Indonesian novelist, poet, critic, and essayist (also writing in English and Dutch), b. 11 Feb. 1908, Natal, North Sumatra

T.'s name is generally prefaced with Sutan, an aristocratic title of the West Sumatran Minangkabau people. After being an undistinguished student in Dutch-language high schools and a failure as a schoolteacher, in 1930 T. joined the editorial staff of the Netherlands Indies Government publishing house Balai Pustaka, a position which he held until the beginning of the Japanese occupation in 1942. Between 1942 and 1950 he was a key figure in the modernization of the Indonesian language, publishing in 1949 what became a standard grammar. Between 1945 and 1949 he was also a member of the interim parliament of the Republic of Indonesia, and from 1957 until 1960 a member of the Indonesian Constituent Assembly. During the 1950s he established and managed a successful publishing firm and lectured in philosophy and literature at a private institution he founded, the National University in Djakarta. Between 1958 and 1962 he studied cultural theory in Europe and the U.S. Finding the political climate of President Sukarno's Indonesia in the early 1960s uncongenial, he remained abroad. In 1963 he became professor and head of the Department of Malay Studies at the University of Malaya in Kuala Lumpur, Malaysia, angering the Indonesian government. He returned to Indonesia in 1968 and reassumed leadership of the National University. With characteristic energy he established the Toyabungkah Art Center on the island of Bali in 1973.

It is doubtful whether any figure in contemporary Indonesian letters is as important as T. In 1933 he became a founding editor of the independent cultural monthly *Pujangga baru,* which, despite its small circulation, exerted a profound influence on the development of modern Indonesian literature. Through the pages of this journal T. initiated a debate on the direction of Indonesia's cultural development. T. held that prior to the appearance in Indonesia of European technology and liberal values, the country had lived in a dark age of ignorance and feudalism that was best forgotten. T. rejected this past as a basis for Indonesia's national identity and cultural development, and argued that in all fields

Indonesia needed to model itself on Europe if it were to have any hope of creating a dynamic and modern future.

In his novel *Layar terkembang* (1936; under full sail) T. attempted a literary formulation of his views. The novel was the first in Indonesian to attempt a thoroughgoing adaptation of the conventions of European realism. Thematically it deals with the contrast between two sisters: one independent, dynamic, and progressive; the other domestic and traditionally feminine. The comparison, while not denigrating the latter, emphatically favors the former. In the novel *Kalah dan menang* (1978; defeat and victory) T. paints a panoramic portrait of Indonesia during the Japanese occupation. He contrasts the ideologies of European bourgeois liberalism, Javanese feudal mysticism, and Japanese fascist militarism. His sympathies lie firmly with the first, and it is not hard to see in the novel an oblique attack on Indonesia's current social and political order, dominated as it is by a military government top-heavy with conservative Javanese officers.

T.'s interest in cultural polemics and the development of a standard Indonesian language is all too evident in his major works of fiction. They are marred by intrusive, tedious, and in many cases decidedly dated debates. Stylistically they are ponderous, pointedly using only the formal register of Indonesian, which T. has consistently promoted as the national standard.

Although it might cause him some consternation, it seems likely that T.'s literary reputation may come to rest primarily on his poetry, represented in two small collections, *Tebaran mega* (1935; scattered clouds) and *Lagu pemacu ombak* (1978; song of a surfboard rider), and on three early prose romances, *Tak putus dirundung malang* (1929; dogged by endless misfortune), *Dian yang tak kunjung padam* (1932; the undimmed flame), and *Anak perawan di sarang penyamun* (written 1920s, pub. 1941; the virgin and the bandits). The romances, all set in Sumatra, have in common the theme of youthful spirit confronting adversity; they are tinged with a pleasantly sentimental sadness. His poetry is notable for an emotively personal touch expressed with a directness and conciseness conspicuously absent in his more ambitious prose works.

FURTHER WORKS: *Kamus istilah* (1945); *Pembimbing ke filsafat* (1945); *Puisi lama* (1946); *Puisi baru* (1946); *Tatabahasa baru Bahasa Indonesia* (1949); *Soal kebudayaan Indonesia di tengah-tengah dunia* (1950); *Museum sebagai alat pendidikan zaman moderen* (1954); *Sejarah Bahasa Indonesia* (1956); *Krisis akhlak pemuda Indonesia* (1956); *Dari per-*

juangan dan pertumbuhan Bahasa Indonesia (1957); *Perjuangan untuk autonomi dan kedudukan adat di dalamnya* (1957); *Indonesia in the Modern World* (1961; rev. expanded ed., *Indonesia: Social and Cultural Revolution*, 1966); *The Failure of Modern Linguistics in the Face of Linguistic Problems of the Twentieth Century* (1965); *Values as Integrating Forces in Personality, Society and Culture* (1966); *Kebangkitan puisi baru Indonesia* (1969); *Grotta Azzura: Kisah cita dan cinta* (3 vols., 1970–71); *Perkembangan sejarah kebudayaan dilihat dari jurusan nilai-nilai* (1975); *Language Planning for Modernization: The Case of Indonesian and Malaysian* (1976); *Dari perjuangan dan pertumbuhan Bahasa Indonesia sebagai bahasa moderen* (1977); *Perjuangan tanggung jawab dalam kesusasteraan* (1977); *Amir Hamzah sebagai penyair dan uraian sajak Nyanyian sunyi* (1978)

BIBLIOGRAPHY: Raffel, B., *The Development of Modern Indonesian Poetry* (1967), pp. 56–61; Sutherland, H., "Pujangga Baru: Aspects of Indonesian Intellectual Life in the 1930s," *Indonesia*, No. 6 (1968), 106–27; Aveling, H., *A Thematic History of Indonesian Poetry: 1920 to 1974* (1974), passim; Friedus, A. J., *Sumatran Contributions to the Development of Indonesian Literature, 1920–1942* (1977), pp. 37–41; Udin, S., ed., *Spectrum: Essays Presented to S. T. A. on His Seventieth Birthday* (1978); Teeuw, A., *Modern Indonesian Literature*, rev. ed. (1979), Vol. I, pp. 31–41, 65–66, and passim, Vol. II, pp. 165–67 and passim

GEORGE QUINN

JAPANESE LITERATURE

As the 20th c. began, the chief impetus in Japanese literature involved a concerted effort to break with older Japanese traditions, an impetus that has had both its positive and negative side. On the positive side, Japanese writers embraced Western literary movements and theories and tried to model some works on particular European or American examples. Although the result in many cases was imitative, the impulse to reach out and to adapt Western literature to native needs was basically constructive, with Western modes of literature imparting fresh vitality. On the negative side, writers pointedly rejected traditional Japanese myths, archetypes, and literary conventions, turning away from their own heritage.

But tradition dies hard in Japan, where the conservative impulse is strong. Older forms of prose, poetry, and drama have survived in 20th-c. Japan, albeit undergoing transformation. Even today traditional forms of lyric poetry, such as the thirty-one-syllable *tanka* (or *waka*) and the seventeen-syllable *haiku* (a 20th-c. term for an independent short poem that emerged from the *haikai)* remain popular along with a modern style of free verse inspired by contact with the West. Traditional modes of drama—Nō, Kabuki, and the Bunraku (the Japanese puppet theater)—flourish together with Western-style realistic plays and postmodernist theater.

Likewise, modern fiction, which has emerged as the principal literary genre, after having overshadowed earlier lyrical and dramatic forms, also remains indebted to an indigenous lineage of narrative prose that goes back to chronicles compiled largely in the Chinese language in the 8th c. and to purely fictional narratives written in Japanese that date from the 10th c. This earlier tradition of narrative prose, often interspersed with thirty-one-syllable lyric poems, culminated in *Genji monogatari* (c. early 11th c.; *The Tale of Genji,* 6 vols., 1925–33; new tr., 1976).

During the first three decades of the 20th c. the modern counterpart of older forms of narrative prose proved particularly amenable to expressing the most significant theme in 20th-c. Japanese literature, namely awareness of the self, and Japanese writers began espousing the ideology of individualism. Thus, a characteristically Japanese version of the novel, the *shishōsetsu* (also called *watakushi-shōsetsu*), literally, "I-novel," came into being. Concurrently, Japanese authors capitalized on newly found freedom to deal with topics that suggested social and political awareness. An exemplar of the early 20th-c. *shishōsetsu* is *An'ya kōro* (serial pub., 1921–28; 2 vols., 1938; *A Dark Night's Passing*, 1976), by Shiga Naoya (q.v.). An example of an early-20th-c. novel that deals with social and political awareness is *Hakai* (1906; *The Broken Commandment*, 1974), by Shimazaki Tōson (q.v.). In the words of Natsume Sōseki (q.v.), a critic as well as an outstanding and widely translated novelist, *Hakai* was "the first [genuine] novel of the Meiji era [1867–1912]."

At the same time that the *shishōsetsu* deserves to be seen as a manifestation of a newfound sense of individual identity, reflecting the process of Westernization, this species of modern Japanese novel also evinces connections with earlier Japanese literary genres such as the *nikki* ("diary") and the *zuihitsu* ("miscellaneous essay"), two forms that involved a conception of self, as distinct from that of group or corporate self. Certain situations in *An'ya kōro*, moreover, call to mind close parallels with *Genji monogatari*, the outstanding achievement of all ages in Japanese literature. Likewise, the idea of a socially committed literature predates *Hakai*, being found, for instance, in late-18th- and early-19th-c. tales and romances by Ueda Akinari (1734–1809) and Takizawa Bakin (1767–1848), both of whose great moral concern betrays an indebtedness to Chinese literature.

Besides the dichotomies of old and new, native and Western, self and other, which permeate 20th-c. Japanese literature, certain other dualities may also be perceived. One of these is the split between the so-called *jun-bungaku* ("pure literature") and *taishū bungaku* (literally, "mass literature," or by extension, "popular literature"). Unavoidably, these terms imply class differences of high and low, just as in earlier times there existed similar distinctions, such as *gabun* ("elegant writings") and *zokubun* ("common writings"). Likewise, *tanka* on the one hand had its aristocratic origin in salons of court poets, and *haiku* on the other hand derived from plebeian groups of ordinary citizens. Despite the modernization of these forms by Masaoka Shiki (q.v.) and the composition of thirty-one-syllable *tanka* on everyday topics in a new, modern idiom by poets such as Ishikawa Takuboku (q.v.), the old associations with a particular social class linger. The earlier dramatic forms of Nō and Kabuki also continue to have overtones of social class, the former being thought to belong to an elite level of society, the latter to the ordinary people. One of the 20th-c. authors most adept at creating both "pure" and "popular" literature was Mishima Yukio (q.v.); his *Shiosai* (1954; *The Sound of Waves*, 1956) is representative of the latter category, and *Kinkakuji* (1956; *The Temple of the Golden Pavilion*, 1959) of the former.

Among other general points that deserve attention, several may be singled out. Centralization of Japanese literary activity in the capital city of Tokyo, for instance, has its earlier counterpart in literary history. The names of literary periods (Nara, Heian, Kamakura, Muromachi, Edo) identify literary activity with centers of political administration. In this sense the 20th c. may well be thought of as the Tokyo period. One of the first 20th-c. Japanese authors to exploit the sense of Tokyo as a distinctive place and of its people as being worthy of literary attention was Nagai Kafū (q.v.), himself a native of the city and heir to the older traditions of Edo. To an unprecedented degree modern novelists, poets, dramatists, and critics live and work in the city of Tokyo and depend on a system of communications centered in the modern capital of Japan.

Closely related to the concentration of literary activity in Tokyo, newspapers and serials in 20th-c. Japan serve as the primary medium of literary publication, having also absorbed the function of promulgating ephemeral forms of literature such as the *kusazōshi* ("chapbooks") of Japan, popular in the late 18th and early 19th cs. (The importance of seasonal celebrations and the seasonal element in traditional Japanese aesthetics also deserves consideration in any analysis of the function of newspaper and serial literature in Japan.) The book version of a novel, for instance, even today often follows its appearance in the daily, weekly, or monthly press. Moreover, literary men and women are public personalities to a greater degree than in English-speaking countries, a fact that gives authors added reason for living and working in the Tokyo area. Izumi Kyōka (q.v.) best exemplifies an early-20th-c. Japanese author who began his career and sustained it by writing popular fiction that appeared serially, that exploited traditional aesthetic sensibilities, and that brought him public acclaim.

One other noteworthy characteristic of 20th-c. Japanese literature is the form of language of most literary works. The modern colloquial Japanese language has become established as the preeminent medium for literary expression. Previously, there existed a much larger gap than now between the linguistic forms used in literary texts and ordinary discourse. Although this change has taken place gradually, two stages may be singled out. The first came late in the 19th c., when efforts to find a suitable idiom for translating Western literature into Japanese began in earnest. Most of all, Futabatei Shimei (q.v.) deserves to be remembered for his efforts to bring literary composition more closely into line with the idiom of everyday speech. The second stage dates from the period following World War II, when from 1948 to 1952 a number of reforms in language and education took place. All the while there has been a decline in the use of Chinese, the earliest literary language in Japan. Natsume Sōseki, for example, is sometimes called the last important 20th-c. author to have left a body of poetry in Chinese. Meantime, literature in translation has flourished. In the late 1970s, for instance, a specialized monthly journal, *Hon'yaku no sekai,* devoted to the theory and practice of translation, appeared.

Fiction

A new era in Japanese literature following the Russo-Japanese war (1904–5) brought fame and popularity to many young writers, and 20th-c. world literature, with all its complexity, took root in Japan. Writers, several of whom remained active into the 1940s and 1950s, felt a surge of inspiration and confidence after Japan forced Russia to sue for peace.

By 1906 Japanese naturalism began supplanting romanticism. Innovations by an intense group of young writers in their thirties hastened the break with tradition. The naturalistic novel was established by Kunikida Doppo (q.v.), Shimazaki Tōson, and Tayama Katai (1871–1930), along with Iwano Hōmei (1873–1919) and Tokuda Shūsei (1871–1943), whose common goal was to depict life as it is, not glossing over its seamier side. Chiefly out of their work arose the *shishōsetsu,* oftentimes a type of autobiographical confessional in which a semifictional hero and an actual writer tend to be identified.

In their efforts to oppose naturalism, Natsume Sōseki and Mori Ōgai (q.v.), both several years older than the above-mentioned writers, rose to prominence. Mori and Natsume still hold a firm place in the Japanese reader's affections. Natsume's crisp conversational style has influenced young writers particularly. In *Kusamakura* (1906; *Unhuman Tour,* 1927; new tr., *Three-Cornered World,* 1965), he taught that the leisure moments one devotes to art and letters offer the sole relief from the unavoidable suffering of existence, an uplifting belief contrary to the naturalists' creed. Natsume's philosophy and theory of literature, in spite of his period of study in England, show an affinity for those of the earlier *haikai* master, Matsuo Bashō (1644–1694). In *Kokoro* (1914; *Kokoro*, 1941; new tr., 1957), written toward the end of his life, he granted man only three equally dreary choices: death, madness, or religion. Natsume's thought therefore combined "art for art's sake" and pronounced Buddhist tenets.

Mori, who began as a romantic, turned to historical fiction and to belief in stoic self-discipline. A prodigious worker, he combined a medical and military career with authorship in the novel, drama, poetry, criticism, translation, scholarship, and philosophy. One edition of his complete works fills fifty-three volumes. During the last decade of his life he devoted his talent to a series of historical stories for which he is best remembered. Many 20th-c. Japanese writers, late in their careers, have similarly immersed themselves in their own national tradition.

Near the end of the Meiji era and into the Taishō era (1912–26), a group of writers who shared their disapproval of the excess of the naturalists published a periodical called *Shirakaba* (1910–23). Humanitarian in outlook and aristocratic in background and temperament, the group's members included Shiga Naoya, Arishima Takeo (1878–1923), Mushakoji Saneatsu (1885–1976), and Satomi Ton (b. 1888). Although the boundary between naturalist and antinaturalist now seems vague, such distinctions at least show how modern writers in Japan have tended to band together into small independent groups. One of the leading writers who first published prior to 1912 is Tanizaki Jun'ichirō (q.v.), who explored human life with daring, sensitivity, and psychological acumen. His writing appeals readily to Western readers, and he rates as one of the eminent literary figures of the 20th c.

Taishō literature usually includes several years of Meiji and the early part of the Shōwa era (1926 to the present). Until recently Japanese commentators have criticized Taishō authors for failing to transcend traditional, feudal, or nationalistic concepts. Nevertheless, the authors of the 1910s and 1920s produced delicately wrought detail and displayed acute perception. Some writers, to be sure, shirked social responsibility and feigned moral decadence, but Western readers may readily discover untranslated literary works that are at once original and part of the 20th-c. *Zeitgeist*. Reevaluation of the contribution of Taishō authors to the creation of a distinctly modern sensibility is just getting under way. In the 1910s Dostoevsky, Tolstoy, the German Nobel Prize winner Rudolf C. Eucken (1846–1926), Henri Bergson, Rabindranath Tagore, and

Maurice Maeterlinck became known in Japan. The art of Cézanne, Van Gogh, and Rodin attracted attention; the aestheticism of Poe, Wilde, and Baudelaire found numerous emulators.

During and after World War I, Romain Rolland, Henri Barbusse, and Vicente Blasco Ibáñez became widely read in Japan. Satō Haruo (1892–1964) and Kikuchi Kan (1888–1948) emerged as part of an avant-garde group that declared that only in society can man achieve individuality. Although the group traced their intellectual origins to Europe, the members never completely abandoned traditional style and sensibility. Kikuchi Kan worked as the iron-handed editor of *Bungei shunjū* (founded 1923), making it a leading Japanese literary monthly.

Other writers, such as Akutagawa Ryūnosuke (q.v.), Yamamoto Yūzō (1887–1974), and Kume Masao (1891–1952), made their debuts in private periodicals. One of these periodicals, *Shin shichō,* founded in 1907, was associated with Tokyo Imperial University students who had literary aspirations. In 1923 Kawabata Yasunari (q.v.) revived this periodical. Together with Yokomitsu Riichi (q.v.) and their followers, in 1924 he was involved in yet another periodical, *Bungei jidai,* which advanced such European causes as futurism, expressionism, and Dadaism. Kawabata's short-lived group, however intuitive, subjective, sensual, and faintly decadent, owed as much to medieval Japanese drama as to modern European "isms." Kawabata was the first Japanese writer to win the Nobel Prize for literature.

For a time in the 1920s it appeared that leftist literature might overshadow the efforts of these avant-garde writers and modernists. Government authorities, however, repressed the proletarian movement, despite the support of many established writers. Two noteworthy leftist authors who failed to survive beyond World War II are Hayama Yoshiki (1894–1945) and Kobayashi Takiji (1903–1933). Leftist writers who lived through government repression and the hardships of war resumed literary activity after Japan's defeat. The most notable of them are Nakano Shigeharu (b. 1902), author of *Muragimo* (1954; nerve), Miyamoto Yuriko (1899–1951), Hirabayashi Taiko (1905–1972), Miyamoto Kenji (b. 1908), and Hayashi Fumiko (q.v.). Miyazawa Kenji's (q.v.) selfless altruism and his active participation in agricultural reform movements suggest a devotion to humanitarian ends similar to that of the proletarians.

Nonleftist writers active during the 1930s included Ibuse Masuji (q.v.) and Hori Tatsuo (1904–1953). Dazai Osamu (q.v.) best typified the immediate postwar period, a time of excruciating self-examination and

extreme nihilism. His autobiographical narratives in some respects anticipated "beat" literature. Many other writers emerged after World War II,
the most notable being Mishima Yukio. His spectacular suicide in the
conventional manner of the Edo-period samurai in 1970, followed by
Kawabata's self-asphyxiation in 1971, startled the world. Other writers
representative of the immediate post-World War II years include Inoue
Yasushi (b. 1907)—author of *Ryojū* (1949; *The Hunting Gun*, 1961),
Tempyō no iraka (1957; *The Roof Tile of Tempyō*, 1976), *Tonkō* (1959;
Tun-huang: A Novel, 1978)—Takeda Taijun (1912–1976), and Noma
Hiroshi (b. 1915), who wrote *Shinkū chitai* (1952; *Zone of Emptiness*,
1956).

In the 1960s new writers continued to appear, and certain established
authors extended their reputation. The work of Abe Kōbō (q.v.), for
example, which has been widely translated, combines a scrupulous attention to the individual's emotional state (a characteristic of much of the
best traditional literature) with a deft appreciation of the present human
predicament. Ōe Kenzaburō (q.v.), active as author, editor, and critic, has
probed into modern youth's confrontation with sex and society. Among
older authors, Ibuse Masuji has published *Kuroi ame* (1966; *Black Rain*,
1969), the best novel about the prolonged suffering and the lingering side
effects that the atomic bomb can cause.

During the 1970s yet other fresh authors contributed to the vibrant
state of Japanese literature. For instance, a fantasy of sex, drugs, and
violence by Murakami Ryū (b. 1952), *Kagirinaku tōmei ni chikai burū*
(1976; *Almost Transparent Blue*, 1977), won a coveted literary prize and
became a spectacular, albeit controversial, best seller. By means of rich
imagery and crude bluntness, a repellent and filthy world in an advanced
state of disintegration, decay, and corruption is projected. Such works
fairly represent one facet of the Japanese literary scene today. Meanwhile, among established authors, Enchi Fumiko (q.v.) published a well-
received and highly praised new translation into modern Japanese of
Genji monogatari in ten volumes. And Endō Shūsaku (b. 1923), a Catholic novelist, has had several of his works translated into English: *Umi to
dokuyaku* (1958; *The Sea and Poison*, 1980), *Chimmoku* (1966; *Silence*,
1969), and *Kuchibue o fuku toki* (1975; *When I Whistle*, 1979).

Poetry

Developments in poetry in Japan during the 20th c. have roughly
corresponded to the pattern set by narrative prose. Shimazaki Tōson

expressed the exuberent recognition of a fresh age in poetry when he wrote, in 1904, "All seemed intoxicated with light, with new tongues, with new imaginings. . . ." An incipient romantic movement soon gave way to symbolism in the early 1900s with the appearance of Ueda Bin's (1874–1916) collection of translations, especially from French poetry, *Miotsukushi* (1905; sound of the tide). The sensuous language of Kitahara Hakushū (1885–1942) in, for example, *Jashūmon* (1909; heretical religion), and the taut yet colloquial idiom of Hagiwara Sakutarō (q.v.), in *Tsuki ni hoeru* (1917; *Howling at the Moon*, 1978) and his subsequent collections, mark the establishment of modern free verse in 20th-c. Japan. Hagiwara, however, who is probably the most widely translated 20th-c. Japanese poet, went on to write in "Nihon e no kaiki" (1938; return to Japan) of abandoning "the mirage of the West across the sea" and of returning "to our ancient country, with its more than two thousand years of history."

Although older lyrical forms have survived, the charge that they are hardly poetry has persisted. The dynamic young nationalistic *haiku* and *tanka* poet Masaoka Shiki led a revolution in *haikai* by insisting that the seventeen-syllable *haiku* must stand as an independent verse. Hitherto all *haiku* were theoretically written for linked verse *(renku,* or *renga).* Masaoka's followers, Takahama Kyoshi (1874–1959) and Kawahigashi Hekigodō (1873–1937), continued the *haiku* revolution begun by Masaoka. Takahama, remaining narrowly loyal to Masaoka's objectives, helped to institute a new orthodoxy in terms of form and technique. Irrepressibly innovative by temperament, Kawahigashi, however, instituted a free style of *haiku,* in which the traditional syllable count, season word, and seasonal topic were no longer held to be essential. Kawahigashi's idea of *haiku* as a form of lyrical expression of an individual sensibility brought this traditional kind of verse closer to modern European-style poetry. A follower of Kawahigashi, Nakatsukasa Ippekiro (1887–1946), on the one hand, carried the free-meter *haiku* to a creative pinnacle, rejuvenating it as a poetic tool to embody the modern experience. On the other hand, Ogiwara Seisensui (1884–1976), another of Kawahigashi's disciples, argued that even the seasonal element, however much it preserved continuity with the past, might be sacrificed for the sake of self-expression. Taneda Santōka (q.v.), who began writing *haiku* as a disciple of Seisensui, also extended the possibilities of free-verse *haiku.* His restless quest for spiritual enlightenment and his search for release from worldly anxiety mark him as kinsman to earlier Japanese poet-monks and followers of Zen Buddhism.

Lest it be thought that the traditionalists were left clinging only to worn-out concepts of an increasingly forgotten past, Takahama Kyoshi's many followers, especially in the periodical *Hototogisu* (founded 1897), argued cogently for an orthodoxy that might be consistent both with modern theories and with the function of literature. A proletarian school of *haiku* also thrived from the 1920s until 1942, when government repression and internal dissension brought the movement to an end. Today, with around one thousand magazines appearing regularly and with a thriving national organization, modern Japanese *haiku* evinces amazing resilience, and a lively international *haiku* movement flourishes outside Japan. No other non-Western literary form has proven as widely influential as the Japanese *haiku*.

Similarly, the thirty-one-syllable *tanka*, prevalent for over twelve hundred years, has retained its supporters and won a growing number of practitioners in the West. During World War II certain extremists urged the exclusion of "decadent" Western poetry in favor of *tanka*. Inspired by the earlier example of Yosano Akiko (1878–1942), Wakayama Boku-sui (1885–1928), and Saitō Mokichi (1882–1953), postwar *tanka* poets of various schools have sustained this lyric art. Ishikawa Takuboku, one of the first modern voices in Japanese poetry, is best remembered for his *tanka*.

Drama

Although in fiction new and old have merged to replace premodern forms, in poetry, perhaps because of its closeness to religion, traditional modes persist alongside modern verse. The same holds true in the drama. Some theatergoers prefer modern plays to the Nō, Kabuki, or Bunraku, but not so much that they completely withhold patronage from the traditional forms. Meantime, well-organized groups and associations preserve the traditional theater, its continuity since the Middle Ages unbroken. Because the conventions of these traditional forms of theater are increasingly remote from modern experience, from time to time new productions of a similar sort are offered to the public, including adaptations from the Western drama and opera. For example, a Japanese version of Yeats's poetic drama *At the Hawk's Well*, at first entitled *Taka no izumi* (perf. 1949; hawk's well) and later revised and called *Takahime* (1969; hawk princess), adapted by Yokomichi Mario (b. 1916) and Nomura Man'nojō (b. 1930), has been presented on Nō stages in Tokyo and Kyoto. Among modern playwrights and theater critics, Kishida Kunio (q.v.) worked assiduously to establish a form of theater that projects the conditions of actual life with originality and psychological acumen. Yashiro Seiichi (b. 1927) is the most recent example of a modern playwright whose work has been performed in English translation. His play *Hokusai manga* (1973; *Hokusai Sketchbooks,* 1979) was staged in Hollywood early in 1981, demonstrating his uninhibited ribaldry drawn straight from Edo culture and portraying the triumphant free expression of a famous creative artist, Hokusai (1760–1849), whose zest for life overcame seemingly insurmountable human adversities.

Abe Kōbō, better known for his surrealistic novels, is also one of the most productive playwrights and imaginative theater directors in Japan. And two of the plays of the prolific Yamazaki Masakazu (b. 1934) have appeared in English translation: *Zeami* (1969; *Zeami,* 1980) and *Sanetomo shuppan* (1973; *Sanetomo,* 1980). Both plays, very much rooted in Japanese culture, deal with the Middle Ages.

Despite the fame of certain modern poets and playwrights, narrative prose writers have probably made Japan's greatest contribution to world literature in the 20th c. Yet, poetry and drama, as well as modern Japanese fiction, command increasing attention from Western readers, not because of their supposedly exotic qualities but because of their literary artistry and attention to problems common to modern life. If some readers may complain of lack of power, others will surely find meaningful comment on human life, death, and love. Nowhere on earth does one encounter a more world-minded literary atmosphere.

The theme that dominates much of modern Japanese literature is the search for the self in society. Toward the end of the Edo era (1603–1867) and in the early Meiji, traditional society collapsed. Old morals, religion, and loyalties proved inadequate. Modern authors, by using all the resources of a rich language with a long literary tradition, have continually groped for solutions to the human predicament. At times some have accepted without question Western ideology, religion, or literary forms, but the best writers have sought original answers to the questions of life, literature, and art. In recent years the search for identity of the self in society continues unabated. Young authors still seek a place for the individual in mass society. They search, so far without success, to find a substitute for the accepted system of duties and obligations that gave structure to traditional society.

Japanese literature reflects the continuing vitality of a prosperous nation of more than a hundred million people. For successful writers the rewards are enormous, both in terms of wealth and public acclaim.

Nevertheless, the current educational system places low emphasis on creative writing, which as an occupation is discouraged, making it all the more of a marvel that so much energy and attention is devoted to this particular human activity.

BIBLIOGRAPHY: Kokusai Bunka Shinkōkai, ed., *Introduction to Contemporary Japanese Literature* (3 vols., 1939, 1959, 1972); Keene, D., *Modern Japanese Novels and the West* (1961); Shea, G. T., *Leftwing Literature in Japan: A Brief History of the Proletarian Literary Movement* (1964); Arima, T., *The Failure of Freedom: A Portrait of Modern Japanese Intellectuals* (1969); Keene, D., *Landscapes and Portraits: Appreciations of Japanese Culture* (1971); Japan PEN Club, *Studies on Japanese Culture* (1973), Vol. I, pp. 157–557; Kimball, A. G., *Crisis in Identity and Contemporary Japanese Novels* (1973); Harper, J., et al., eds., *An Invitation to Japan's Literature* (1974), pp. 5–9, 33–40, 96–154; Kijima, H., and Miller, R. A., introductory essays in Kijima, H., ed., *The Poetry of Postwar Japan* (1975), pp. xi–xlix; Tsuruta, K., and Swann, T. E., eds., *Approaches to the Modern Japanese Novel* (1976); Ueda, M., *Modern Japanese Writers and the Nature of Literature* (1976); Ueda, M., Introduction to *Modern Japanese Haiku: An Anthology* (1976), pp. 3–25; Takeda, K., ed., *Essays on Japanese Literature* (1977); Rimer, J. T., *Modern Japanese Fiction and Its Traditions: An Introduction* (1978); Yamanouchi, H., *The Search for Authenticity in Modern Japanese Literature* (1978); Bowring, R. J., *Mori Ōgai and the Modernization of Japanese Culture* (1979); Peterson, G. B., *The Moon in the Water: Understanding Tanizaki, Kawabata, and Mishima* (1979); Takaya, T., ed., Introduction to *Modern Japanese Drama: An Anthology* (1979), pp. ix–xxxvii; Walker, J. A., *The Japanese Novel of the Meiji Period and the Idea of Individualism* (1979); Keene, D., tr., Introduction to *The Modern Japanese Prose Poem: An Anthology of Six Poets* (1980), pp. 3–57; Lippit, N. M., *Reality and Fiction in Modern Japanese Literature* (1980)

LEON M. ZOLBROD

ABE Kōbō

Japanese novelist, short-story writer, and dramatist, b. 7 March 1924, Tokyo

The son of a doctor practicing in Shenyang, Manchuria, A. attended school there and in Tokyo. He was exempted from military service during World War II because of a respiratory illness; he finished medical school in 1948, but decided against a medical practice in favor of a writing career. He allied himself with a literary group, led by Kiyoteru Hamada (b. 1909), that was committed to the goal of fusing the techniques of surrealism with Marxist ideology. Using an avant-garde, experimental style that quickly won the praise of the younger generation of readers, A. began to write stories, novels, and plays that expose the emptiness of life in modern society.

His short stories, published first in journals, established a special place for him in postwar Japanese literary life. He received coveted prizes in Japan for his three stories, "Akai mayu" (1950; "Red Cocoon," 1966), "Kabe" (1951; wall), and "S. Karuma-shi no hanzai" (1951; Mr. S. Karuma's crime). In the last mentioned, which is really a short novel, the style and subject matter are reminiscent of Kafka. The narrator loses his name, and hence, access to normal relations with other human beings. As a result, however, he is mysteriously able to communicate with certain animals in the zoo and also with inanimate objects, such as store mannequins, which seem to come to life.

One of A.'s best-received short stories is "Chinnyūsha" (1951; intruders). An allegorical satire on democracy in postwar Japan, it tells how a group of people invades the narrator's one-room apartment and, by insisting on the democratic rule of the majority, enslave him.

A. is one of the most productive writers for the Japanese stage. His prize-winning play *Tomodachi* (1967; *Friends,* 1969) focuses on the members of one family, whose actions are predatory and cruelly destructive, although they claim to be devoting themselves to social good, to respect for life, and to the responsibilities of human brotherhood. The play *Omae nimo tsumi ga aru* (1978; *You, Too, Are Guilty,* 1979), set in a modern apartment, explores with sardonic humor the possible bond between the living and the dead. A. has also written film scripts and radio plays. His theater troupe has toured the U.S. and performed in New York City (1979).

A.'s international reputation rests largely on his novels and on the films based on them. In his masterpiece, *Suna no onna* (1962; *The Woman in the Dunes,* 1964), a conflict between two concepts of home emerges: the place where one is born as opposed to the place where one must actually live, the second being one's true home in an existential sense. The protagonist is a schoolteacher who, on a holiday expedition, happens on a village in danger of being buried by massive sand dunes that have accumulated around it. The schoolteacher accepts shelter from a woman who lives alone in one of the threatened houses. He is pressed to help her and the villagers in their constant struggle to keep the area free of sand. When a chance to escape comes, he refuses to take advantage of it. Seemingly, he has come to accept his strange life with the woman amid the constantly shifting, unpredictable sand, which at times seems to flow like water in slow motion. The woman represents the ability to adjust to life, while the sand is a symbol of reality, always changing in shape and inexorably demonstrating the power to move men and women, however reluctant they may be to respond.

In *Hako otoko* (1973; *The Box Man,* 1974) A. describes modern man's attempt to escape from himself. His protagonist does so by cutting a peephole in an empty cardboard carton, placing the box over his head, and walking away from his anxieties. The only danger to him lies in the possibility of meeting another "box man." A. has said of this novel, "Being no one means at the same time that one can be anyone." Aversion to bourgeois existence and the question of what is genuine and what is counterfeit here are expressed by means of a symbol—the box as a shield from the world—that represents disposability and concealment. For readers attuned to the traditions of Japan, the mask of the Nō actor, a thing of exquisite beauty to be treasured forever, has given way to a device that serves its utilitarian purpose and may then be abandoned.

In *Mikkai* (1978; *Secret Rendezvous,* 1979) A. has written a surrealistic detective story about an unidentified man searching for his wife at a hospital, to which she has been unaccountably taken in the middle of the night. The hospital seems like a bizarre laboratory, where the patients and staff alike are sexual cripples. The plot resonates with classical myths and Freudian symbolism.

A number of themes constantly recur in A.'s work: the individual's search for the "roots of existence," which may stabilize his identity; the difficulty people have in communicating with one another; and the discrepancy between inner and outer reality. By juxtaposing ordinary events and absurd ones A. compels his readers (or audience) to believe that his misshapen world is really Everyman's.

For three decades A. has detached himself to an unusual degree from the literary traditions of Japan. His writing, often stiff and formal, reveals his preoccupation with ideas rather than style. A. uses concepts and expressions drawn from science and philosophy for his criticisms of society. Allegory, irony, and satire all serve to delineate his principal theme—that of the outsider in modern society.

FURTHER WORKS: *Mumei shishū* (1947); *Owarishi michi no shirube ni* (1948); *Ueta hifu* (1952); *Kiga dōmei* (1954); *Kabe atsuki heya* (1954); *Āru rokujū-ni gō no hatsumei* (1956); *Mōken no kokoro ni keisanki no te o* (1957); *Kemono-tachi wa kokyō-o mesasu* (1957); *Tōō o yuku: Hangariya mondai no haikei* (1957); *Hakareru kiroku* (1958); *Daishi kampyōki* (1959; *Inter Ice Age 4*, 1970); *Yūrei wa koko ni iru* (1959); *Ishi no me* (1960); *Mukankei na shi* (1964); *Tanin no kao* (1964; *The Face of Another*, 1966); *Moetsukita chizu* (1967; *The Ruined Map*, 1969); *Bō ni natta otoko* (1969; *The Man Who Turned into a Stick*, 1975); *A. K.-shū* (1970); *A. K. gikyoku zenshū* (1970); *A. K. zen-sakuhin* (15 vols., 1972–73); *Warau tsuki* (1978). FURTHER VOLUME IN ENGLISH: *Four Stories by K. A.* (1973)

BIBLIOGRAPHY: Ōta, S., and Fukuda, R., eds., *Studies on Japanese Culture*, I (1974), pp. 401–5, 477–82; Kimball, A., *Crisis in Identity and Contemporary Japanese Novels* (1973), pp. 115–39; Hardin, N. S., "An Interview with A. K.," *ConL*, 15 (1974), 438–56; Levy, A., "The Box Man Cometh," *NYTMag*, 17 Nov. 1974, 36ff.; Beasley, W. G., ed., *Modern Japan* (1975), pp. 166–84; Tsuruta, K., and Swann, T. E., eds., *Approaches to the Modern Japanese Novel* (1976), pp. 1–18; Rimer, J. T., *Modern Japanese Fiction and Its Traditions* (1978), pp. 261–70; Yamanouchi, H., *The Search for Authenticity in Modern Japanese Literature* (1978), pp. 153–74

LEON M. ZOLBROD

AKUTAGAWA Ryūnosuke

(born Niibara) Japanese short-story writer, b. 1 March 1892, Tokyo; d. 24 July 1927, Tokyo

"Heredity, environment, and chance—these three ultimately determine our fate," wrote A., obviously with his own case in mind. Because he was born when his parents were at ages considered ill-omened, he was made a foundling—an old ritual that would, it was believed, protect him from evil. Furthermore, shortly after his birth, his mother became insane; as a result, he was raised and eventually adopted by his maternal uncle Akutagawa, whose name he took. While still a student at the Tokyo Imperial University, A. became active in literary circles, and with "Hana" (1916; "The Nose," 1930), a comic story about a Buddhist monk's frustration with his oversize nose, he won the praise of Natsume Sōseki (q.v.).

Although A.'s career was cut short by his suicide, it was an intensely creative one. Thoroughly grounded in literature, old and new, he rejected the native school of the pseudonaturalistic confessional novel in favor of modern European models. Always insistent on the primacy of critical intelligence, he fostered the intellectual tradition in modern Japanese literature. In thus helping to transform it into something richer—at once Oriental and Occidental—he followed closely in the footsteps of Natsume Sōseki.

A.'s short stories, some 150 in all, generally reflect the three phases of his development as a writer. His aesthetic phase began with "Rashō-mon" (1915; "Rashomon," 1920)—Kurosawa's celebrated film version combined it with "Yabu no naka" (1922; "In a Grove," 1952)—and culminated with "Jigokuhen" (1918; "The Hell Screen," 1936–37), depicting the madness of a painter who sacrifices his only daughter in order to complete his masterpiece: the sight of her burning to death inspires him to paint the flames of hell on a screen. Many of his early stories are set in ancient Japan—historical tales with modern insights. During the ensuing phase, however, A. turned toward realism, in such stories as "Aki" (1920; "Autumn," 1928), registering the quiet resignation of a woman who yields her lover to her own younger sister; "Niwa" (1922; "The Garden," 1964), depicting the struggle of a once-wealthy family against the ravages of time; and "Ikkai no tsuchi" (1924; "A Clod of Soil," 1957), portraying the loneliness of an old peasant woman who survives her son and daughter-in-law.

During his last phase A., all the while wrestling with thoughts of suicide, managed to produce an astonishing variety of writings. His critical eye was at its best in "Bungeitekina amarini bungeitekina" (1927; literary, too literary)—knowledgeable, candid, and original. His realism found its final expression in "Genkaku sanbō" (1927; "The House of Genkaku," 1961), the pitiless portrait of a man facing a slow death. So did his satiric spirit, in "Kappa" (1927; "Kappa," 1947), a savage assault on human civilization. At the end of his life A. quite willingly laid his soul bare. In "Haguruma" (1927; "Cogwheels," 1965) he saw in himself the image of modern man wandering in his own private hell. And in both "Aru ahō no isshō" (1927; "The Life of a Fool," 1961), a series of vignettes recapitulating his own career, and "Seihō no hito" (1927; "Man of the West," 1961), another series, tracing the life of Jesus, A. sought to discover at last some definitive pattern that would justify his own existence as man and as artist.

Highly versatile and experimental, A. refused to repeat himself; relentlessly self-critical, he aspired to perfection. He was a prose stylist with the soul of a poet. Always a favorite with the Japanese, he is considered one of the greatest national writers. With his increasing accessibility in translation, A. is finding his niche in world literature.

FURTHER WORKS: *A. R. zenshū* (4 editions: 10 vols., 1934–35; 20 vols., 1954–55; 8 vols., 1964–65; 11 vols., 1967–69). FURTHER VOLUMES IN ENGLISH: *Tales Grotesque and Curious* (1930); *The Three Treasures, and Other Stories for Children* (1944); *Hell Screen. and Other Stories* (1948); *Rashomon, and Other Stories* (1952); *Japanese Short Stories* (1961); *Exotic Japanese Stories* (1964); *A Fool's Life* (1970)

BIBLIOGRAPHY: Arima, T., "A. R.: The Literature of Defeatism," *The Failure of Freedom: A Portrait of Modern Japanese Intellectuals* (1969), pp. 152–72; Hibbett, H. S., "A. R. and the Negative Ideal," in Craig, A. M., and Shively, D. H., eds., *Personality in Japanese History* (1970), pp. 425–51; Tsuruta, K., "A. R. and I-Novelists," *MN*, 25 (1970), 13–27; Yu, B., *A: An Introduction* (1972); Ueda, M., *Modern Japanese Writers and the Nature of Literature* (1976), pp. 111–44; Yamanouchi, H., *The Search for Authenticity in Modern Japanese Literature* (1978), pp. 87–106

BEONGCHEON YU

DAZAI Osamu

(pseud. of Tsushima Shūji) Japanese novelist and short-story writer, b. 19 June 1909, Aomori; d. 13 June 1948, Tokyo

D. was the tenth of eleven children born into a wealthy land-owning family in northern Honshu. He enrolled in Tokyo University in 1930 to study French literature but did not complete his studies.

D. wrote in a simple and colloquial style. His best stories are based on his own experiences and thus fall into that category of Japanese fiction known as *shishōsetsu*, or autobiographical/confessional fiction. Given the facts of his life, the mood could have been lugubrious, but it is not. As D. studied himself from all angles in his stories he resorted to humor, irony, and subtle shifts in language to keep the tone light. In this respect, he learned much from Ibuse Masuji (q.v.), a writer famed for his humor and light touch.

D. first attracted attention in 1933 when his short stories began to appear in magazines. These were later collected in *Bannen* (1936; twilight years). The best-known stories in it are "Omoide" (recollections) and "Dōke no hana" (the essence of clowning), in which he dealt with an attempted suicide. D. was to turn to suicide as a theme in many of his stories, including "Tokyo hyakkei" (1941; one hundred views of Tokyo).

Two of D.'s best short stories before the end of World War II are "Fugaku hyakkei" (1943; one hundred views of Mount Fuji) and "Tsugaru" (1944; Tsugaru). The first, written in a lyrical style but melancholy in tone, has the writer-narrator settling down to work in a bucolic setting and observing a group of prostitutes out having a picnic in the foothills. In the second D. evokes the flavor and character of his native region, Tsugaru, as he made an attempt to go back home again.

For a brief period after the end of the war, D. came into his own when he published his most famous work, *Shayō* (1947; *The Setting Sun*, 1956), which deals with the fall of an aristocratic family. A mother and daughter are evacuated from Tokyo during the war and suffer privations, but they look hopefully to the return of the son from southeast Asia. He does return, but as a drug addict. He attempts to adjust to postwar conditions by joining the entourage of a dissolute writer but is unable to sever the ties with the life his mother represents, and when she dies, he commits suicide. The daughter gives herself to the writer and bears his child. She has made a complete break with the past and will survive the impending changes.

"Viyon no tsuma" (1947; "Villon's Wife," 1956) is probably D.'s best short story. The first-person narrator, a famed poet's wife, virtually abandoned by her husband, finds meaning in her existence by taking a job for a tavern keeper her husband has stolen money from. Nothing—retarded child, rape, or her husband's endless self-delusion—can crush her new-found determination to survive.

In *Ningen shikkaku* (1948; *No Longer Human*, 1958), a novel of profound pessimism, D. merged a number of earlier themes: distrust of self and of others, inability to compromise, the rape of an overly trusting wife, drug addiction, confinement in a mental institution.

Like all Japanese intellectuals since 1868, when Japan emerged from a self-imposed state of isolation that had lasted three centuries, D. tried to cope with the problem of discerning some sense of order in a society that had been torn from its moorings by enormous forces of change and that was becoming increasingly fragmented. This sense of dislocation continued for D. up to Pearl Harbor and the war in the Pacific, when national mobilization pressured writers into complying with state policy. After the war, D. lapsed into an even more virulent despair. His sardonic observation of those who had supported the militaristic regime before and during the war and who were now embracing democracy with equal fervor contributed to his sense of alienation. On June 13, 1948, D. killed himself.

FURTHER WORKS: *Nijusseiki kishu* (1937); *Kyokō no hōkō* (1937); *Ai to bi ni tsuite* (1939); *Joseito* (1939); *Onna no kettō* (1940); *Shin Hamuretto* (1941); *Seigi to bishō* (1942); *Udaijin Sanetomo* (1943); *Sekibetsu* (1945); *Otogizōshi* (1945); *Shin shokokubanashi* (1945); *Pandora no hako* (1946); *Fuyu no hanabi* (1946); *Kyōshin no kami* (1947); *Nyoze gabun* (1948); *Jinushi ichidai—Mihappyō sakuhin shū* (1949); *D. O. zenshū* (10 vols., 1952); *D. O. zenshū* (12 vols., 1955–56)

BIBLIOGRAPHY: Keene, D., *Landscapes and Portraits: Appreciations of Japanese Culture* (1971), pp. 186–203; Miyoshi, M., "Till Death Do Us Part: D. O.—*The Setting Sun,*" *Accomplices of Silence* (1974), pp. 122–40; Lyons, P., "Women in the Life and Art of D. O." *LE&W*, 18 (1974), 44–57; O'Brien, J., *D. O.* (1975); Ueda, M., *Modern Japanese Writers and the Nature of Literature* (1976), pp. 145–72; Wagatsuma, H., and DeVos, G., "A *Kōan* of Sincerity: O. D.," *HSL*, 10 (1978), 156–81

FRANK T. MOTOFUJI

ENCHI Fumiko

Japanese novelist and short-story writer, b. 2 Oct. 1905, Tokyo

E. was the second daughter of the well-known Japanese linguist Ueda Kazutoshi (1867–1937). Sickly and precocious as a child, E. often stayed home from school, and instead read voraciously, thereby familiarizing herself with both modern and classic literary works. This early exposure to literature, plus frequent trips to the Kabuki theater and many hours of listening to tales told by her grandmother, helped forge E.'s own views on love. In her early teens E. was fascinated by the aesthetically sensuous descriptions prevalent in the works of Tanizaki Jun'ichirō and

Nagai Kafū (qq.v.). She also enjoyed reading such Western writers as Oscar Wilde and Edgar Allan Poe. Frustrated and unchallenged, she quit high school after the tenth grade and studied English, French, and classical Chinese at home under tutors.

E. began her literary career by publishing a short drama at the age of twenty-one. At twenty-three another of her plays was produced on the stage. After her marriage two years later and the subsequent birth of her only child, E. found that writing plays did not provide her enough freedom to express what was in her mind. Turning to fiction, she attempted to bring out the complexities of human psychology. Her career as a novelist, however, did not have an easy start. Not until twenty years later, at the age of forty-eight, with the publication of her short story "Himojii tsukihi" (1953; the starving years), did E. finally gain recognition. She was awarded the sixth Women's Literary Award for this work in the following year. Her literary activities have been vigorous since then.

Onnazaka (1957; *The Waiting Years,* 1971) is probably the best known of E.'s works. It is also her only novel translated into English so far. Unlike many of her stories, which are admixtures of reality and fantasy, *Onnazaka* is strictly realistic, and has none of E.'s usual "amoral" topics (adultery and seduction). Neither does it deal with eroticism of middle-aged woman, E.'s recurrent theme. Instead, Tomo, the stoic heroine, endures long years of humiliation by her lustful husband, who keeps two mistresses—all three women under the same roof. She vents her spite in curt, strikingly revengeful words spoken on her deathbed, which makes a powerfully effective conclusion. The Noma Literary Prize was awarded this work in 1957.

E.'s autobiographical trilogy, *Ake o ubau mono* (1957; one who steals red), *Kizu aru tsubasa* (1962; the injured wing), and *Niji to shura* (1968; rainbow and carnage), is probably more representative of her work. In these novels she depicts a woman's loveless, acrimonious marriage and her relationships with other men. The heroine's intense frustration as a novelist undoubtedly parallels E.'s own experience before she established herself as a writer. She received the fifth Tanizaki Jun'ichirō Award for the trilogy in 1969.

It is in many of her short stories that E. often exhibits her profound knowledge of classical Japanese literature by weaving elements from it into contemporary settings, which become fascinating combinations of reality and fantasy, actuality and apparition. For example, in "Nise no enishi: shūi" (1957; the conjugal ties: gleanings), she borrows the theme of a mysterious tale with the same title by Ueda Akinari (1734–1809), in which a man long dead returns to life, to create a bizarre story about a woman who gives herself over to wild fantasies.

One of E.'s latest accomplishments is the translation into modern Japanese of *The Tale of Genji*, the long 11th-c. tale by the court lady Murasaki Shikibu; E. succeeds well in reproducing the sensitivity of the original.

Now in her mid-seventies, E. is highly respected by critics for her profound knowledge of classical Japanese literature, her careful choice of words, and her literary versatility. Yet her work is also loved by the general public for being neither overintellectual nor too theoretical.

FURTHER WORKS: *Aki no mezame* (1958); *Onnamen* (1958); *Watashi mo moete iru* (1960); *Aijō no keifu* (1961); *Hanachirusato* (1961); *Minami no hada* (1961); *Onna no mayu* (1962); *Onna obi* (1962); *Tsui no sumika* (1962); *Shishijima kidan* (1963); *Yukimoe* (1964); *Komachi hensō* (1965); *Namamiko Monogatari* (1965); *Azayaka na onna* (1965); *Kakeru mono* (1965); *Senhime shunjūki* (1966); *Saimu* (1976); *Shokutaku no nai ie* (1979)

YOKO MCCLAIN

FUTABATEI Shimei

(pseud. of Hasegawa Tatsunosuke) Japanese novelist and translator, b. 4 April 1864, Tokyo; d. 10 May 1909, on shipboard in the Bay of Bengal

Born into the samurai class, F. entered the Russian division of the Tokyo School of Foreign Languages in 1881 and fell passionately in love with Russian literature. He made his reputation early with translations of stories by Turgenev and with *Ukigumo* (1887–89; *Ukigumo*, 1967), Japan's first modern novel. Despairing of surviving as a professional writer, he entered the government bureaucracy in 1889. He was also subsequently employed as a teacher and journalist. He resumed publication of translations in 1897, and two final works of fiction appeared early in the 20th c.: *Sono omokage* (1906; *An Adopted Husband*, 1919) and *Heibon* (1907; *Mediocrity*, 1927). He died on shipboard of an illness while returning home from Russia.

In constructing *Ukigumo* (whose title literally means "drifting clouds"), F. introduced limitations of time, space, and character previously unknown in Japanese fiction. Confining his novel to a detailed study of four characters within a two-week period, and limiting the action to a minute geographical area, he concentrated on probing into his characters' lives with an intensity generally absent in earlier fiction. Their problems are such as might be shared by any of his contemporaries, and the language they speak in internalized comments and to each other is the language of his time. Readers were able to approach F.'s narrative without the special knowledge required for much of the earlier fiction of Japan, and they responded eagerly to this new accessibility. It was a novel for and about the emerging, more equalitarian Japan, and it provided a model for subsequent generations.

Sono omokage deals with the agonies of an intellectual adopted into his wife's family, and *Heibon* is actually a series of short sketches— seemingly autobiographical—reflecting the weary and frustrated tone of the Japanese naturalist school.

In all of his fiction F. maintained an attractive balance between bittersweet humor and pathos. There are no major tragedies nor is there sustained slapstick. The reader finds instead a sense of appropriateness. Emotions are confined within plausible boundaries, and actions are no more or less than his contemporaries are likely to have experienced.

The language in which F. wrote his translations and fiction is remarkably vibrant and contributed significantly to the development of modern Japanese prose. Just as F.'s Russian models portrayed their own class and society—with all its limitations—so F. sought to hold the mirror of fiction up to his compatriots in Japan.

FURTHER WORKS: *Zenshū* (16 vols., 1953–54)

BIBLIOGRAPHY: Ryan, M. G., *"Ukigumo": Japan's First Modern Novel* (1967); Ryan, M. G., *The Development of Realism in the Fiction of Tsubouchi Shōyō* (1975)

MARLEIGH GRAYER RYAN

HAGIWARA Sakutarō
Japanese poet, essayist, and literary theorist, b. 1 Nov. 1886, Maebashi; d. 11 May 1942, Tokyo

The son of wealthy parents, H. was able even as a young man to devote himself full time to writing poetry. He never finished college, but studied Western authors on his own and was especially attracted to Poe,

Nietzsche, Schopenhauer, and Dostoevsky. His first collection of poems, *Tsuki ni hoeru* (1917; *Howling at the Moon*, 1978), immediately established him as a highly imaginative poet. During the next twenty-five years he published five volumes of poetry, eight collections of essays, four books of aphorisms, one novelette, and three treatises on poetry. He also helped to found several literary magazines, and taught at Meiji University in Tokyo from 1934 until the year of his death.

Tsuki ni hoeru gained lavish critical acclaim because it represented the first successful attempt to give, in colloquial Japanese, a poetic form to existential anxiety. The poems skillfully articulated what H. called a "physiological fear," a fear that, lying deep in man's physical existence, ceaselessly threatens his mental well-being. A modern man afflicted with this fear feels something rotten in the core of his being and vainly looks up toward the sky for salvation. In H.'s metaphor man is a dog fearful of his own shadow and forever howling at the moon.

In H.'s second collection of poems, *Aoneko* (1923; *Blue Cat*, 1978), this anxiety gives way to ennui, gloom, and despair. The central image of the book is a tired, melancholy cat sitting lazily and indulging in fantasies. Man, having lost all hope in life, no longer howls at the dream world; he is completely within it. The nihilism pervading the book was partly derived from Schopenhauer, but in giving verbal expression to it H. made masterful use of a dull rhythm characteristic of colloquial Japanese.

Hyōtō (1934; the iceland), H.'s last major book of poetry, marks a return from the dream world to the realities of daily life. The predominant tone of these poems is neither fear nor melancholy; it is the anger of a man ostracized by contemporary society because of his extrasensitivity as a poet. For H., this anger was too intense to express in colloquial Japanese. Making effective use of sonorous literary Japanese, he vented his rage at the people who failed to understand him. Modern Japan seemed like an iceland.

As he grew older, H. turned increasingly to prose. In *Nekomachi* (1935; *The Cat Town*, 1948) he tried to bridge the gap between poetry and prose; in his words, he created a novelette "in the form of a prose poem." The experiment, however, was not entirely successful. Describing a journey into an imaginary land, the book is much like *Aoneko,* but without its evocative power.

H. fared better in writing aphorisms and critical essays. An avid reader of classical poetry, he compiled the anthology *Ren'ai meika shū* (1931; a treasury of love poems), in which he provided his own interpretive analysis of each poem. The analysis was most successful in dealing with poems that sang of longing for a remote, metaphysical lover. His study of an 18th-c. haiku poet, *Kyōshū no shijin Yosa Buson* (1936; Yosa Buson, the poet of nostalgia), likewise is a personal interpretation of poems of longing and nostalgia.

H.'s talent for literary theory found its best expression in *Shi no genri* (1928; principles of poetry). "Through a uniquely dreamlike method," he wrote, "poetry articulates the essence of the self that looms in the twilight zone of consciousness." "A uniquely dreamlike method" meant symbolic representation ("imagerization" was H.'s equivalent for it), and H. considered the Japanese language as lending itself especially well to the symbolist mode, because it was imagistic by nature. On the other hand, he lamented the paucity of musical qualities in modern Japanese.

H. made two major contributions to modern Japanese poetry. First, with his consummate skill with words he demonstrated that vernacular Japanese could be used in an artistically satisfying way. Other poets before him had made use of the vernacular in their works, yet their diction was essentially little different from everyday speech. With H., modern Japanese became a *poetic* language for the first time. Second, he was the first Japanese author who successfully created poetry out of the existential anxiety typical of a modern intellectual. Nietzsche and Schopenhauer had been known in Japan before his time, but no one else had taken their pessimism so much to heart as H. did. For better or for worse, Japanese poetry has come markedly closer to that of Europe through H.'s effort.

FURTHER WORKS: *Atarashiki yokujō* (1922); *Chō o yumemu* (1923); *Junjō shōkoyoku shū* (1925); *Shiron to kansō* (1928); *Kyomō no seigi* (1929); *Junsei shi ron* (1935); *Zetsubō no tōsō* (1935); *Rōka to shitsubō* (1936); *Shijin no shimei* (1937); *Mu kara no kōsō* (1937); *Nippon e no kaiki* (1938); *Shukumei* (1939); *Kikyōsha* (1940); *Minato nite* (1940); *Atai* (1940). FURTHER VOLUME IN ENGLISH: *Face at the Bottom of the World, and Other Poems* (1969)

BIBLIOGRAPHY: Piper, A., "Das Shi als Ausdruck des japanischen Lebensgefühls in der Taishōzeit: H. S. und Takamura Kōtarō," *Nachrichten der Gesellschaft für Natur- und Völkerkunde Ostasiens*, 77, 79–80 (1955–56), 8–21, 110–30; Wilson, G., Introduction to *Face at the Bottom of the World, and Other Poems* (1969), pp. 11–32; Tsukimura, R.,

"H. and the Japanese Lyric Tradition," *JATJ*, 11 (1976), 47–63; Sato, H., Introduction to *Howling at the Moon* (1978), pp. 11–26

MAKOTO UEDA

HAYASHI Fumiko
Japanese novelist, short-story writer, and poet, b. 31 Dec. 1904, Shimonoseki; d. 2 June 1951, Tokyo

Daughter of an itinerant peddler, H. spent most of her childhood traveling from town to town, living always in flea-ridden inns. What she remembered most vividly about those days was perpetual hunger. She found solace, however, in writing poetry and reading. H. managed to put herself through high school by working as a factory hand and as a maid. Upon graduating, she went to Tokyo, only to experience the most bitter hardships of her life. Since childhood, roving had become almost second nature; she never settled in one place and constantly switched jobs (waitress, clerk, peddler, maid). She changed lovers just as swiftly.

Between her jobs and love affairs she found time to write poetry and children's stories. She also kept a diary, excerpts of which were serialized in the women's literary magazine *Nyonin geijutsu*, in 1928, under the title *Hōrōki* (journal of a vagabond). When *Hōrōki* was published in book form in 1930 it immediately attained tremendous popularity. It depicts a young heroine who manages to live with impressive honesty and cheerfulness in the lowest stratum of society. It is candidly narrated, devoid of pessimism and sentimentality. The montagelike sequence of diary entries creates a natural time flow of events, and H.'s style is compellingly vivid and intensely lyrical.

The success of *Hōrōki* put an end to H.'s precarious mode of life; she was able to travel to China and, in 1931, to Europe. She spent much time in Paris frequenting museums, concert halls, and theaters. Returning home in 1932, she wrote a number of short stories that gradually established her place in literary circles.

In 1935 H. wrote her first successful novel, *Inazuma* (lightning), whose characters were modeled on the members of her own family. During the Second Sino-Japanese War (1937–45), she was dispatched to China as a special correspondent by the newspaper *Mainichi*. She also served as a member of the Japanese wartime press corps in the South Pacific in 1942. These experiences gave further scope and depth to her later writings. During the remainder of the war she lived in the country and concentrated on writing children's stories.

In 1948 H. published one of her finest stories, "Bangiku" ("Late Chrysanthemum," 1960). It delineates with consummate skill the subtle, shifting moods of a retired geisha who is visited by a former lover. But on arrival the man confides that the purpose of his visit is to solicit financial assistance. Struggling to hold onto her receding romance, she receives a second blow on learning that the money is for extricating him from a tangled affair with a young woman.

Ukigumo (1951; *Floating Cloud,* 1957) was acclaimed as H.'s major work. The heroine Yukiko leaves for Indochina, trying to forget a rape incident. There she falls in love with Tomioka, and together they return to Japan. Spurned by him, she vainly tries to revive Tomioka's affection and gradually degenerates to the point of prostitution. Tomioka, having failed in business, leaves for Yaku Island. Enfeebled with tuberculosis, Yukiko follows him to the island only to die while he is away in the mountains. Just before her death Yukiko abandons herself to beautiful memories of their days in Indochina. A dark pessimism prevails in this work, but H.'s controlled detachment and penetrating insight into the fallen, wandering Yukiko generate a genuine pathos and an added dimension to the world of H.'s hobo protagonists.

Few of her contemporaries can rival H.'s skill in vividly evoking a particular atmosphere. Perhaps more important, she felt and understood the loneliness of displaced women, creating female characters, alienated but always alive, who speak with a universal voice that transcends their milieu and their homeland.

FURTHER WORKS: *Hatō* (1939); *Shitamachi* (1948; *Tokyo,* 1957); *Chairo no me* (1949); *Meshi* (1951); *H. F. zenshū* (23 vols., 1951–52)

BIBLIOGRAPHY: Morris, I., ed., *Modern Japanese Stories* (1962), pp. 349–50; Janeira, A. M., *Japanese and Western Literature: A Comparative Study* (1970), pp. 172–74; Johnson, E. W., "Modern Japanese Women Writers," *LE&W,* 18 (1974), 98–99

KINYA TSURUTA

IBUSE Masuji

Japanese novelist, short-story writer, essayist, and poet, b. 15 Feb. 1898, Kamo

Born into an old family of independent farmers, I. spent his childhood in the country. In 1917 he moved to Tokyo and for several years studied literature and painting. Although he specialized in French literature, he became interested in Russian writers, chiefly in Tolstoy and Chekhov.

In 1923 I. published his first successful story, "Yūhei" (confinement). The story, a satirical allegory of intellectual and artistic pretense, is better known by its revised title, "Sanshōuo" ("Salamander," 1971). In another early story, "Yofuke to ume no hana" (1925; "Plum Blossom at Night," 1971), I. blended a self-mocking humor with a dreamy, symbolist mood.

The allegorical or symbolist overtones of these early works suggest Western influences, but in 1926, with "Koi" ("Carp," 1971), I. turned to the more traditional techniques of his homeland. Using the highly subjective Japanese "I-novel" mode, in which narrator and author are one, he interwove fiction and reality, literary symbols and actuality. In sharp contrast, however, with other I-novelists who concentrate solely on expressing their own feelings, he used the technique as a means of restraining the emotion-filled memories precipitated by a friend's death.

During the 1930s, I.'s thematic interest shifted to the rustic countryside of southern Japan where he was born. A painstaking craftsman, he had always spent more time revising and polishing his stories than taking sides in ideological polemics.

The symbolic return to his native soil inspired some of I.'s best stories and novellas, such as "Tangeshitei" (1931; "Life at Mr. Tange's," 1971), a loving, humorous evocation of two colorful rustics, master and servant, in a remote mountain valley.

In these works, I.'s expression acquired its full, mature flavor. Skillful use of dialect, subtle contrasts in dialogue, nuances of mood and setting, a wry humor and sparse characterization through gesture and manner of speech, are the distinguishing traits of this style.

As the military clique rose to power and Japan was moving toward World War II, I. steadily worked on the most remarkable of his works on historical themes, *Sazanami gunki* (1930–38; a war diary). The historical background of the novella is the actual escape and the final defeat of the Heike clan in the 12th c.; the story itself portrays the initiation of a sensitive young Heike samurai into a brutal world.

I.'s last major prewar work, the novella *Tajinko mura* (1939; "Tajinko Village," 1971), presents a broad portrayal of the life of a village; it is also a fond farewell to a gentler way of life that cannot last.

I. did not write much during the war; his unwilling induction into the army as a war correspondent probably inspired his biting satire of the debilitating influence of army drills in "Yōhai taichō" (1950; "Lieutenant Lookeast," 1971).

Although I. returned to publishing short stories and novellas in the years following World War II, he was preparing for his longest and most important novel, *Kuroi ame* (1966; *Black Rain*, 1969), which deals with the atomic ordeal of Hiroshima. A quiet elegy for a city and its population, *Kuroi ame* emerges as a significant work of art distinct from the many sentimental or political accounts of the bombing.

I. avoided portraying the disaster in its totality, but rather set the beauty of the southern landscape, the ancient customs of the people, their colorful foibles, the little, everyday details of their lives, against the absurd brutality of the atomic holocaust. All his previous techniques and thematic interests served him well here. He needed not only his characteristic sympathy for the simple life and an intimate knowledge of popular lore, but also the calm tone and detached poise of a chronicler that he had acquired in his earlier historical writings. He also needed the skill to handle a vast documentary montage of eyewitness accounts and authentic journals.

Using the rich resources of his literary tradition, I. cautiously experimented with a number of prose techniques and styles, trying to expand the limits of the novel. He enlivened the conventional I-novel, grafted onto the ancient stock of romantic nature-lyricism a robust, epic quality, and introduced a dry, original humor into the often too serious and sometimes too sentimental art of modern Japanese prose writing.

FURTHER WORKS: *Shigotobeya* (1931); *Kawa* (1932); *Zuihitsu* (1933); *Keirokushū* (1936); *Shūkin ryokō* (1937); *John Manjirō hyōryūki* (1937; *John Manjiro: The Cast-Away, His Life and Adventures,* 1940); *Shiguretō jokei* (1941); *I. M. zuihitsu zenshū* (3 vols., 1941); *Chūshū meigetsu* (1942); *Gojinka* (1944); *Wabisuke* (1946); *Magemono* (1946); *Oihagi no hanashi* (1947); *I. M. zenshū* (9 vols., 1948); *Kashima ari* (1948); *Shibireike kamo* (1948); *Honjitsu kyūshin* (1950); *Kawatsuri* (1952); *I. M. sakuhinshū* (5 vols., 1953); *Hyōmin Nanakamado* (1955); *Usaburō* (1956); *Kanreki no koi* (1957); *Ekimae ryokan* (1957); *Nanatsu no kaidō* (1957); *Chinpindo shujin* (1959); *Tsurishi, Tsuriba* (1960); *Kinō no kai* (1961); *Shuzai ryokō* (1961); *Bushū hachigatajō* (1963); *Mushinjō* (1963); *I. M. zenshū* (12 vols., 1964); *Gendai bungaku taikei* (1966); *Shinchō nihon bungaku* (1970); *Tsuribito* (1970); *I. M. zenshū* (14 vols., 1975). FURTHER VOLUME IN ENGLISH: *Lieutenant Lookeast, and Other Stories* (1971)

BIBLIOGRAPHY: Lifton, R., "*Black Rain*," *Death in Life* (1967), pp. 543–55; Kimball, A., "After the Bomb," *Crisis in Identity and Contemporary*

Japanese Novels (1973), pp. 43–59; Liman, A. V., "I.'s *Black Rain,*" in Tsuruta, K., and Swann, T., eds., *Approaches to the Modern Japanese Novel* (1976), pp. 45–72

ANTHONY V. LIMAN

ISHIKAWA Takuboku

Japanese poet, critic, and diarist, b. 20 Feb. 1886, Hinoto village, Iwate prefecture; d. 13 April 1912, Tokyo

The only son of a Zen priest in a rural community in northern Japan, I. developed a strong, individualistic personality. From his student days on, he engaged in literary activity, dropping out of school in 1902 in order to go to Tokyo to become a writer. His first verses, in the form of *tanka* (or *waka*, thirty-one-syllable poems), were published in the influential periodical, *Myōjō,* and I. benefited from the tutelage of the editor, Yosano Tekkan (1873–1935), and his wife, the poet Yosano Akiko (1878–1942). In February 1903, I. became ill and was forced to return to his home in northern Japan. From this time until his death from tuberculosis, he struggled against abject poverty and failing health.

I.'s first collection of verse, *Akogare* (1905; longing), demonstrated a strong romantic bent, but thereafter his poetry took on an independent direction. With *Ichiaku no suna* (1910; *A Handful of Sand,* 1934) he established himself as a leading writer of *tanka,* to which he imparted a new tone of realism. He endeavored to write "poems that are down to earth, poems with feelings unremoved from actual life," and he abhorred all traces of imitativeness. The 551 verses of *Ichiaku no suna* were integrated to form a unified whole, imparting a sense of growth and progression to the collection and giving somewhat the effect of a spiritual autobiography in verse. Through *Ichiaku no suna* and his posthumously published book of verse, *Kanashiki gangu* (1912; sad toys), I. infused a powerful new current of life into the old tradition of *tanka.* His verses continue to be anthologized in Japanese school texts, and later *tanka* poets have accepted his innovations, which changed the very nature of this form of poetry.

In the last years of his life, after the trial behind closed doors and execution (which followed immediately) of the Japanese anarchist philosopher Kōtoku Shūsui (1871–1911), I. was increasingly moved by socialist ideals, as verses such as the following reveal: "Still quite far away/I believed it all to be;/But the terrorists'/Plaintive and heart-rending cry/ Day by day now draws nearer." In 1910–12, in association with Toki

Zemmaro (1885–1980), *tanka* poet, essayist, and scholar of Japanese literature, I. attempted to publish a socialist literary magazine. The venture failed, but their friendship, ardor for socialism, and efforts to establish a proletarian *tanka* group continued undiminished. One week before I.'s death, Toki Zemmaro delivered the manuscript for *Kanashiki gangu* to the publisher and used the twenty-yen advance to buy medicine to comfort his dying friend.

I.'s diaries and miscellaneous writings, as well as his verse, are admired for the stark revelation of his search for love and his struggle against poverty, despair, and death. His *Romaji nikki* (1948–49; partial tr., *The Romaji Diary,* 1956), the especially noteworthy journal that I. kept in the spring of 1909, stands out as one of the memorable works of 20th-c. Japan. It reveals a completely modern three-dimensional man, capable of introspection and displaying fierce, self-destructive honesty.

One of the first modern voices in Japanese poetry, I. is best remembered for the way in which he utilized the traditional *tanka* form to articulate new problems of the modern age. Despite the brevity of his life, I.'s subsequent influence on *tanka* poets such as Saitō Mokichi (1882–1953), Nishimura Yōkichi (1892–1959), and Watanabe Junzō (1894–1972) marks him as one of the significant innovators and as one of the enduring voices in 20th-c. Japanese literature. I.'s writings reveal not a tranquil world of soft rain sounds and delicate relations but rather the shrill outcry of a tortured young soul, pouring forth a red-hot stream of uncontrollable passion.

FURTHER WORKS: *Yobiko to kuchibue* (1913); *Takuboku zenshū* (8 vols., 1978). FURTHER VOLUMES IN ENGLISH: *The Poetry of I. T.* (1959); *Takuboku: Poems to Eat* (1966)

BIBLIOGRAPHY: Takamine, H., *A Sad Toy: A Unique and Popular Poet, Takuboku's Life and His Poems* (1962); Keene, D., *Landscapes and Portraits* (1971), pp. 131–70; Hijiya, Y., *I. T.* (1979)

LEON M. ZOLBROD

IZUMI Kyōka

(pseud. of Izumi Kyōtarō) Japanese novelist and dramatist, b. 4 Nov. 1873, Kanazawa; d. 7 Sept. 1939, Tokyo

I.'s native city of Kanazawa was one of the great centers for the flourishing arts and crafts of Japan throughout the Edo period (1603–1868). I.'s family was very much a part of this traditional world; his mother had deep ties with the Nō theater, and his father was a craftsman specializing in metal engraving. This ambience of traditional culture and art proved to be a major source of I.'s literary background. His writing is enriched by the traditions of *gesaku* (popular) fiction, the Kabuki theater, the art of the storytellers, and local legends. Of particular importance were the prose and poetry of the Nō texts.

Like other aspiring writers of the period, he went to Tokyo, where in 1891 he apprenticed himself to Ozaki Kōyō (1867–1903) and began to learn the writer's craft. By 1895 he had achieved a position in the literary establishment, and his first important works began to appear, at the same time as the rise of Japanese romanticism.

Kōya hijiri (1900; *The Kōya Priest*, 1959–60) is I.'s best and most representative work of this period. It displays the full range of his commitment to romanticism, fantasy, and beauty. Central to the story is his depiction of the disturbingly beautiful seductress, a figure who appears in many of his works and whom critics view as a nostalgic evocation of his mother who died when he was nine. The story is replete with the Buddhist notions of sinful passion and salvation by grace, while its style, called *gembun-itchi*, is a mixture of the classical and the colloquial languages, rich with Chinese words, yet supple and musical in its rhythms.

Just as I. reached this peak of literary development, naturalism came to full flower in Japan, and he found himself increasingly isolated within the literary world. He never wavered, however, in his commitment to romantic writing. In an age when other writers were rushing forward to embrace new styles and to use literature as a vehicle for the expression of the "self," I. remained steadfast in his old-fashioned style of writing. At this time he published *Uta andon* (1910; the paper lantern of poetry), one of the masterpieces of his mature period. This work draws significantly on the literary heritage of both the Nō and Kabuki theaters as well as on Edo travel fiction. At one level it can also be seen simply as a celebration of artistic beauty. It is written in the elegant *gembun-itchi* style that immediately sets this story apart from the spare, clinical narratives of the naturalist writers.

I.'s final work, *Rukō shinsō* (1939; a web of crimson thread) appeared a few weeks before his death. This novel combines all the elements for which I.'s work is known: ghosts from the past, the beautiful temptress, the distorting power of passion, and the redeeming power of mercy.

I. has been greatly admired by such modern writers as Kawabata Yasunari and Mishima Yukio (qq.v.). In a literary career of fifty years, I. recognized that the literature of the present is necessarily based on the literature of the past. And so he looked to the old Edo culture and spun his elaborate, dreamlike fantasies, and with this web of dreams he built a link with the past.

FURTHER WORKS: *Yushima mōde* (1899); *Muyūju* (1906); *Nanamotozakura* (1906); *Aika* (1906); *Shikibu kōji* (1907); *Kusa meikyū* (1908); *Onna keizu* (1908); *Shinsaku* (1909); *Koinyōbo* (1913); *Nihonbashi* (1914); *Oshidorichō* (1918); *Yukari no onna kushige shū* (1921); *Rindō to nadeshiko* (1924)

STEPHEN W. KOHL

KAWABATA Yasunari
Japanese novelist, b. 11 June 1899, Osaka; d. 16 April, 1972, Kamakura

K. lost all his closest relatives by the age of fourteen. His diary, virtually his first literary product, published only in 1925 as *Jūrokusai no nikki* (the diary of a sixteen-year-old-boy), records the boy's observation of his dying grandfather (the "sixteen" in the title refers to the old style of reckoning age). As a middle-school student well versed in the Japanese classics, K. chose to become a writer and soon began to contribute short stories to a local paper. In 1924 he became a leading member of the "New Perceptionist" group of young writers interested in the literary and art trends from the West. During this experimental period K.'s works revealed the modernist influence. Soon after his reaffirmation of his inheritance of Japan's literary tradition K. began to publish in serial form the celebrated *Yukiguni* (1935–48; *Snow Country,* 1956); this work was succeeded by numerous serialized novels that appeared after the defeat of Japan. K. was also noted as an acute critic and discoverer of new talents. He won the Nobel Prize for literature in 1968. Four years later he took his own life.

Izu no odoriko (1926; *The Izu Dancer,* 1955) established K.'s reputation. On a journey a young student encounters a fourteen-year-old dancer, a member of a family of traveling entertainers. The youth appreciates their kindness and feels a genuine innocent love for the girl. The autobiographical hero, a receptive observer, foreshadows his fictional successors. This simple story ends with a separation, as in most of K.'s novels.

K. generates a pervasive sadness not with the depiction of catastrophic conflicts, but with great subtlety, as best exemplified in *Yukiguni*, a story about a country geisha, Komako, who falls in love with Shimamura, a dilettante from Tokyo. This novel demonstrates K.'s remarkable style, uniquely his own, and characterized by refined simplicity and evocative images. Lyric descriptions of nature are central to the narrative progression in K.'s novels. Their basically episodic form emerges through the allusive links of successive scenes, not according to a well-defined plot structure. As is often pointed out, this form echoes the Japanese poetic tradition, especially that of *renga,* linked verse.

The traditional Japanese sensibility discerns the quality of evanescence in beautiful objects. The search for and admiration of beauty are dominant Kawabata themes. Beauty in K. is not unattainable absolute beauty; it is manifested in the innocence and purity of a girl or in the warmth of a woman's love, or in a kind of devotion exemplified by the hero in *Meijin* (1954; *The Master of Go,* 1972). Pursuit of such beauty cannot be isolated from an awareness of deprivation or from the encroachment of fatigue, degeneration, and death.

Sembazuru (1952; *Thousand Cranes,* 1959) and *Mizuumi* (1954; *The Lake,* 1974) explore the degradation and guilt into which man is liable to be led through the attraction of beauty. *Sembazuru,* centering on the tea ceremony, recalls the karmic, incestuous relationships in the famous 11th-c. Japanese novel *The Tale of Genji. Mizuumi,* with few references to the tradition, is perhaps the most experimental among K.'s postwar novels. Hallucinations, stream-of-consciousness, and free associations in the complex shifts of time are used to portray an ex-teacher's impelling desire to follow beautiful women. In spite of the character's grotesquely ugly degeneration, this exploration into the dark subconscious is again permeated with lyrical pathos.

Direct human relationships are avoided in *Kinjū* (1933; *Of Birds and Beasts,* 1969), whose hero, rejecting human affection, raises birds and dogs, and in *Nemureru bijo* (1961; *House of Sleeping Beauties,* 1969), a bizarre, but nonetheless masterfully controlled story of an old man who visits an establishment to sleep for a night with drugged girls. This evasion is carried to an extreme in a strange story, *Kataude* (1964; *One Arm,* 1969), in which a human relationship exists only through a severed arm. These works might be read as satires on dehumanizing alienation,

JAPANESE LITERATURE   105

but again the lyrical and often reflective note implicitly calls for the recovery of a wholesome communion.

K.'s most important work, *Yama no oto* (1954; *The Sound of the Mountain*, 1970), subtly embodies his profound understanding of human nature and suggests the possible achievement of such a communion. This difficult task is undertaken in the spiritual chaos following Japan's defeat. The aging protagonist, Shingo, is deeply concerned about the marital crises of his two children and tries, as much as he can, to assist. The novel attempts to redeem and reaffirm that traditional Japanese sensibility that enjoys communion with nature and caring human relationships. Stylistically as well, this novel is K.'s finest achievement. The dialogue, which exhibits his accomplished ease in creating scenes from daily life, is skillfully interwoven with the hero's dreams, recollections, and reflections. The poetic descriptions of nature, often consisting of extremely evocative one-sentence paragraphs, are suggestive of the psychological state of the protagonist. At the same time these passages also allow the reader's participation in the hero's communion with nature.

K.'s works represent a rare combination of tradition and modernity. The quiet realism, the seeming formlessness, and above all the poetic intensity in K., while testifying to the tenacious literary legacy of Japan, suggest to the West many innovative possibilities.

FURTHER WORKS: *Kanjō sōshoku* (1926); *Asakusa kurenaidan* (1930); *Hana no warutsu* (1940); *Maihime* (1951); *Hi mo tsuki mo* (1953); *Tokyo no hito* (1955); *Niji ikutabi* (1955); *Onna de aru koto* (1957); *Kaze no aru michi* (1959); *Koto* (1962); *Kawa no aru shitamachi no hanashi* (1962); *Utsukushisa to kanashimi to* (1965; *Beauty and Sadness*, 1975); *Rakka ryūsui* (1966); *Gekka no mon* (1967); *Utsukushii Nihon no watakushi* (1969; *Japan the Beautiful and Myself*, 1969); *Bi no sonzai to hakken* (1969; *The Existence and Discovery of Beauty*, 1969)

BIBLIOGRAPHY: Tsukimura, R., "A Thematic Study of the Works of K. Y.," *JATJ*, 5 (1968), 22–31; Seidensticker, E. G., "K.," *HudR*, 22 (1969), 6–10; Tsukimura, R., "Theme and Technique in *Mizuumi*," in Japan PEN Club, ed., *Studies on Japanese Culture* (1973), Vol. I, pp. 433–39; Miyoshi, M., *Accomplices of Silence: The Modern Japanese Novel* (1974), pp. 95–121; Ueda, M., "The Virgin, the Wife, and the Nun: K.'s *Snow Country*," in Tsuruta, K., and Swann, T. E., eds., *Approaches to the Modern Japanese Novel* (1976), pp. 73–88; Tsuruta, K., "Two Journeys in *The Sound of the Mountain*," in Tsuruta, K., and

Swann, T. E., eds., *Approaches to the Modern Japanese Novel* (1976), pp. 89–103; Ueda, M., *Modern Japanese Writers and the Nature of Literature* (1976), pp. 173–218; Tsuruta, K., "The Colour Scheme in *House of the Sleeping Beauties*," in Tsukimura, R., ed., *Life, Death and Age in Modern Japanese Fiction* (1978), pp. 21–34; Tsukimura, R., "The Symbolic Significance of the Old Man in *The Sound of the Mountain*," in Tsukimura, R., ed., *Life, Death and Age in Modern Japanese Fiction* (1978), pp. 45–54

REIKO TSUKIMURA

KISHIDA Kunio
Japanese dramatist and critic, b. 2 Nov. 1890, Tokyo; d. 5 March 1954, Tokyo

Born into a samurai family, K. went through military school and received a commission, He disappointed his father, a military officer, however, by resigning in order to take up the study of French literature at Tokyo University in 1916 instead of carrying on the family tradition. He left the university before graduation and went to France in 1920, determined to learn the craft of playwriting. In Paris he studied with the famous director Jacques Copeau at the Théâtre du Vieux Colombier.

K. returned to Japan in 1922 to try to create a truly modern Japanese drama based on the creation of poetic and psychologically accurate dialogue he found in the European works he discovered while living in Paris. K.'s efforts to replace a Japanese drama still heavily dependent on more traditional means of expression also led him into drama criticism, theater management, and stage direction, but all these activities shared the same purpose: to create a contemporary drama responsive to the psychological realities that he felt were crucial to portray if the Japanese theater were to become a viable form of modern literary expression.

K.'s early one-act plays are marked by a highly effective fusion of realistic dialogue and elegant fantasy. *Chiroru no aki* (1924; autumn in the Tyrol) places a Japanese protagonist in a European setting, in which he develops an affection for a European woman staying in the same small Austrian hotel. *Buranko* (1925; the swing) shows a young Tokyo couple coming to grips with the shifting roles of sense and sensibility in a marriage. The most successful of his early plays, *Kamifūsen* (1925; paper balloon), is a more lyrical examination of the same predicament.

By the late 1920s K.'s reputation had grown to the point that he was asked to write full-length plays for production in Tokyo, and much of his best work dates from this period. *Ochiba nikki* (1927; diary of fallen leaves) remains one of K.'s most poignant statements about the meaning of his French experience. The protagonist of the play is an elderly Japanese woman, of great wit and charm, whose son had married a French woman some years before; her granddaughter, Henriette, now stays with her. K.'s grasp of the nuances of the differences in cultures and his genuine ability to create effective stage personality makes the old lady, whose death scene concludes the play, one of his most moving creations. France figures again in *Ushiyama hoteru* (1929; Ushiyama Hotel), which chronicles in a sardonic, almost nihilistic fashion, the lives of a group of Japanese living in a dingy hotel in Vietnam, then a French colony.

After a long series of experiments, K. reached the final phase of his development in *Sawa shi no futari musume* (1935; Mr. Sawa's two daughters), which combines evocative dialogue with trenchant commentary on the social and psychological climate of the time. Like the characters in the earlier plays of K., those presented here are sophisticated and worldly (Mr. Sawa himself has lived in Europe), but their attempts at self-understanding are altogether Japanese.

By the beginning of World War II, K. had stopped writing, although he continued certain theatrical and cultural activities until 1944. After the end of the war he wrote a few short pieces but was hampered by ill health and heavy duties with the Bungakuza, an important acting troupe. He died while directing a play for the Bungakuza.

K.'s plays remain among the most respected modern classics of the Japanese stage and are still admired for their subtle dialogue, vivid atmosphere, and an emphasis on the centrality for the drama of individual psychology, a concept at variance with the Marxist dramaturgy popular in influential theater circles in Tokyo before the government suppression in the late 1930s. The Kishida Prize, the most important drama award in Japan, indicates the esteem in which K.'s work is still held. K.'s plays provide the best theatrical record of the Japanese in search of their own spiritual identity during the difficult decades between the two world wars.

FURTHER WORKS: *Furui omocha* (1924); *Hazakura* (1925); *Mura de ichi ban kuri no ki* (1926); *Mama sensei to sono otto* (1930); *Asamayama* (1931); *Shokugyō* (1935); *Saigetsu* (1935); *Fūzoku jihyō* (1936); *Zenshū* (10 vols., 1955)

BIBLIOGRAPHY: Japan UNESCO Commission, ed., *Theatre in Japan* (1963), pp. 213–41; Ortolani, B., "Shingeki: The Maturing New Drama of Japan," in Roggendorf, J., ed., *Studies in Japanese Culture* (1963), pp. 163–85; Rimer, J. T., *Toward a Modern Japanese Theatre: K. K.* (1974)

J. THOMAS RIMER

KUNIKIDA Doppo

(pseud. of Kunikida Tetsuo; known as Doppo) Japanese short-story writer, b. 15 July 1871, Chōshi; d. 23 June 1908, Chigasaki

K. grew up with a sense of pride in his samurai heritage mingled with an awareness that samurai ideals were ill suited to the competitive modern age; due in part to his father's financial insecurity, he was unable to finish college, and he supported himself as a teacher and then as a war correspondent.

K. is remembered for his literary works (including some marginally successful experiments in modern verse), but in fact he spent the greater part of his brief professional life as a journalist, distinguishing himself initially with lively accounts of his shipboard experiences during the Sino-Japanese War of 1894–95. He met his first wife, a willful "modern" woman who shared his Christian faith, at a reception for newly returned war correspondents, and when she deserted him after six months of marriage, both his religious faith and the romanticized view of love he had absorbed from his reading in the English romantics were destroyed. Perhaps as a result of this early disillusionment, he became the first writer of his generation to break away from puerile sentimentalism.

From his earliest attempt at fiction, the prose-poem "Takibi" (1896; "The Bonfire," 1970), to his last important story, "Take no kido" (1908; "The Bamboo Gate," 1972), there is a remarkable consistency of theme and imagery in K.'s writing. Lonely wanderers or figures in the distance symbolize the endless stream of humanity drifting into and out of the world, but individually leaving no mark upon it. Early stories, such as "Gen oji" (1897; "Old Gen," 1955) and "Wasureenu hitobito" (1898; "Unforgettable People," 1972), and the lyrical essay "Musashino" (1898; Musashino) express this theme in a voice close to song, while later stories, such as "Shōjikimono" (1903; "An Honest Man," 1972) and "Take no kido," attempt to invest the symbolic characters with individual personalities and place them in a dramatic context.

Turgenev's *Sportsman's Sketches* first provided K. with a Western model of poetic fiction, while the example of Maupassant brought to his later work a greater command of detached narration. In contrast to the so-called naturalists, with whom he is usually grouped, however, K. never relinquished the view of the moral nature of man he learned from his reading of Wordsworth. He was being praised as a pioneer naturalist near the end of his life (he died young of tuberculosis), but he firmly rejected the label.

As much as K. owed to his Western models, he left an entirely original and coherent body of works that draw from his own experience and imaginative power. Written in a period of Japanese literature that was primarily transitional and derivative, his stories not only served as models for such later masters as Shiga Naoya and Akutagawa Ryūnosuke (qq.v.) but they continue to be read and enjoyed in their own right.

FURTHER WORKS: *Musashino* (1901); *D.-shū* (1905); *Unmei* (1906); *Tōsei* (1907); *Byōshōroku* (1908); *D.-shū dai-ni* (1908); *Azamukazaru no ki* (2 vols., 1908–9); *Aitei tsūshin* (1908); *Nagisa* (1908); *K. D. zenshū* (10 vols., 1964–67)

BIBLIOGRAPHY: McClellan, E., "The Impressionistic Technique in Some Modern Japanese Novelists," *ChiR*, 57 (1965), 48–60; Rubin, J., "Five Stories by K. D.," *MN*, 27 (1972), 273–341

JAY RUBIN

MASAOKA Shiki

(pseud. of Masaoka Tsunenori) Japanese poet, diarist, critic, essayist, and journalist, b. 14 Oct. 1867, Matsuyama; d. 19 Sept. 1902, Tokyo.

After studying philosophy and Japanese literature for two years at the University of Tokyo, M. left to become the haiku (traditional seventeen-syllable verse form) editor of the newspaper *Nippon,* from whose pages he launched his reform of the haiku in 1892. In 1895 he went to China as a war correspondent for *Nippon* but became so ill (with tuberculosis) on the return trip that he nearly died. For the rest of his life M. was an invalid.

Nevertheless, he managed to lead a very active literary life from his sickbed. In 1897, he and his disciples founded the literary journal *Hoto-togisu.* The next year he launched a reform of the tanka (traditional thirty-one-syllable verse form) similar in aim to his earlier reform of the haiku, and also turned his attention to autobiographical essays.

When M. began his career, the haiku and the tanka had come to be regarded as frivolous pastimes incapable of expressing the complexities of modern life. The necessary premise of M.'s haiku reform, as well as his most important contribution as a critic, was his insistence on the potential of the haiku and the tanka as serious literature. The second pillar of M.'s haiku reform was his commitment to realism as the aim of literature. His reevaluation of the 18th-c. poet Yosa Buson (1716–1783) in the light of the ideal of realism was responsible for Buson's reputation today as one of the greatest haiku poets. His most important writings on haiku are *Dassai sho-oku haiwa* (1892; talks on haiku from the otter's den), *Haikai taiyō* (1895; the essence of haikai), and *Haijin Buson* (1897; the haiku poet Buson).

At first M.'s poems (both his haiku and tanka) were derivative. Later they became efforts to depict real scenes from nature or daily life, and finally, in the last few years of his life, he created a literary persona, a semifictional "I," who became the central character of his most affecting works while he still retained the realism of his earlier works. The recurring theme of his later work, especially of the two diaries that he published in his last two years, *Bokujū itteki* (1901; partial tr., "A Drop of Ink," 1975) and *Byōshō rokushaku* (1902; a six-foot sickbed), is the juxtaposition of M.'s own suffering mortality with the ongoing life of nature and the human world. The prose style he used in these works had been developed through his experiments with the short essay beginning in 1898 and later influenced a significant number of Japanese novelists, including Natsume Sōseki and Shiga Naoya (qq.v.). Thus, as well as having brought haiku into the modern age and having established the dominant tone of the modern tanka, M. was instrumental in the evolution of modern Japanese prose style.

There is no room to doubt M.'s crucial importance as a critic and charismatic literary figure who inspired an entire generation of haiku poets. On the other hand, there has been a wrong-headed tendency for critics and scholars (now beginning to change) to question his merits as a poet and virtually ignore the diaries and essays. M.'s excellence as a writer lies in neither his poetry nor his prose but in writing that is on the border between the two. The two diaries mentioned above best exemplify this style, in that they combine qualities of the classical Japanese poetic diary with the self-revelation of modern autobiography.

FURTHER WORKS: *Shiki zenshū* (25 vols., 1975–78). FURTHER VOLUME IN ENGLISH: *Peonies Kana: Haiku by the Upsasak Shiki* (1972)

BIBLIOGRAPHY: Brower, R. H., "M. S. and Tanka Reform," in Shively, D. H., ed., *Tradition and Modernization in Japanese Culture* (1971), pp. 379–418; Keene, D., "*Shiki* and Takuboku," *Landscapes and Portraits: Appreciations of Japanese Culture* (1971), pp. 157–70; Beichman-Yamamoto, J., "M. S.'s *A Drop of Ink*," *MN*, 30 (1975), 291–302; Ueda, M., "M. S.," *Modern Japanese Haiku: An Anthology*, pp. 3–8, 25; Beichman, J., *M. S.* (1982)

JANINE BEICHMAN

MISHIMA Yukio

(pseud. of Hiraoka Kimitake) Japanese novelist, short-story writer, dramatist, and essayist, b. 14 Jan. 1925, Tokyo; d. 25 Nov. 1970, Tokyo

M., the son of a government official, was raised mainly by his paternal grandmother, who hardly permitted the boy out of her sight. This fact has frequently been cited to explain both his fragility and oversensitivity as an adolescent.

In 1944, the year in which he entered Tokyo University, his first book, *Hanazakari no mori* (the forest in full bloom), was published. In 1945 he took his physical examination for military service, but was rejected.

In 1946 M. met Kawabata Yasunari (q.v.). The older novelist took an interest in his work and not only introduced him to the literary world but recommended his stories to important magazines. M. continued his law studies at Tokyo University, but found after graduation in 1947 that he could not combine a career as a civil servant with that of a writer; he resigned his post in the finance ministry in 1948 to devote himself entirely to his writings. M. was not an avant-garde writer and showed relatively little interest in the work of foreign contemporary writers; he drew greater inspiration from premodern literature, both Japanese and Western. His absorption with classical Japanese literature sets him off from other writers of his generation.

Kamen no kokuhaku (1948; *Confessions of a Mask*, 1968) was the novel that established M.'s literary reputation. In the opinion of some critics, this is his best work. It describes in thinly disguised form M.'s childhood memories, his life as a student, and his wartime experiences. It is a record of the significant steps in the development of the narrator's awareness that he would have to wear a mask before the world because of his abnormal sexual preferences.

The central character of M.'s next major novel, *Ai no kawaki* (1950; *Thirst for Love*, 1969), is Etsuko, a woman who has become the mistress of her late husband's father. M. admitted that he had written this novel under the influence of François Mauriac, and it is not difficult to detect similarities between Etsuko and various Mauriac protagonists. But the climactic moments when Etsuko gashes the back of the young man she loves as he cavorts at a festival, or when in the final scene she kills him, continue the mood of *Kamen no kokuhaku*. Etsuko's victim is the strong, sunburned youth untroubled by intellectual concerns who seemed to embody for M. the most attractive aspect of traditional Japan.

Perhaps M.'s finest novel is *Kinkakuji* (1956; *The Temple of the Golden Pavilion*, 1959). The central incident, the burning of the celebrated temple by a deranged monk, was inspired by an actual event of 1950. M.'s concern here was not with uncovering the facts but with establishing circumstances that would make the act seem logical and even inevitable.

Many of M.'s later novels were intended as experiments. In the unsuccessful *Kyōko no ie* (1959; Kyoko's house) he apportioned different aspects of his life among the four main characters in the detached manner of a "study in nihilism," to use his description. He followed this with the less ambitious but nearly flawless *Utage no ato* (1960; *After the Banquet*, 1963), a story so closely based on the personal life of a well-known politician that M. lost the ensuing suit for invasion of privacy.

Even as he was writing these novels, M. wrote many short stories and novellas. His best novella, *Yūkoku* (1960; *Patriotism*, 1966), describes the suicides of a young army officer and his wife. This was the first manifestation of M.'s absorption with the February 26, 1936, army coup, when young officers attempted to wrest power from the politicians in the name of the emperor. M. contrasted the purity of their motives with the greed of the old politicians and businessmen. His fascination with their ideals led him to emulate them.

His plays, especially those included in *Kindai nōgaku shū* (1956; *Five Modern Nō Plays*, 1957), were the finest written in Japan in the postwar years. M.'s plays were cast in many idioms, and their contents ranged from contemporary events to themes inspired by the Nō dramas and the tragedies of Euripides and Racine. His best full-length play was *Sado kōshaku fujin* (1965; *Madame de Sade,* 1967), of which he wrote: "I felt obliged to dispense entirely with the usual, trivial stage effects, and to control the action exclusively by dialogue; collisions of ideas had to create the shape of the drama, and sentiments had to be paraded throughout in the garb of reason." The play was clearly in the tradition of Racine, M.'s favorite among Western dramatists. Each of the six women of the play stands for a particular kind of feminine personality as it reacts to the offstage presence of the Marquis de Sade.

M.'s last work of fiction, the tetralogy *Hōjō no umi* (1969–71; the sea of fertility), is loosely based on an 11th-c. Japanese tale of dreams and reincarnation. In his own opinion, this was the grand summation of his work as a novelist. The first volume, *Haru no yuki* (1969; *Spring Snow,* 1972), evoked the world of the aristocracy in 1912. This story, told with exceptional beauty of style and detail, was an expression of the feminine ideals of Japan. The second volume, *Homba* (1969; *Runaway Horses,* 1972), by contrast, describes the masculine ideals of the way of the Japanese warrior. It takes place in the 1930s, and its protagonist, the stern young Isao, is the reincarnation of the rather effeminate protagonist of *Haru no yuki.* In *Homba* M. gave his most powerful expression of the themes of loyalty and devotion to Japanese ideals that had occupied him since *Yūkoku.*

The third volume, *Akatsuki no tera* (1970; *The Temple of Dawn,* 1973), is divided into two parts: the first is set in southeast Asia, where we first see the Thai princess who is the reincarnation of Isao; the second takes place in Japan after World War II, when the old values of society have been corrupted. The last volume, *Tennin gosui* (1971; *The Decay of the Angel,* 1974), carries the story into the future, and describes the conflict between the reincarnation of the Thai princess and the one man who has observed the four transformations of the being whose decay presages his end. The novel concludes with a superbly written scene that casts doubt on the reality of the events described in the four volumes. In the end we discover that the "sea of fertility" may be as arid as the region of that name on the moon, although it seems to suggest infinite richness.

On the day that M. delivered the final instalment of *Tennin gosui* to his publisher he and members of his private "army" broke into the headquarters of the Japanese Self-Defense Force. He unsuccessfully harangued a crowd of soldiers, and soon afterward committed *seppuku* in the traditional manner, apparently in the hopes of inducing the Japanese to reflect on what they had lost of their cultural heritage. The incident created an immense sensation, but M.'s reputation was to be determined not by this act but by the brilliant works in many genres he wrote during his short life. Long before his suicide he had established himself as the first Japanese writer whose fame was worldwide.

FURTHER WORKS: *Kinjiki* (1951–53; *Forbidden Colors,* 1968); *Manatsu no shi* (1953; *Death in Midsummer,* 1966); *Yoru no himawari* (1953; *Twilight Sunflower,* 1958); *Shiosai* (1954; *The Sound of Waves,* 1956); *Shizumeru Taki* (1955); *Shiroari no su* (1956); *Shi wo kaku shōnen* (1956; *The Boy Who Wrote Poetry,* 1977); *Bitoku no yoromeki* (1957); *Rokumeikan* (1957); *Bara to kaizoku* (1958); *Ratai to ishō* (1959); *Yoroboshi* (1960; *Yoroboshi: The Blind Young Man,* 1979); *Kemono no tawamure* (1961); *Utsukushii hoshi* (1962); *Gogo no eikō* (1963; *The Sailor Who Fell from Grace with the Sea,* 1965); *Watakushi no henreki jidai* (1964); *Kinu to meisatsu* (1964); *Mikumano mōde* (1965); *Eirei no koe* (1966); *Suzaku-ke no metsubō* (1967); *Hagakure nyūmon* (1967; *The Way of the Samurai,* 1977); *Wa ga tomo Hittorā* (1968; *My Friend Hitler,* 1977); *Taiyō to tetsu* (1968; *Sun and Steel,* 1970); *Bunka bōei ron* (1969)

BIBLIOGRAPHY: Keene, D., *Landscapes and Portraits: Appreciations of Japanese Culture* (1971), pp. 204–25; Kimball, A. G., *Crisis in Identity and Contemporary Japanese Novels* (1973), pp. 75–93; Keene, D., "The Death of M.," in Dillon, W. S., ed., *The Cultural Drama: Modern Identities and Social Ferment* (1974), pp. 271–87; Nathan, J., *M.: A Biography* (1974); Miyoshi, M., *Accomplices of Silence: The Modern Japanese Novel* (1974), pp. 141–80; Scott-Stokes, H., *The Life and Death of Y. M.* (1974); McCarthy, P., "M. Y.'s *Confessions of a Mask,*" in Tsuruta, K., and Swann, T. E., eds., *Approaches to the Modern Japanese Novel* (1976), pp. 112–28; Ueda, M., *Modern Japanese Writers and the Nature of Literature* (1976), pp. 219–59; Yamanouchi, H., *The Search for Authenticity in Modern Japanese Literature* (1978), pp. 137–52

DONALD KEENE

MIYAZAWA Kenji

Japanese poet and writer of children's stories, b. 27 Aug. 1896, Hanamaki; d. 21 Sept. 1933, Hanamaki

M. went to an agricultural college and taught at an agricultural school. Both institutions had been established to meet the special need of his region, Iwate, which suffered from chronic crop failures because of the harsh climate and backward agricultural methods. A devout Buddhist of an activist sect, M. resigned from his school in 1926 and turned to farming to put his teachings into practice. During the next few years he forced himself to subsist on a poorer diet than even the local farmers were used to, and ruined his health.

M.'s scientific training, Buddhist vision, and concern for the plight of the local farmers, combined with his hallucinatory imagination, sense of drama, and humor, resulted in a highly distinctive body of work. His poems are laced with precise technical terms and vivid descriptions, but they seldom become trivial or simply curious, supported as they are by a larger view of life, a combination of Buddhist pantheism and the belief that science can solve all problems. At the center of his poetic world is the poet himself, presented as an *asura* (a Sanskrit word), in Buddhist belief a contentious, arrogant, malevolent giant somewhere between a human and a beast. As described in the title poem of his first book, *Haru to shura* (1924; spring and asura), M.'s *asura* is unenlightened and restless. Still, M.'s poetic self is far from being egotistic. Even when he describes himself, he externalizes the description. More often, he is concerned with people and phenomena: his dead sister, a bull enjoying himself in the night mist, a horse that died from overwork, a tired farm boy, the movement of clouds, a rainstorm, a country doctor. It is the depth and range of M.'s mind apparent in such poems that make him outstanding.

The stories M. wrote for children share similar qualities, here often extended in a fantastic way. M. describes a great variety of animals and objects, such as a slug, a cat, a fox, a nighthawk, a lark, an ant, a frog, a birch tree, a constellation, and an electric pole, as if he let them project their qualities onto himself, rather than projecting his emotions onto them. The stories are often stark, sometimes brutal. Even where compassion is the theme, the resolution of the conflict of the story is usually realistic and credible.

M. wrote prolifically, and although he revised many of his poems and stories, a good number of them give the impression of being rough-hewn and unfinished. Not widely known while alive, he is now considered one of the three or four greatest poets, and surely the most imaginative writer of children's stories, of 20th-c. Japan.

FURTHER WORKS: *M. K. zenshū* (15 vols., 1973–77); *M. K. zenshū* (16 vols., 1979–80). FURTHER VOLUMES IN ENGLISH: *Winds from Afar* (1972); *Spring and Asura: Poems of K. M.* (1973)

HIROAKI SATO

MORI Ōgai

(pseud. of Mori Rintarō) Japanese novelist, short-story writer, and critic, b. 17 Feb. 1862, Tsuwano; d. 9 July 1922, Tokyo

M. followed his father by taking up a career in medicine, studying new Western scientific techniques, largely imported from Germany, which were taught in Tokyo in the 1870s. After joining the army, M. was sent to Germany to observe hygienic practices. He remained in Europe from 1884 to 1888, and on his return, fired by a new-found love for German literature and philosophy, began to pursue a double career as a writer and a bureaucrat that was to continue throughout his life. M. eventually obtained the rank of Surgeon General of the Japanese army, but his creative writing activities put him, along with his contemporary, Natsume Sōseki (q.v.), in the forefront of the writers of his generation.

Shortly after his return from Germany, M. wrote a trilogy of stories about his German experiences. The first of these, "Maihime" (1890; "The Girl Who Danced," 1964), chronicles the activities of a young Japanese in Europe who falls in love and then abandons his German mistress. The story, for all of its romantic trappings, concentrates on the conflict between self-fulfillment and social duty, a theme that finds repercussions in virtually every important M. work.

M.'s enthusiasms then turned to the preparation of a series of translations of works by Hans Christian Andersen, Goethe, Heine, and Kleist, among many others. He also did research in German aesthetic theory. M. wrote a number of stories and essays in the years that followed, but his first sustained period as a writer began in 1909, when, late in his forties, he began a series of novels and stories that allowed him to explore his own experience against the background of a rapidly modernizing society. The first of them, *Vita sexualis* (1909; *Vita Sexualis*, 1973), sketches with trenchant irony his development of feelings for the opposite sex. The second, *Seinen* (1910; youth), recounts the spiritual adventures of a young man struggling to become a novelist in modern Tokyo. In the third novel, *Gan* (1911; *Wild Geese*, 1959), M. creates as his heroine a woman caught between traditional and modern ways of behavior. She and the protagonist, a young student bound for study in Germany, are attracted to each other but never manage to meet in any meaningful way; her loneliness forces the woman to come alive to the forces of life that well up within her.

The protagonist of *Seinen* declares that art can only grow from a sense of the past, and by 1912 M. showed his commitment to this position in a series of historical stories and novels usually judged as his finest work. Among these, "Sanshō dayū" (1914; "Sanshō Dayū," 1952), a moving story, set in medieval times, of two children taken into slavery, shows M.'s ability to infuse traditional narrative with acute psychological and philosophical insight. Another notable story, "Kanzan Jittoku" (1915; "Han Shan and Shi Te," 1971) tells the legend of two Chinese Zen recluses with humor and wisdom. M.'s masterpiece is doubtless *Shibue Chūsai* (1916; Shibue Chūsai), the biography of a Confucian scholar and doctor who lived from 1805 to 1858, the period just prior to the modernization of Japan. M. reconstructs the details of the scholar's life, and, as he does so, shows his own affinities with this earlier figure, revealing both his and his subject's views on life in an intimate and compelling fashion.

M. continued to write and translate important works from European literature, including a number of Ibsen plays and Goethe's *Faust.* Although failing health caused him to curtail his activities, he continued to do research and writing until shortly before his death.

M.'s reputation is founded not only on his literary and critical works but also on a widespread admiration for the quality of the life that he led. His understanding of modern European culture, with its restless search for truth in an era when science was replacing metaphysics, helped him delineate the same changes in Japan. M.'s ironic detachment, which led him to an austere and poetic sense of philosophical resignation, reveals an atmosphere of moral courage that combines traditional Confucian virtue with modern sophistication.

FURTHER WORKS: *Omokage* (1889); *Utakata no ki* (1890; *Utakata No Ki,* 1974); *Kamen* (1909); "Hannichi" (1909; "Half a Day," 1974); "Hanako" (1910; "Hanako," 1918); *Ikutagawa* (1910); "Asobi" (1910); "Mōsō" (1911; "Delusion," 1970); *Hyaku monogatari* (1911); "Ka no yo ni" (1912; "As If," 1925); "Sakai jihen" (1914; "The Incident at Sakai," 1977); "Yasui Fujin" (1914; "The Wife of Yasui," 1977); *Oshio Heihachirō* (1915); "Takasebune" (1915; "Takase-bune," 1918); *Izawa Ranken* (1916); *Zenshū* (53 vols., 1951–56)

BIBLIOGRAPHY: Miyoshi, M., *Accomplices of Silence: The Modern Japa-

nese Novel (1974), pp. 38–54; Rimer, J. T., *M. Ō.* (1975); Johnson, E. W., "Ōgai's *The Wild Goose*," in Tsuruta, K., and Swann, T., eds., *Approaches to the Modern Japanese Novel* (1976), pp. 129–47; Rimer, J. T., *Modern Japanese Fiction and Its Traditions* (1978), pp. 138–61; Bowring, R., *M. Ō. and the Modernization of Japanese Culture* (1979)

J. THOMAS RIMER

NAGAI Kafū

(pseud. of Nagai Sōkichi) Japanese novelist, short-story writer, essayist, and critic, b. 3 Dec. 1879, Tokyo; d. 10 April 1959, Tokyo

As a young man, N. was sent by his father to the U.S. and to France to learn the banking trade, but his love of the traditional Kabuki theater and of Japanese and French literature caused him upon his return to Japan in 1908 to take up a career as novelist, professor of French literature, literary editor, and translator, most notably of French symbolist poetry.

In an early masterpiece, the novel *Sumidagawa* (1909; *The River Sumida,* 1965), N. already shows certain of the hallmarks of his mature style, which include an ability to create an ironic view of the present reflected through an appreciation of the beauties of traditional urban Japanese culture, an elegant and elegiac prose style, and an interest in the nuances of the erotic lives of his characters, many of them from the demimonde. N. came to write about such supposedly degraded persons because he felt they represented the truth about society; for him, middle-class respectability represented an essential falsehood.

From the beginning of his career, N. showed great skill in capturing nuances in characterization and setting. In *Sumidagawa,* N. achieved a consonance of setting, mood, and character that set him apart and ahead of all other writers of his generation. In that novel, the sections on the Kabuki theater are particularly vivid. N. continued to adapt certain elements from this theatrical form to his fiction, including the use of surprising happenings and of characters with unusual and colorful personalities.

In 1916 N., increasingly disillusioned with the reactionary policies of the Japanese government, abandoned public life after the death of his father, never again assuming any kind of public position. He continued to write about the byways of contemporary Japanese culture, finding lyric impetus in the erotic world of the geishas and mistresses who functioned in perhaps the only area of life that remained resistant to change in a rapidly modernizing Japan. In an oblique fashion, N. served as a sort of cultural critic through his evocation, half lyrical, half ironic, of a vanishing lifestyle that represented for him a time when Japanese culture had been of a piece. In this one regard, his attitude of irony and detachment resembles that of his mentor, the novelist Mori Ōgai (q.v.).

Of N.'s many pre-World War II works, *Bokutō kidan* (1937; *A Strange Tale from East of the River,* 1965) is perhaps the finest, a remarkable evocation of the atmosphere of a poor section of Tokyo, written as a story within a story, in which the protagonist, a novelist, has an affair with a prostitute while composing his own story about an affair with a prostitute. A brilliant command of detail combined with a sense of evanescence allows N. to produce a striking evocation of psychology, time, and place. N.'s treatment of the liaison mixes introspection, literary reference, and acute observation with an expression of his own intense disdain for the forces of order in society.

During the war years N. refused to cooperate with the government authorities; because of his fiercely independent attitude he became something of a culture hero after 1945. In his short stories written during the postwar period, N. continued to examine changes in Japan with an aristocratic and acerbic eye.

N. continues to be appreciated for his brilliant, evocative style as well as for the special atmosphere and psychological insight of all his works. In spite of the charges of decadence that have often been brought against him, he is, in his own way, a moralist.

FURTHER WORKS: *Amerika monogatari* (1908); *Furansu monogatari* (1909); *Kazagokochi* (1912); *Udekurabe* (1917; *Geisha in Rivalry,* 1963); *Okamezasa* (1918); *Ame shōshō* (1921); *Enoki monogatari* (1931); *Odoriko* (1944); *Towazugatari* (1945); *Zenshū* (24 vols., 1948–53). FURTHER VOLUME IN ENGLISH: *Kafū the Scribbler: The Life and Writings of N. K., 1879–1959* (1965)

BIBLIOGRAPHY: Seidensticker, E., *Kafū the Scribbler: The Life and Writings of N. K., 1879–1959* (1965); Ueda, M., *Modern Japanese Writers and the Nature of Literature* (1976), pp. 26–53; Rimer, J. T., *Modern Japanese Fiction and Its Traditions* (1978), pp. 138–61

J. THOMAS RIMER

NATSUME Sōseki

(pseud. of Natsume Kin'nosuke) Japanese novelist, b 5 Jan. 1867, Tokyo; d. 9 Dec. 1916, Tokyo

N. (usually called Sōseki) was born to a family that had fallen on hard
times as a result of the Meiji Restoration. His parents were embarrassed
at having a child late in life and tried unsuccessfully to have him
adopted, and he was left permanently with a feeling of being unwanted.
After a brilliant career as a student of English at Tokyo Imperial University, he abandoned his native city and accepted a series of rural teaching
positions. In 1900 the government sent him to England for further study
of English. He returned to Japan in early 1903, after having suffered a
nervous breakdown. Nerves and ulcers were to plague him for the rest of
his life. Although he decided, while in England, to become a creative
writer rather than a literary scholar, he took a position as professor of
English literature at Tokyo University, succeeding the American writer
Lafcadio Hearn (1850–1904). In 1907 N. resigned his professorship to
become literary editor of the newspaper *Asahi shimbun*. The ensuing
decade was a period of intense literary activity until the very moment of
his death from ulcers in 1916.

N.'s work can be divided into several groups representing stages in
his developing philosophy. He began with experimental works, trying
several fictional techniques. His first major work was *Wagahai wa neko
de aru* (1905; *I Am a Cat*, 1961), a satire depicting modern Japanese
society as seen from the point of view of a cat. The idea for this story
was apparently derived from E. T. A. Hoffmann's (1776–1822) *Kater
Murr*. At the time he wrote this book N. was still developing his narrative style, and it is not so much a unified novel as a loosely related series
of amusing episodes poking fun at many aspects of Japan's modernization.

Another work from this experimental phase is *Kusamakura* (1906;
Unhuman Tour, 1927; new tr., *Three-Cornered World*, 1965). N. said this
was intended as a novel in the manner of a haiku. In one sense he uses
the work to contrast Western and Eastern aesthetic values, arguing that
the West emphasizes the individual while the East denies individuality.
N. also said that his broader intention with *Kusamakura* was simply to
leave an impression of beauty in the reader's mind.

Shortly after joining the newspaper staff and devoting himself to
writing full time, there appeared his first trilogy, composed of *Sanshirō*
(1908; *Sanshiro*, 1977), *Sorekara* (1909; *And Then*, 1978), and *Mon*
(1909; *Mon*, 1972). In these works he introduced themes he consistently

used throughout his career. One is initiation, usually taking the form of a youth who comes to Tokyo and learns to deal with adult life in the modern world. As these young men struggle to come to terms with life, they end up making decisions or taking actions, and then have to live with their consequences for the rest of their lives. Usually the consequence is feeling guilty of having been greedy or selfish. Where, asks N., can man find solace to assuage this feeling of guilt? In this trilogy he suggests love and religion to relieve the burden of guilt.

N.'s second trilogy consists of *Higan sugi made* (1910; until after the spring equinox), *Kōjin* (1912–13: *The Wayfarer*, 1967), and *Kokoro* (1914; *Kokoro*, 1941; new tr., 1957). In these works the mood is darker, as N. probes more deeply the themes of loneliness, alienation, and guilt. The avenues of relief he offers here are much less hopeful than the ones presented in earlier works. In *Kōjin*, Ichirō, the central figure, declares that the only solutions to modern man's dilemma are suicide, insanity, and religion. In exploring insanity, N. more clearly defines his philosophy: man must learn to surrender his own self to something larger.

Kokoro is probably the best and certainly the most widely read of all of N.'s novels. Here again he shows that mistrust and selfishness lead to betrayal, guilt, and alienation, which are the normal condition of modern man. N. also reflects on the merits of suicide as a means of atonement, and the theme of initiation is prominent, as in earlier works. N.'s narrative technique here is still fragmentary, but it is also highly imaginative. The first part tells of the youthful narrator going to college in the city and being exposed to modern life. The second part shows the youth at home in the country caring for his dying father, and traditional Japanese life is contrasted to the modern. The third part is in the form of a long letter and suicide note from Sensei, the youth's mentor and also a surrogate father figure. With stark simplicity N. presents the unendurable loneliness of the modern intellectual, which cannot be breached either by the ties of love and family or by intellectual companionship.

At the time of his death N. had completed several hundred pages of the novel *Meian* (1916; *Light and Darkness*, 1971). Since the work is incomplete, we have no way of knowing for certain how he would have ended it. Critical opinion is sharply divided. Some feel that the characters are headed for the same sort of gloomy dilemma we see in N.'s earlier works. Others say that he had come to terms with life by developing his philosophy of "sokuten kyoshi," which means to seek heaven by abandoning the self. Certainly, egoism or the burden of self-consciousness is at the heart of all the problems N.'s characters struggle with.

It is no exaggeration to say that N. has been the single most popular writer in Japan in the 20th c. Not only do his works give expression to the social and moral problems faced by Japan as it became Westernized and modernized; he also introduced a philosophical approach to literature. This represents a remarkable development, since traditionally fiction had been considered only frivolous and entertaining. N. raised it to the level of a serious medium for artistic expression and philosophical thought.

FURTHER WORKS: *Botchan* (1906; *Botchan,* 1970); *Yokyoshu* (1906); *Gubijinso* (1908); *Kusa awase* (1908); *Shihen* (1910); *Garasudo no naka* (1915); *Michikusa* (1915; *Grass on the Wayside,* 1969)

BIBLIOGRAPHY: McClellan, E., "An Introduction to Sōseki," *HJAS,* 20 (1959), 150–208; Viglielmo, V. H., "An Introduction to the Later Novels of N. S.," *MN,* 19 (1964), 1–36; Eto, J., "N. S.: A Japanese Meiji Intellectual," *ASch,* 34 (1965), 603–19; McClellan, E., *Two Japanese Novelists: Sōseki and Tōson* (1969), pp. 3–69; Yu, B., *N. S.* (1969); Miyoshi, M., *Accomplices of Silence: The Modern Japanese Novel* (1974), pp. 55–92; Doi, T., *The Psychological World of N. S.* (1976); Jones, S., "N. S.'s *Botchan:* The Outer World through Edo Eyes," in Tsuruta, K., and Swann, T., eds., *Approaches to the Modern Japanese Novel* (1976), pp. 148–65; Viglielmo, V. H., "Sōseki's *Kokoro:* A Descent into the Heart of Man," in Tsuruta, K., and Swann, T., eds., *Approaches to the Modern Japanese Novel* (1976), pp. 166–79; McClain, Y., "Sōseki: A Tragic Father," *MN,* 33 (1978), 461–69

STEPHEN W. KOHL

ŌE Kenzaburō
Japanese novelist, short-story writer, and essayist, b. 31 Jan. 1935, Ōsemura (now Uchiko-cho)

Ō. was born and raised in an isolated rural region of the small island of Shikoku. He made his literary appearance in 1957 while still a student at Tokyo University. His early works, published between 1957 and 1963, express his sense of the degradation, humiliation, and disorientation caused by Japan's surrender at the end of World War II. Since 1964 his writing has focused on themes of madness and idiocy, themes that give expression to his personal experience as the father of a brain-damaged child and that are metaphors for the human condition. Ō. has a strong sense of social involvement, which began with the anti-American Security Treaty protests in 1960, and which encompasses his role as an antinuclear spokesman, involvements in radical causes, and numerous essays on political and social topics. Given Ō.'s commitment to social action as a way of authenticating his existence, it is not surprising that his literary mentors include Jean-Paul Sartre, Albert Camus, and Norman Mailer.

One of the finest of Ō.'s early stories is "Shiiku" (1958; "Prize Stock," 1977), in which the hero is propelled from the innocent world of childhood into adulthood by various acts of madness ranging from the madness of war to the temporary insanity of his father, who murders a prisoner of war with an ax. Other early stories, such as "Kimyō na shigoto (1957; an odd job) and "Shisha no ogori" (1957; "Lavish Are the Dead," 1965), also have protagonists who are alienated and disoriented in a world where gratuitous degradation and abuse are commonplace. Ō.'s heroes fight back with hostility and rebellion, or escape into fantasies and perverse sex.

In 1964 Ō. simultaneously published *Kojinteki na taiken* (1964; *A Personal Matter*, 1968) and *Hiroshima nooto* (1964; Hiroshima notes), both dealing with madness-producing events. The latter is an essay about the public madness of nuclear warfare. The former is more personal, a fictional account of coming to terms with the birth of a brain-damaged son. This novel was followed by several stories outlining other possible relationships between the corpulent father and the idiot son.

Although many would argue that Ō. is the finest writer in Japan today, he has been criticized by those who feel his rage against complacency is out of line in view of Japan's prosperity. Others criticize his style for being so rough it sometimes sounds as though his novels have been ineptly translated into Japanese from some other language. These complaints aside, Ō. has achieved and maintained an impressive level of literary excellence.

FURTHER WORKS: *Megumushiri kouchi* (1958); *Warera no jidai* (1959); *Seinen no omei* (1959); *Sakebigoe* (1962); *Nichijō seikatsu no bōken* (1963); *Man'en gannen no futtobōru* (1967; *Silent Cry*, 1974); *Warera no kyōki o iki nobiru michi o oshieyo* (1969; *Teach Us to Outgrow Our Madness*, 1972); *Kōzui wa waga tamashii ni oyobi* (1973); *Pinchiranna chōsho* (1976)

BIBLIOGRAPHY: Rabson, S., "A Personal Matter," in Tsuruta, K., and Swann, T., eds., *Approaches to the Modern Japanese Novel* (1976), pp.

180–98; Iwamoto, Y., "The 'Mad' World of Ō. K.," *JATJ*, 14 (1979), 66–83; Wilson, M. N., "Ō.'s Obsessive Metaphor, Mori the Idiot Son: Toward the Imagination of Satire, Regeneration, and Grotesque Realism," *JJS*, 7 (1981), 23–52

STEPHEN W. KOHL

SHIGA Naoya

Japanese short-story writer and novelist, b. 20 Feb. 1883, Ishimaki; d. 21 Oct. 1971, Tokyo

S. was raised in a family that had prospered during the Meiji Restoration. Indeed, it was his father's wealth and social standing that made it possible for S. to attend the exclusive Peers' School, where he first became involved in literature. It was also this family wealth that allowed him the leisure to pursue his artistic interests and his association with other artists in the White Birch group.

S.'s writing career passed through various stages. He began writing at a time when the Japanese variant of naturalism was at its peak, and his early works tend to focus on the extreme conditions of insanity and suicide. He quickly outgrew this period of experimentation, however, and concentrated on works that emphasized psychological development. Many of his early stories deal with family situations, and a significant number of them resulted from his seventeen-year estrangement from his father. Although willing to live on his father's money, S. felt that his father was vulgar, philistine, grasping, and insensitive. Independence as an individual and as an artist is one of the chief characteristics of S. This was so much the case that he defined morality in terms of freedom, saying in one of his works: "My likes and dislikes are the basis of my personal sense of good and evil." This independence kept him aloof from every sort of literary or political ideology and dogma. Thus, although S. was a founding member and a leader of the White Birch group, it was such a diverse collection of artists and scholars that he always felt free to pursue his own artistic directions without inhibition.

During the middle years of his career S. attempted to capture the tranquillity of nature and of men who are able to live harmoniously with nature and with their fellow man. Typical of these works is the story "Kinosaki nite" (1917; "At Kinosaki," 1956), a lyrical reflection on death in which the narrator learns to come to terms with his own inevitable end as he encounters death in nature. Since death cannot be avoided, it must be accepted with tranquillity.

Another representative story of this period is "Takibi" (1920; "The Bonfire," 1975). Here the need for dramatic conflict and resolution gives way to an evocation of shared emotions. Again, the story is a lyric about man immersed in nature. Although some have condemned it for being meandering and pointless, it is vintage S. His intention was to evoke a mood, to express the tranquillity of mind and harmony with nature he had always sought. While it is true that he violates most Western concepts of acceptable literary form—there is no organized plot, no dramatic conflict, no climax and resolution, and no characterization—nevertheless, the story has its own integrity and great beauty, and it has been extravagantly admired by Japanese writers and readers alike.

S.'s best-known work and his only novel is *An'ya kōro* (1937; *A Dark Night's Passing*, 1976). Here he brings the two basic strands of his work together. On the one hand, he depicts difficult family relationships; on the other, he uses loose structure to evoke emotions and the final harmonious unity with nature. His concern, S. said, was not so much with what happened as with what it felt like when it happened.

After the mid-1930s S. continued to write works of great skill and carefully polished style, but few of them achieved the intensity of his earlier creations. Still, a few works stand out, such as "Haiiro no tsuki" (1945; "The Ashen Moon," 1977), a brilliant evocation of Japan immediately after World War II.

Not widely known outside Japan, S. is considered one of the finest Japanese writers of the 20th c. He is called "the god of fiction," and was greatly admired by such diverse authors as Akutagawa Ryunosuke (q.v.) and Kobayashi Takiji (1903–1933), both of whom sought to use S.'s work as models for their own writing.

FURTHER WORKS: *S. N. zenshū* (14 vols., 1973–74)

BIBLIOGRAPHY: Mathy, F., *S. N.* (1974); Kohl, S. W., et al., *The White Birch Society (Shirakabaha): Some Sketches and Portraits* (1975), pp. 28–41; Kohl, S. W., "S. N. and the Literature of Experience," *MN*, 32 (1977), 211–24; Sibley, W. F., *The S. Hero* (1979)

STEPHEN W. KOHL

SHIMAZAKI Tōson

Japanese poet, novelist, short-story writer, dramatist, and essayist, b. 25 March 1872, Magome; d. 22 Aug. 1943, Higashi-Koiso

Born into a prominent family living in a remote mountain village, S. was sent to Tokyo to study in 1886. In 1887 he entered a Protestant missionary academy and was baptized. Upon graduation he began teaching, translating, and writing poetry, plays, and book reviews. His highly romantic poetry kept the rhythms of traditional verse while bringing in fresh ardor and passion. After winning acceptance, he published the first collection of his verse, *Wakana-shū* (1897; young leaves), which earned him lasting fame as the first important poet of modern Japan.

During the first decade of the 20th c. S. turned to fiction, which became his preferred genre. *Hakai* (1906; *The Broken Commandment,* 1974), his most widely known work, deals openly with the social problems of members of the outcast minority group known as Eta; consequently, S. had to publish the novel at his own expense. Indeed, the Japanese are still reluctant to discuss the position of these "base people," who traditionally worked as scavengers, tanners, and executioners, and who were prohibited from mingling with ordinary citizens. The hero of the novel, Ushimatsu, is one of the earliest characters in modern Japanese fiction who conveys a sense of deeply lived personal experience. *Hakai* may be thought of as the first novel of the inner life in 20th c. Japanese literature.

During this period the trend toward naturalism was growing stronger in Japan; S., along with authors such as Tayama Katai (1871–1930), added impetus to the movement. S.'s next two novels mark the apex of Japanese naturalism. *Haru* (1908; spring), an autobiographical account, foreshadowed his mature style. *Ie* (1911; *The Family,* 1976), his best naturalistic work, is a chronicle of a household that is paradoxically destroyed by the desire to save it.

Shinsei (1919; a new life) tells the story of a man (in reality, S. himself) who, having lost his wife, takes up with a niece. She becomes pregnant, and he, fearing a scandal, flees to France. But his wartime experiences lead him to reflect on where he really belongs, and in the end he recognizes his responsibilities as a father and returns. By publicly confessing his secret, the protagonist hopes to begin a new life. Although often criticized for disregarding accepted standards of respectability, the novel nevertheless skillfully exploited the change in literary fashion, which was now concerned with a protagonist's spiritual growth.

S.'s last and most ambitious novel, *Yoakemai* (serial pub., 1929–35;

before the dawn), impresses the patient reader with its grandeur, restraint, and genuine sense of tragedy. Set in the author's native village, Magome, the story opens in the 1850s, during the waning years of the Tokugawa period (1600–1868). The hero, Aoyama Hanzō, is modeled on S.'s father. Sympathetic to the movement to revive national institutions, he becomes actively involved in political affairs. But as village headman, as the community's wholesale merchant, and as keeper of the inn designated for travelers on official business, he finds himself trapped between the farmers and the samurai. Although his own party, favoring restoration of the power of the emperor (Meiji restoration, 1868), prevails, he is unable to cope with the rapid changes; he turns to drink, incurs large debts, and eventually goes insane. He is placed in a makeshift cell behind his house, where he dies, "without ever seeing the sun again." Nowhere in modern Japanese fiction does one find a more compelling account of the process of transformation from the old to the new.

The central theme in S.'s writing—how a new Japan after the Meiji restoration grew out of the decay of the old, but only at a cost of grievous personal suffering and loss—is made poignant by the autobiographical and historical material that illustrates and documents his theme. Yet another theme that runs throughout S.'s writings involves the new ideal of individualism, which entered Japan from the West at the beginning of the 20th c., with all of its humanistic and positive implications.

FURTHER WORKS: *Natsugusa* (1898); *Hitohabune* (1898); *Rakubai-shū* (1901); *T. shishū* (1904); *Ryokuyō-shū* (1907); *Shin-katamachi yori* (1909); *T. shū* (1909); *Chikuma-gawa no suketchi* (1911); *Shokugo* (1912); *Bifū* (1913); *Sakura no mi no jukusuru toki* (1919); *Furusato* (1920); *T. zenshū* (12 vols., 1922); *Osana monogatari* (1924); *Haru o machitsutsu* (1932); *Tōhō no mon* (1943); *T. zenshū* (18 vols., 1966–71)

BIBLIOGRAPHY: Kokusai Bunka Shinkōkai, ed., *Introduction to Contemporary Japanese Literature* (1939), pp. 300–311; Roggendorf, J., "S. T.: A Maker of the Modern Japanese Novel," *MN*, 7 (1951), 40–46; McClellan, E., *Two Japanese Novelists: Sōseki and Tōson* (1969); Morita, J. R., "S. T.'s Four Collections of Poems," *MN*, 25 (1970), 325–69; Yamanouchi, H., *The Search for Authenticity in Modern Japanese Literature* (1978), pp. 20–39; Walker, J. A., *The Japanese Novel of the Meiji Period and the Ideal of Individualism* (1979), passim

LEON M. ZOLBROD

TANEDA Santōka

(pseud. of Taneda Shōichi) Japanese poet, b. 3 Dec. 1882, Hōfu; d. 11 Oct. 1940, Matsuyama

Son of a well-to-do landowner in western Japan, T. became interested early in traditional haiku poetry, with its five-seven-five-syllable pattern. In 1902 he was admitted to Waseda University in Tokyo to study literature, but he dropped out of school after a year because of a serious drinking problem, which was to plague him throughout his life.

In 1911 T. came under the influence of Seisensui Ogiwara (1884–1976), the leader of the New Tendency School of haiku, which discarded the traditional seasonal imagery and the fixed syllabic pattern for a freer verse form. While T. contributed sporadically to Seisensui's poetry journal *Sōun,* he drifted from job to job and in 1924 tried to commit suicide, an action that led to his taking vows as a Zen priest the following year. Thereafter known in Japan by his Buddhist priest's name Santōka, he spent the remaining fifteen years of his life wandering through Japan, writing free-verse haiku about his experiences.

T.'s literary reputation derives from this final quarter of his life, when he walked thousands of miles as a mendicant priest and wrote thousands of poems, sometimes only two or three words long and few longer than ten words, describing the natural scenes he encountered and how he related to them. In 1930 he began publishing a poetry journal, *Sambaku,* named after a boardinghouse in Kumamoto City, and in 1932, with the financial backing of other poets, he published his first book of poems, *Hachi no ko* (the begging bowl).

T. evinces in his poetry the deeply ingrained Japanese tradition of seeking in nature a release from anxieties caused by society and an entry into spiritual enlightenment. Like the great 12th-c. priest-poet Saigyō and the early-19th-c. Zen master Ryōkan, T. sees nature both as a place of serenity and as an arena in which to do battle with his inner conflicts. In some of his poems T. exorcises the demons within himself by surrendering to the inevitable cycles of the natural world.

While they follow a much-trodden literary path, T.'s poems are free from the literary allusions and multilayered images that can make traditional Japanese poetry so abstruse. Although T. in 1936 did retrace the route taken by the famous haiku poet Bashō (1644–1694) in *Narrow Road to the Deep North,* his poetry remains firmly fixed in the 20th c. Like walking and drinking sake, T. said, writing haiku was a cathartic experience through which he transcended his personal flaws in search of more permanent truths. He dreamed of taking the artifice out of art, of making his poems sing "like the floating clouds, like the flow of water, like a small bird, like the dancing leaves."

Unknown outside of a small circle during his lifetime, T. has gained a wide following in the past twenty years. Readers admire both his use of nature as the principal image and his probings of the tensions of modern man. T. was both possibly the last in a thousand-year-old tradition of roving priest-poets and a pioneer in the use of unadorned, profoundly simple free-verse haiku.

FURTHER WORKS: *Sōmokutō* (1933); *Sangyō suigyō* (1935); *Zassō fūkei* (1936); *Kaki no ha* (1938); *Kōkan* (1940); *Karasu* (1940). FURTHER VOLUME IN ENGLISH: *Mountain Tasting: Zen Haiku by S. T.* (1980)

BIBLIOGRAPHY: Blyth, R. H., *A History of Haiku* (1964), Vol. II, pp. 173–88; Abrams, J., "Hail in the Begging Bowl: The Odyssey and Poetry of Santōka," *MN*, 3 (1977), pp. 269–302; Stevens, J., Introduction to *Mountain Tasting: Zen Haiku by S. T.* (1980), pp. 9–29

JAMES ABRAMS

TANIZAKI Jun'ichirō

Japanese novelist, short-story writer, essayist, and dramatist, b. 24 July 1886, Tokyo; d. 30 July 1965, Yūgawara

Eldest surviving son of a declining merchant family in Tokyo, T. was in his formative years while Japan was emerging as a world power. Owing to his father's business failure and the family's precarious economic situation, he received schooling only through the charity of friends and relatives and the encouragement of teachers who recognized his talent. Having previously studied law and English, he entered Tokyo University's Department of National Literature in 1908 with the intention of becoming a writer. This was "the most convenient way of slacking off my school work," he later wrote. In 1910 he was expelled from the university for failure to pay tuition. Following the great earthquake of 1923, in a move symbolic of a return in spirit to traditional Japan, T. rejected his native city of Tokyo and retreated to the quieter, old-fashioned world of the Kansai area, around Kyoto and Osaka, where some of his most characteristic works were written. After World War II, once again living near Tokyo, T. had a final outburst of creativity.

Although most important for his fiction, T. early in his career also wrote many plays—particularly between 1911 and 1924—and in 1920 he became a consultant for a budding motion picture company, for which he wrote scenarios.

In 1910 T. published the best known of his early stories, "Shisei" ("The Tattoo," 1914), a tale that reveals in embryonic form his central theme, which he was to develop for more than half a century: beauty is feminine, beauty is strength. During the years that immediately followed, he devoted himself to writing and found his literary identity. "Who was it," he wrote in "Itansha no kanashimi" (1917; the sorrows of a heretic), an autobiographical story, "that created in me the strange propensity to be more deeply concerned not about what is good but rather what is beautiful?"

The tale "Manji" (1928; whirlpool) portrays a femme fatale, a beautiful young art student who is the model for a drawing of a Buddhist saint. Her actual character, however, is perverse, deceptive, and destructive, as she seduces both a mild-mannered lawyer and his aggressive wife. The Osaka setting, rich with the flavor of old Japan, and the feminine Osaka dialect help to evoke the languorous charm of traditional culture, which is juxtaposed to a bizarre confession. In several ways "Manji" foreshadowed the novel *Tade kuu mushi* (serial pub. 1928–29; *Some Prefer Nettles*, 1955), which is about a hopeless marriage and a conflict between the old and new ways of life, also set in the Kansai area. Both works deal with contrasting concepts of the idealized woman, on the one hand, and the everyday woman of reality, on the other.

Representative of the most polished and skillful of the tales that T. wrote is the novella *Shunkinshō* (1933; *The Story of Shunkin*, 1936; later tr., *A Portrait of Shunkin*, 1963), which tells of how a devoted servant blinds himself in order to perfect his art and remain always with his beloved mistress, who is a blind musician. The tale is a psychological study of how devotion may curdle into a neurotic fixation. T.'s long essay *In'ei raisan* (serial pub. 1933–34; *In Praise of Shadows*, 1977), which celebrates his rejection of Tokyo and his retreat to the more traditional world of Kyoto and Osaka, expresses his view that classical Japanese art flourished in the shade and that the dazzle of the modern world destroys it. Therefore one must dim the lights.

At the peak of his creative powers, T. published serially (1939–41) a modern version of the 11th-c. classic *The Tale of Genji*, the greatest work in Japanese literature.

Sasame Yuki (3 vols., 1946–48; *The Makioka Sisters*, 1958), an elegy to a vanished era and his longest novel, stands out not only among

T.'s works but also from the whole corpus of 20th c. Japanese literature. He had actually begun to publish it serially in 1943, but it was suppressed at the time by the military authorities. Within an old but declining merchant family, which clings to the belief that suitably arranged matches preserve one's heritage and social position, two unmarried sisters, the younger of four, display conflicting styles of life. The older of the pair, Yukiko (literally, "Snow-Child," the heroine denoted in the Japanese title), emerges as a quiet, traditional woman. The younger, Taeko, scandalously impulsive and modern, indulges in various escapades and adventures. It is as if T.'s prototypical woman has split into two; she who is outwardly strong and she who is outwardly feminine. Yet, ironically, the willful Taeko dies and the apparently placid Yukiko survives.

Kagi (1956; *The Key,* 1961) is a study of adultery and middle-aged depravity set in Kyoto. In this novel, a complex web of reality and fantasy, the parallel diaries of a husband and wife, largely about their sexual experiences, convey surprising narrative rhythms and a distinctive tone. One of T.'s last novels, *Fūten rōjin nikki* (1962; *The Diary of a Mad Old Man,* 1965), presents the satirical portrait of an ill but unruly patriarch, revealing a childish and obdurate sensibility long attuned to art, to the nuances of sexuality, and to the imminence of death.

Nothing that occurred in the world around T. deterred him from his quest for the "eternal woman" of traditional Japan, whom he deified. Concurrently, he wrote with fondness of the past and of the losses suffered in the course of modernization. Translating the conflict between old and new from the world of thought into the realm of feeling, he reduced it to sexual terms. A prolific writer and painstaking craftsman, he desired to entertain, enlighten, and shock his audience. The alarming implications of his art and his skill in revealing disturbing truths to the reading public evoked wide attention. T. explored human life with daring, sensitivity, and psychological acumen. His writing appeals readily to Western readers, and he deserves to be remembered as one of the preeminent writers of the 20th c.

FURTHER WORKS: *Shisei* (1911); *Akuma* (1913); *O'Tsuya-goroshi* (1915; *A Springtime Case,* 1927); *Itansha no kanashimi* (1917); *Haha o kōru ki* (1919); *Kyōfu jidai* (1920); *Mumyō to Aizen* (1924); *Chijin no ai* (1924–25); *Jōzetsuroku* (1930); *Yoshino kuzu* (1931; *Arrowroot,* 1982); *Mōmoku monogatari* (1932; *A Blind Man's Tale,* 1963); *Ashikari* (1932; *Ashikari,* 1936); *Seishun monogatari* (1933); *Bushū-kō hiwa* (1935; *The Secret*

History of the Lord Musashi, 1982); *Neko to Shōzō to futari no onna* (1937); *Yōshō-jidai* (1957); *Yume no ukihashi* (1960; *The Floating Bridge of Dreams,* 1963); *Mitsu no baai* (1961); *Daidokoro taiheiki* (1963); *Nihon no bungaku: T. J.* (1964); *T J. zenshū* (28 vols., 1966–70). FURTHER VOLUME IN ENGLISH: *Seven Japanese Tales by J. T.* (1963)

BIBLIOGRAPHY: Olson, L., "*The Makioka Sisters,*" *American Universities Field Staff: East Asia,* 9, 5 (1964), 533–41; Chambers, A., "T. J.'s Historical Fiction," *JATJ,* 8 (1972), 34–44; Fernandez, J., "A Study of T.'s *The Key,*" and Tsukimura, R., "The Sense of Loss in *The Makioka Sisters,*" in Tsuruta, K., and Swann, T. E., eds., *Approaches to the Modern Japanese Novel* (1976), pp. 215–40; Gangloff, E. J., "T.'s Use of Traditional Literature," *JATJ,* 11 (1976), 217–34; Ueda, M., *Modern Japanese Writers and the Nature of Literature* (1976), pp. 54–84; Rimer, J. T., *Modern Japanese Fiction and Its Traditions* (1978), pp. 22–37; Petersen, G. B., *The Moon in the Water: Understanding T., Kawabata, and Mishima* (1979), pp. 44–120; Lippit, N. M., *Reality and Fiction in Modern Japanese Literature* (1980), pp. 55–69, 82–103; Chambers, A. H., "A Study of T.'s *Yoshino kuzu,*" *HJAS,* 41 (1981), 483–505; Merken, K., "T. J.: 'Tattoo,' 'The Tale of Shunkin,' 'The Bridge of Dreams,' " in Swann, T. E., and Tsuruta, K., eds., *Approaches to the Modern Japanese Short Story* (1982), pp. 319–38

LEON M. ZOLBROD

YOKOMITSU Riichi

Japanese novelist and short-story writer, b. 17 March 1898, Fukushima; d. 30 Dec. 1947, Tokyo

Y. grew up in a family with no intellectual or cultural pretensions. From the age of twelve he was obliged to spend much of his time away from home: his father worked in Korea for a number of years and Y.'s mother went with him, leaving the youth with relatives or in lodging houses. These lonely adolescent years perhaps account for the desperate tone of much of his work. He had no other career except that of a professional writer. He was married twice, his first wife dying when she was only twenty, an event of great impact on his writing: it seems to have put an end to his literary experimentalism.

Y. made his literary debut with a stylistically experimental novella, *Nichirin* (1923; the sun in heaven), at a time when European modernism was being introduced into Japan. In 1924, with Kawabata Yasunari (q.v.) and others, he founded the magazine *Bungei jidai*, which during its two-and-a-half-year existence published the writings of the Shinkankakuha (New Sense-Impression Group), whose theoretical aim was to describe the world in terms of the sense impressions as they are directly received, rather than as mediated by the mind or the emotions. This group, in fact, represented the one significant attempt in Japanese literature in the 1920s to write a modernist prose, and Y. was the only member of it who did so with any real vigor.

This modernism was only short-lived, since proletarian writing soon came to dominate the literary scene, but Y.'s second collection of short stories, *Haru wa basha ni notte* (1927; spring riding in a carriage), reestablished his reputation. When he came to write his first long novel in 1927–28, *Shanghai* (1932; Shanghai), he was already famous. This novel shows a gradual abandoning of the impressionistic, brisk sentences of his earlier experimental work, a stylistic change completed in his most famous short story, "Kikai" (1930; "Machine," 1962), in which Y. uses long, convoluted sentences in an attempt to reveal the devious and obscure inner workings of the mind. "Kikai" is also typical of his writing in that it has a hero whose habit of self-reflection reveals little about himself. Y. thus creates a nightmarish image of man's inability to grasp the truth of existence—that human life is dominated by a deterministic "machine" beyond human control. This theme is the keynote of his serious writing.

The result of Y.'s experiments with psychological fiction was a series of long novels written during the 1930s in which he shows a growing concern with the division between "pure" and "popular" literature, attempting to create an amalgam of the two, although these works look, at least at first, more popular than serious.

A six-month stay in Europe in 1936 produced (or intensified) a sense of alienation from the spiritual Westernization that he presumed Japan had undergone, and he devoted much of the next ten years to the long, uncompleted, serially published novel, *Ryoshū* (1937–48; travel sadness), an attempt to debate this question in terms of the story of two men, one representing the Japanese, the other the Westernized spirit, and the women they love. After the 1945 defeat, Y. refused to swing with the reversal of the intellectual current, which now favored democracy and criticized the emperor worship and anti-Western views of the war years. Thus, he fell totally out of favor with the literary world, and so he remained until his death.

Y. was perhaps the leading Japanese novelist during the 1930s, but since his death he has been mainly ignored, his work overshadowed by that of his contemporary and close friend Kawabata. There are now signs, however, that some kind of reappraisal of his writings is about to take place. Even if his only truly accomplished work is seen as a handful of short stories, his central importance in the history of the Japanese novel during the experimental interwar years is beyond question.

FURTHER WORKS: *Onmi* (1924); *Hanabana* (1931); *Shin'en* (1932); *Monsho* (1934); *Tokei* (1934); *Seisō* (1935); *Tenshi* (1935); *Kazoku kaigi* (1935); *Haruzono* (1937); *Mi imada juku sezu* (1938); *Keien* (1941); *Yoru no kutsu* (1947). FURTHER VOLUMES IN ENGLISH: *Time, and Others* (1965, bilingual); *Love, and Other Stories of Y. R.* (1974)

BIBLIOGRAPHY: Keene, D., Introduction to *Love, and Other Stories* (1974), pp. ix–xxii; Keene, D., *Y. R.: Modernist* (1980)

DENNIS KEENE

KOREAN LITERATURE

The appearance of the first truly modern literature in Korea was preceded by the transitional dominance of a "new literature" of enlightenment. The modern literary movement was launched by Ch'oe Nam-sŏn (1890–1957) and Yi Kwang-su (1892–?). The "new poetry" movement dates back to the publication of a "Hae esŏ pada ege" (1908; "From the Sea to the Children," 1964), by Ch'oe Nam-sŏn in *Sonyŏn,* the first literary journal aimed at producing cultural reform by introducing Western civilization to the masses. Inspired by Byron's *Childe Harold's Pilgrimage,* Ch'oe celebrates, in clean masculine diction, the strength of the young people who will carry out the necessary social and literary revolution. However, neither Ch'oe nor his contemporaries succeeded in going beyond the bounds of traditional prosody, with its set alternation of four and three syllables, or in modernizing traditional forms of speech and allusion. In his stories, Yi Kwang-su adopted a prose style that approximated the everyday speech of the common people. Yet his stories, which dealt with the enlightened pioneers who championed Western science and civilization, still followed the conventional theme of the "reproval of vice and promotion of virtue."

In 1919, shortly before the unsuccessful movement for independence from Japan, translations from such Western poets as Paul Verlaine (1844–1896), Remy de Gourmont (1858–1915), and Fyodor Sologub (1863–1927) began to exert a powerful influence on Korean poetry. The indirection and suggestiveness of French symbolism were introduced by Kim Ŏk (1895–?), the principal translator. Against the didacticism of the age Kim set Mallarmé (1842–1898); against its rhetoric and sentimentality he set Verlaine, concluding in the process that free verse was the supreme creation of the symbolists. Kim's fascination with symbolism culminated, in March 1921, in the publication of *Onoe ŭi mudo* (dance of anguish), the first Korean collection of translations from Western poetry. Kim's translations from English, French, Esperanto, as well as from Japanese, were written in a mellifluous, dreamy style. The exotic and melancholy beauty of autumn, as well as expressions of ennui and anguish, all appealed to poets who sought to express their frustration and despair at the collapse of the independence movement of 1919.

The movement for literary naturalism was launched in the 1920s by a group of young writers who rallied around a new definition of universal reality in hopes of rectifying defects of form and content in fiction. Yŏm Sang-sŏp (1897–1963), the first to introduce psychological analysis and scientific documentation into his stories, defined naturalism as an expression of awakened individuality. Naturalism's purpose, Yŏm asserted, was to expose the sordid aspects of reality, especially the sorrow and disillusionment occurring as authority figures are debased and one's idols are shattered. Many works of naturalist fiction were first-person narratives. A desire to portray reality led writers to touch upon certain problems, but only those encountered by the writers, members of the intelligentsia, who were offering themselves as the subjects of case studies. Most stories written in this vein dealt with the miseries of the urban poor, or with the characters' attempts to cope with socioeconomic pressures. The disharmony between the writer and his society often induced the writer to turn to nature; and the land and the simple folk furnished themes and motifs for some of the better Korean stories in the Zolaesque tradition, among them "Pul" (1925; "Fire," 1974) by Hyŏn Chin-gŏn (1900–1943) and "Kamja" (1925; "Potato," 1974) by Kim Tong-in (1900–1951). But the most persistent theme in these stories is the assault on orthodox moral codes.

Naturalism in Korea was never a unified literary movement. Naturalist writers were productive over a span of several decades and wrote works that diverged widely in their treatment of basic themes. "Nalgae" (1936; "Wings," 1974) by Yi Sang (1910–1937), which traces the ceaseless activity of the hero's mind, is a stream-of-consciousness story. Others wrote panoramic novels, case studies of emancipated women, or historical novels.

The 1920s produced several major poets. Han Yong-un (1879–1944), revolutionary, reformer, monk, poet, and prophet, published *Nim ŭi ch'immuk* (1926; the silence of love) comprising eighty-eight meditative poems. Han and succeeding poets of resistance against the Japanese were constantly aware of their country's plight. Han sought insights into the terrible fate he and his country faced, and he found Buddhist contemplative poetry the lyric genre most congenial to this pursuit. Kim So-wŏl (1902–1934), a nature and folk poet, used simplicity, directness, and terse phrasing to good effect, as in his "Ch'ohon" (1925; "Summons of the Soul," 1964), an impassioned plea to his love that she return to him.

Many of his poems in *Chindallaekkot* (1925; *Azaleas,* 1980) were set to music.

The Manchurian incident of 1931 and the Japanese invasion of China in 1937 induced the military authorities to impose wartime restrictions. The grinding poverty of the lower classes at home and abroad, especially in the Korean settlements in southern Manchuria, was the chief concern of the writers of the "new tendency" movement, a movement in opposition to the romantic and decadent writers of the day, which later became proletarian in spirit. Writers of the class-conscious Korean Artist Proletariat Federation (KAPF), organized in 1925, asserted the importance of propaganda and regarded literature as a means to the political ends of socialism. The movement also attracted fellow travelers, who emerged from the shadows with the Russian slogan *V narod* ("To the people") on their lips.

Modern Korean literature attained its maturity in the 1930s through the efforts of a group of extraordinarily talented writers. They drew freely upon European examples to enrich their art. Translation of Western literature continued, and works by I. A. Richards, T. S. Eliot, and T. E. Hulme were introduced. This artistic and critical activity was a protest against the reduction of literature to journalism by influential magazines of the day, and to its use as propaganda by leftist writers.

The first truly successful poet of modern Korea was Chŏng Chi-yong (b. 1903), a master of his medium and a continuing presence. A student of Blake and Whitman, Chŏng rendered details with imagistic precision. His first published collection of poems, *Chŏng Chi-yong sijip* (1935; the poems of Chŏng Chi-yong), was followed by *Paengnoktam* (1941; White Deer Lake), which marks the high point of his career. The collection symbolically represents the progress of the spirit to lucidity, the fusion of man and nature.

A poetry of resistance, voicing a sorrow for the ruined nation with defiance but without violence or hatred, is the legacy of Yi Yuksa (1904–1944) and Yun Tong-ju (1917–1945). In such poems as the posthumously published "Kwangya" (1946; "The Wide Plain," 1980) and "Ch'ŏngp'odo" (1939; "Deep-Purple Grapes," 1980) Yi Yuksa sang of his winter of discontent and trial, and of his hopes for Korea's future. The poetry of Yun Tong-ju, an unimpassioned witness to Korea's national humiliation, expresses sorrow in response to relentless tyranny.

Korean fiction of the 1930s took shape in the void created by the compulsory dissolution of KAPF in 1935. Barred from all involvement with social or political issues, writers became preoccupied with technical perfection and the pursuit of pure art. Some, such as Yi Hyo-sŏk (1907–1942), returned to nature and sex; others retreated to the labryinth of primitive mysticism, superstition, and shamanism, for example Kim Tong-ni (b. 1913); still others sympathetically portrayed characters born out of their time, defeated and lonely. Narrative sophistication and subtlety were achieved through a denial of the writer's commitment to his art or to himself. A notable exception was Yŏm Sang-sŏp (1897–1963), who produced a document of the time in his novel *Samdae* (1932; three generations), a dialogue between liberalism and socialism and a study in the disintegration of traditional values and social classes.

The early 1940s brought disaster to all branches of Korean literature, as the Japanese suppressed all writings in Korean. The Sino-Japanese war extended into the Pacific in 1941. Censorship, which had begun with the Japanese annexation of Korea in 1910, was intensified. Korea was liberated on August 14, 1945, and the Republic of Korea (South Korea) was born on August 15, 1948. On the literary scene the controversy between left and right that had raged in the late 1920s and early 1930s was revived. There were frantic groupings and regroupings, and most of the hardcore leftist writers, such as Yi Ki-yŏng (b. 1896) and Han Sŏr-ya (b. 1900), had gone to North Korea by 1948.

Some poets who came of age in the 1940s also went north, while others gave up writing entirely. In general, though, the liberation of 1945 produced a flowering of poetry of all kinds. Some poets, like Pak Tu-jin (q.v.), Shin Tong-yŏp (1930–1969), and Hwang Tong-gyu (b. 1938), were determined to bear witness to the events of their age. Some, like Sŏ Chong-ju (q.v.), Pak Mogwŏl (1916–1978), and Shin Kyŏng-nim (b. 1936), sought to further assimilate traditional Korean values. Still others, like Kim Su-yŏng (1921–1968), Kim Ch'un-su (b. 1922), Hwang Tong-gyu, and Chŏng Hyŏn-jong (b. 1939), have drawn variously on Western traditions to enrich their work. All have sought to voice their own authentic testimony regarding the moments of crisis their culture has known.

The single overwhelming reality in Korean fiction since the Korean War has been the division of the country. As a symbol not only of Korea's trials but of the division of mankind and his alienation from himself and his world, the thirty-eighth parallel torments the conscience of every protagonist in modern Korean fiction in search of his destiny. Among South Korean writers, Hwang Sun-wŏn (b. 1915) and O Yŏng-su (b. 1914) have attempted to capture the images of the people in lyrical prose. Sŏnu Hwi (b. 1922) shows historical consciousness in his works,

while Chŏn Kwang-yong (b. 1919) depicts a hapless human type all too
common during Korea's years of servitude. Son Ch'ang-sŏp (b. 1946)
has delved relentlessly into the conscience of the lost generation of the
Korean War, Kim Sŭng-ok (b. 1941) into the inaction, self-deception,
and boredom of the alienated generation of the 1960s. Yi Pŏm-sŏn (b.
1920) has studied the defeat and disintegration of good people; Sŏ
Chŏng-in (b. 1938), the frustration of the educated; Yi Ho-ch'ŏl (b.
1932), the ways in which modern society negates man's freedom and
individuality. Noteworthy writers of the roman-fleuve include Hwang
Sun-wŏn, An Su-gil (b. 1911), and Pak Kyŏng-ni (b. 1927), the mother-
in-law of the poet Kim Chi-ha (b. 1941). Pak's multivolume *T'oji* (1969
ff.; land) has been acclaimed for its commanding style and narrative
techniques. In general, these works explore complex contemporary realities and universal human types.

The "new" drama movement, which began in 1908, saw the rise and
fall of small theater groups, such as the T'owŏrhoe, organized in 1923
by a group of Korean students studying in Tokyo, and finally the Kŭk
Yesul Yŏn'guhoe (Theatrical Arts Research Society), organized in 1931
(dissolved by the Japanese in 1938) by members of a Western literature
research society. Through their experimental theater, the members of the
society staged contemporary Western plays and encouraged the writing
of original plays, such as Yu Ch'i-jin's (b. 1905) *T'omak* (1933; clay
hut). The paucity of first-rate playwrights and actors, the dearth of plays
that satisfy dramatic possibilities, and the general living standards of the
audience have caused the relative inactivity in the field. Domestic plays
and historical pieces continue to be written and staged, but the future of
the dramatic arts in contemporary Korea is uncertain.

In the 20th c. a number of Koreans have written in Western languages or in Japanese. Li Mirok (1899–1950), who wrote in German,
and Younghill Kang (1903–1972) and Richard E. Kim (b. 1932), writing
in English, have produced autobiographical accounts of their formative
years. *The Diving Gourd* (1962), a novel, and *Love in Winter* (1969), a
collection of short stories, by Yong Ik Kim (b. 1920) combine traditional
subjects and modern techniques in portrayals of the farmers and fisher-
folk of the south. Among Korean writers born or residing in Japan, Yi
Hoe-sŏng (b. 1935; known in Japan as Li Kaisei) is outstanding. His
story "Kinuta o utsu onna" (1970; "A Woman Who Ironed Clothes,"
1977), a kind of short *Bildungsroman*, won the coveted Akutagawa Prize
in 1972.

Modern South Korean writers are constantly occupied with the complex realities of modern urban life, and with the lives and emotions of a people enduring continuous uncertainty and repression. That lively literary activity continues in such a setting attests to the resilience, strength, and tenacity of 20th-c. Korean writers.

BIBLIOGRAPHY: Lee, P. H., *Korean Literature: Topics and Themes* (1965), pp. 101–19; Lee, P. H., Introduction to *Flowers of Fire: Twentieth-Century Korean Stories* (1974), pp. xiii–xxv; Pihl, M. R., "Engineers of the Human Soul: North Korean Literature Today," *Korean Studies*, 1 (1977), 63–110; Kim, C., "Images of Man in Postwar Korean Fiction," *Korean Studies*, 2 (1978), 1–27; Lee, P. H., Introduction to *The Silence of Love: Twentieth-Century Korean Poetry* (1980), pp. xi–xix; Lee, P. H., "Literature and Folklore," in Kim, H., ed., *Studies on Korea: A Scholar's Guide* (1980), pp. 165–75

PETER H. LEE

PAK Tu-jin

South Korean poet, essayist, and critic, b. 10 March 1916, Ansŏng

After graduating from a local high school, P. worked as a company employee. He made his literary debut in 1939 with a group of nature poems. Between 1941 and 1945, in response to Japanese repression and the prohibition of the use of the Korean language, he refused to write anything. In 1949 P. published his first poetry collection, *Hae* (the sun). In addition to eleven volumes of poetry, he has written essays and literary criticism, including interpretations of his own poems. P. is currently a professor of Korean literature at Yonsei University in Seoul. He is also an accomplished calligrapher. His many awards include the Free Literature Prize (1956), the Culture Prize of the City of Seoul (1962), the March First Literature Prize (1970), and the Korean Academy of Arts Prize (1976).

P. is credited with having imparted a new direction to modern Korean poetry through skillful use of such elemental images as mountains, rivers, stars, the sun, the sea, and the sky. He inspires hope for a new life, a prelapsarian cosmos of perfect harmony. During the Japanese occupation (1910–45), such a world symbolized not only moral perfection of men but also independence and freedom for Korea and the Koreans. But to P., nature has always been "the source of God's love, light, truth, goodness, and beauty," and his paeans to the beauty of the created world and his Blakean innocence became imbued with a moral vision as he came to view the world in terms of moral conflict. As political corruption and repression increased in South Korea, P.'s moral consciousness came to the fore, and his poems from the mid-1960s on are imbued with a strong historical and cultural consciousness that bears testimony to contemporary reality.

P. is capable of a wide range of moods—angry accusation, fierce honesty, visionary serenity—and his language and style impart a distinctive tone to his Christian and nationalistic sentiments. Sonoric intricacies and incantatory rhythms, achieved by sporadic repetition of key words, are the hallmark of P.'s poetry. Of late, he has withdrawn into nature to perceive its creative power in water-washed stones, the topic of some two hundred of his poems. An authentic inheritor of the East Asian eremitic tradition, P. has consistently rejected the false allegiances demanded by a corrupt society.

FURTHER WORKS: *Ch'ŏngnok chip* (1946, with Pak Mogwŏl and Cho Chihun); *Odo* (1953); *P. T. sisŏn* (1956); *Ingan millim* (1963); *Kosan singmul* (1973); *Sado haengjŏn* (1973); *Susŏk yŏlchŏn* (1973); *Sok susŏk yŏlchŏn* (1976). FURTHER VOLUME IN ENGLISH: *Sea of Tomorrow: Forty Poems of P. T.* (1971)

BIBLIOGRAPHY: Lee, P. H., ed., *The Silence of Love: Twentieth Century Korean Poetry* (1980), pp. xviii–xix, 136

PETER H. LEE

SŎ Chŏng-ju
South Korean poet and essayist, b. 18 May 1915, Koch'ang

As a youth, S. went through a period of aimless wandering until he entered a monastery to study Buddhism. He continued his studies at the Central Buddhist College (now Tongguk University) and then again led the life of a vagabond in southern Manchuria during the dark days of the Japanese occupation. After the liberation (1945), he worked for newspapers and taught at high schools and universities. Currently, he is a professor of literature at Tongguk University. In addition to his volumes of poetry, which have earned him the Freedom Literature Award (1955) and the Korean Academy of Arts Award (1967), he has written literary criticism.

S. has been dubbed the Korean Baudelaire. His early poetry in *Hwasa* (1938; the flower snake), was characterized by sensuality and diabolism in a specifically Korean setting. With *Kwich'okto* (1948; the cuckoo) S. returned to broader East Asian themes and emotions, seeking eternal life and championing poetry for life's sake as opposed to art's sake. In *Silla ch'o* (1961; Silla sketches) he presented a vision of an idealized Silla (an ancient Korean kingdom) in which man and nature were one. S. forged the themes of Buddhist tales and legends into new entities with a sure touch. He has continually presented a view of life imbued with a dark, mysterious stillness, akin to the feeling associated with Zen meditation, and enhanced by skillful use of Buddhist metaphors, as in *Tongch'ŏn* (1968; winter sky). His most recent works show him delving into native shamanism to transform intractably unpoetic elements into works of art.

S. is credited with exploring the hidden resources of the Korean language, from sensual ecstasy to spiritual quest, from haunting lyricism to colloquial earthiness. Some consider S. the most "Korean" of contemporary poets. Yet he appears to have remained untouched by historical forces, even though he attempted suicide during the Korean War.

FURTHER WORKS: *S. C. sisŏn* (1956); *S. C. munhak chŏnjip* (5 vols., 1972); *Chilmajae sinhwa* (1975); *Ttŏdori ŭi si* (1976)

BIBLIOGRAPHY: Hwang Tong-gyu, Critical Introduction to *Selections from S. C.* (1981), pp. 221–44; Kim, U., Foreword to "S. C." [translations], *Quarterly Journal of Literature*, 22 (1981), 7–12

PETER H. LEE

LAO LITERATURE

Lao literature, which had its beginnings in poetry, reached its heights in the 16th and 17th cs. with the production of such epic poems as *Sin Xay* (partial tr., "The Sin Xai," 1967) by Thao Pangkham (fl. 1650). These poems were designed to be sung or chanted to the accompaniment of music. They contained descriptions of landscapes and accounts of love scenes and great battles.

Lao literature in the 20th c. reflects the major political changes during this period. During the first third of the century, when Laos was under French control, the *mohlam,* or traditional singers, continued to create and carry on the traditions of Lao poetry. In the 1930s and 1940s a new era in Lao literature was ushered in by young intellectuals who wrote articles in French about their own culture, language, and religion. Following the publication by Katay Don Sasorith (1904–1959) of *Comment joue-t-on le phay-tong?* (1931; *The Game of Phay-Tong,* 1959), a string of articles by Lao authors appeared in French publications. Others who wrote in French included Prince Phetsarath Ratanavongsa (1890–1959), Prince Souphanouvong (b. 1912), Prince Souvannaphouma (b. 1901) and Nhouy Abhay (b. 1909).

With the rise of Lao nationalism in the 1940s, many writers began publishing prose in their native language. Such important authors as Maha Sila Viravong (b. 1904), Thao Kéne (dates n.a.), Phouvong Phimmasone (b. 1911), and Somchine Pierre Nginn (b. 1892) wrote in Lao. By 1953 the Lao Literary Committee had begun publication of *Wannakhadisan,* a magazine devoted to articles on Lao language and culture.

During the 1940s and 1950s—both before and after independence (1954)—works appeared chronicling political events from the point of view of the Lao, albeit the elite. Prince Phetsarath published an important work in Thai, *Chao Phetsarat: Burut lek haeng Ratcha'anachak Lao* (1956; *Iron Man of Laos: Prince Phetsarath Ratanavongsa,* 1978), which provided a view of the life of a person actively involved in the modern history of Laos.

The publication in Paris of Sisouk Na Champassak's (b. 1928) *Tempête sur le Laos* (1961; *Storm over Laos,* 1961), written from the royalist point of view, added a major work of political journalism to the literature by the Lao elite in the French language.

Phoumi Vongvichit (dates n.a.), as secretary-general of the central committee of the Lao Patriotic Front (a component of the communist Pathet Lao), provided a different view of the political situation in his *Le Laos et la lutte victorieuse du peuple lao contre le néo-colonialisme américain* (1968; *Laos and the Victorious Struggle of the Lao People against United States Neo-colonialism*, 1969).

Much of the poetry composed from the late 1950s to the present reflected Lao political struggles. Poets of the major sides in the fight for Laos—communists, royalists, and neutralists—appealed to the people to join them, frequently referring to Buddhist literature and to Lao myths and legends to support their positions. Poems were also written by Lao in western languages. An interesting collection of poems written in Lao, French, and English by Khamchan Pradith (b. 1930) was called simply *Mes poèmes* (1960; my poems).

A great amount of technical literature in Lao was produced in the 1960s, primarily to support an educational system that was now teaching more subjects in the Lao language. Textbooks were written on agriculture, education, home economics, Lao language and literature, mathematics, and science. And Buddhist works were published by the monks of Vat Phonpranao.

Popular fiction in Lao came into its own in the late 1960s and early 1970s. A group of young writers in the Vientiane area attempted to encourage reading and writing in the Lao language; the major themes of their short stories were love, the trials of war, and Lao nationalism. Much of their writing appeared in two new magazines, *Phay nam* (from June 1972) and *Nang* (from December 1972), the latter a magazine written primarily by and for women. Characteristic of the works of this group is Leng Phouphangeum's (dates n.a.) *Sivit ni khy lakhon kom* (1968; this life is like shadow theater), and Panai (a pseudonym, dates n.a.) and Douangchampa's (a pseudonym, dates n.a.) *Thale sivit* (1971; ocean of life).

At the same time, socialist writers were producing works emphasizing the sufferings and struggles of Lao villagers and guerrillas in the areas of the country controlled by the Lao Patriotic Front. Such writing can be found in the short-story anthology *Kay pa* (1968; *The Wood Grouse*, 1968).

In the late 1970s two major types of publications appeared: (1) works produced in Laos under the new Lao People's Democratic

Republic, including collections of short stories such as *Siang oen khong phay* (1978; whose cry for help), and collections of poems in traditional *lam* styles such as *Kon lam pativat* (1977; songs of the revolution); (2) writings by Lao refugees in the countries to which they had moved, including newsletters in Lao and English containing information about life in a new country, and articles written in English or French on Lao culture.

During the 20th c. the major innovation in Lao literature was the introduction and acceptance of the short story; the major theme was the consequences of political disruption of life in Laos.

BIBLIOGRAPHY: Phimmasone, P., "Cours de littérature lao," *Bulletin des Amis du Royaume Lao,* Nos. 4–5 (1971), 5–70; Lafont, P.-B., "La littérature politique lao," in Lafont, P.-B., and Lombard, D., eds., *Littératures contemporaines de l'Asie du sud-est,* Colloque du XXIXe Congrès International des Orientalistes (1974), pp. 40–55; Phinith, S., "Contemporary Lao Literature," *JSSB,* 63 (1975), 239–50; Compton, C. J., *Courting Poetry in Laos: A Textual and Linguistic Analysis,* Northern Illinois University, Center for Southeast Asian Studies Special Report No. 18 (1979); Nguyen N., "Lao Literature through History," in Social Science Committee of Vietnam (Hanoi), *History and Culture of South East Asia: Studies on Laos* (1981), pp. 35–48

CAROL J. COMPTON

MALAYSIAN LITERATURE

In Malay

Fiction

Modern writing in the Malay language began in the 19th c. with the works of Abdullah bin Abdul Kadir Munshi (1796–1854), but it was not until the 1920s that truly modern literature took shape. Short stories and novels appeared that were no longer the classical *hikayat* fairy tales of princes and princesses but works depicting true-to-life characters facing the problems of contemporary society. *Hikayat Faridah Hanum* (1925; the story of Faridah Hanum) by Syed Sheikh al-Hady (1867–1934) was the prototype of early Malay novels. An adaptation of an Egyptian novel, the characters and setting were therefore not Malayan. Still, it focused on the chief preoccupation of the Malayan elite at the time: to resolve the sociocultural conflicts arising from the confrontation between traditional culture and modern Western civilization. The main message was that the ethics of Islam, especially pertaining to relationships between the sexes, could not be compromised.

Many Malay novels until the outbreak of war in the Pacific in 1942 carried a similar message: the best defense against the problems of modern life is strict observance of the Islamic moral code. While there continued to be novels with foreign settings, Malay fiction had shifted to local scenes and situations. A love story is set against the background of urban life, often portrayed as full of evil. Surprisingly, criticism of old customs and outdated beliefs did not find fertile ground among Malay novelists, as it did among Indonesian novelists writing in Malay (Indonesian) at the same time.

During the 1930s publication of novels in Malay became widespread. About half were short penny-novels telling romantic stories. Many were more serious, concerned with moral questions and national aspirations. *Putera Gunung Tahan* (1936; the prince of Mount Tahan) by Ishak Haji Muhammad (b. 1910) and *Mari kita berjuang* (1940; let us struggle) by Abdullah Sidik (1913–1973) are representative. *Putera Gunung Tahan* satirizes the attitudes of the British colonial rulers toward their subjects. *Mari kita berjuang* is a straightforward narrative aimed at inspiring young Malayans to be self-reliant economically and politically.

The rise of the short story in the 1920s and 1930s coincided with the proliferation of magazines and newspapers in Malay. Many were simple romantic tales interlaced with moral teachings. The leading short-story writer of the period was Abdul Rahim Kajai (1894–1943).

During the Japanese occupation (1942–45) literary production almost ceased. The end of the war ushered in a period of nationalist struggle, first for cultural identity and later for political independence. New importance was placed on Malay language and literature. At first, however, novels continued prewar traditions. The moralistic novels of Ahmad Lutfi (1911–1966), like *Bilik 69* (1949; room 69) and *Joget moden* (1949; modern dance) were reminiscent of *Hikayat Faridah Hanum,* although they presented contemporary situations and spicy bedroom scenes. Ahmad Bachtiar (1902–1961) continued the prewar trend of the historical novel with nationalist overtones, while Salleh Ghani (dates n.a.) in *Seruan merdeka* (1949; the call of freedom) and Hamdan (dates n.a.) in *Barisan Zubaidah* (1950; the Zubaidah movement), treated nationalism in a more contemporary way.

A truly fresh approach to the novel did not appear until the late 1950s, and during the 1960s writing became more sophisticated. Abdul Samad Said (b. 1935), for instance, wanted to make Malay writing more realistic. His graphic portrayal of Singapore slum life in *Salina* (1961; Salina) brought a new dimension to fiction: the purpose of the novel is not to moralize but to capture contemporary society. While *Hikayat Faridah Hanum* and the novels of Ahmad Lutfi reflected fears that Malay traditions were losing out to the modern way of life, the new novels lay bare contemporary social injustices. *Tak ada jalan keluar* (1962; there is no way out) by Suratman Markasan (b. 1930) presents a typical moral compromise: a divorcée resorts to prostitution so that her children can have a better future. *Desa pingitan* (1964; nurturing village) by Ibrahim Omar (b. 1936) and *Angin hitam dari kota* (1968; dark wind from the city) by A. Wahab Ali (b. 1941) are two prize-winning novels that deal with the conflicts between urban and rural values.

A prolific writer in the 1960s, who by the 1970s had become the leading fiction writer, is Shahnon Ahmad (q.v.). His novels mostly deal with controversial issues of the day. *Rentong* (1965; burned to ashes) and *Ranjau sepanjang jalan* (1966; *No Harvest but a Thorn,* 1972) are about the hard life of rural rice farmers, while *Protes* (1967; protest) raises touchy religious issues.

Women writers brought a new perspective to Malay fiction. Salmi

Manja's (b. 1936) youthful novel *Hari mana bulan mana* (1960; which day, which month) depicts a woman's everyday experiences in a changing society. Adibah Amin's (b. 1934) *Seroja masih di kolam* (1968; the lily is still in the pond) focuses on the difficulties women face in trying to eschew traditions. Khadijah Hashim's (b. 1945) novel *Merpati putih terbang lagi* (1971; the white dove flies again) rearticulates the age-old Malayan ideal of honesty and goodness surmounting all obstacles.

While novelists have grappled with language and narrative techniques, they have not been able to deal successfully with new social experiences: the multiethnicity of the Malaysian population, political processes, and economic problems are hardly touched on.

The short story has played a more important role than the novel. Moralizing tales yielded to new trends during the 1950s, spurred on by a radical group known as Asas '50 (generation of the 1950s). Writers like Keris Mas (b. 1922), Awam-il-Sarkam (b. 1918), Wijaya Mala (b. 1923), Hamzah Hussein (b. 1927), and Asmal (pseud. of Abdul Samad bin Ismail, b. 1924), began to deal realistically with social problems. Anticolonial sentiments also appeared, but the main concern was the injustices suffered by the urban poor, rural peasants, and fishermen. The members of Asas '50 were political activists, but they were also concerned with the improvement of literary techniques and a more penetrating approach to themes.

The influence of Asas '50 continued into the mid-1960s. Asmal's "Ingin jadi pujangga" (1959; aspiring poet) is a self-caricature of the young writers who, in trying to live up to the ideals of serious writing, fall prey to their own artificialities. Asmal's "Ah Kau masuk syurga" (1959; Ah Kau goes to heaven) exposes the tendency of Malayans to accept symbols rather than substance. Keris Mas's collection *Patah tumbuh* (1962; continuity) shows not only the progress in Malay short-story writing after the war but also the writer's view of events that led to independence.

By the mid-1960s, the leading short-story writers were Abdul Samad Said and Shahnon Ahmad. Themes were still mainly social, but now set against the problems of a newly independent nation. Short-story writers portrayed emergent types: corrupt politicians, status-conscious civil servants, university-educated social climbers. Younger writers like Mohd. Affandi Hassan (b. 1940), S. Othman Kelantan (b. 1938), Ali Majod (b. 1940), Azizi Abdullah (b. 1942), and the women writers Khadijah Hashim and Fatimah Busu (b. 1943) have broadened the horizons of the short story and evinced a more polished technique. Since the late 1960s social themes have been balanced by a more introspective and penetrating look at human life.

Poetry

The first attempts to break away from traditional *syair* and *pantun* verse forms were made in the early 1930s. The new poetic expression, collectively called *sajak,* was influenced by the rise of modern poetry in Indonesia in the 1920s and 1930s. Although it took hold slowly, *sajak* bloomed after World War II. The early *sajak* poems often expressed Malayan nationalism in romantic terms.

Asas '50 viewed the *pantun* and the *syair* as too rigid for the philosophy the group advocated: they favored the free-verse expression of the *sajak.* The *sajaks* of Usman Awang (q.v.) and Mahsuri Salikon (b. 1927) became models for younger writers. Usman Awang's collection *Gelombang* (1961; waves) is representative of modern poetry of the time. The early *pantun* forms, the later free verse, his preoccupation with freeing himself from the shackles of tradition, his opposition to colonialism, and his concern for social justice are clearly arrayed chronologically in this volume. His second collection, *Duri dan api* (1969; thorns and fire), shows his ease with the free-verse forms and at the same time his widening vision, moving beyond his homeland.

There was a time when some poets thought that free verse was a license to experiment without constraint; this concept brought about the phenomenon of *sajak kabur* (obscure poems) in the 1950s and early 1960s. *Sajaks* proliferated: there was hardly a magazine or newspaper that did not print them.

Poets debuting since the late 1960s and the 1970s have had the advantage of greater education, including some knowledge of foreign literatures. Muhammed Haji Salleh (b. 1942), Firdaus Abdullah (b. 1944), Kassim Ahmad (b. 1933), Latif Mohidin (b. 1941), Zurinah Hassan (b. 1949), and Baharuddin Zainal (b. 1939) are among those who have written serious works of poetry. Poetry has moved away from social and political problems, concentrating instead on personal, philosophical, and aesthetic themes. A woman poet, Zanariah Wan Abdul Rahman (b. 1940), using traditional imagery, has written about the dilemmas of a young girl in love. Even in religious poems, thunderous exhortations and evangelistic fervor have given way to a more philosophical expression.

Drama

Malay drama in the 20th c. has had varied sources: it springs from folk-ritualistic drama, from the traditional shadow play, from the popular theater called the *bangsawan* (plays on romantic or historical themes interspersed with songs and comic sketches), and from the Western plays that were introduced through the schools. Before World War II the *bangsawan* was the main form of urban theater and the main expression of the rising urban culture. Traditional folk performances continued to thrive in the villages.

Modern Malay theater started with school performances, during the colonial period of Shakespeare and other European dramatists. During the Japanese occupation *sandiwara* plays, similar to *bangsawan* but with contemporary themes, to some extent replaced the *bangsawan;* this form of theater was inspired by Indonesian drama. Not until the 1950s was there a deliberate effort to create truly Malayan (later Malaysian) plays. The result was not only plays with modern social themes, but also, following the *bangsawan*, themes drawn from the historical and legendary past. The latter is usually referred to as *purbawara*. Shahrum Hussein (b. 1919) has written plays about past heroes, such as *Si bongkok Tanjung Puteri* (1961; the hunchbacked warrior of Tanjung Puteri) and *Tun Fatimah* (1964; Tun Fatimah [the woman warrior of old Malacca]). Mustapha Kamal Yassin (b. 1925) has dealt with contemporary subjects. His *Atap genting atap rembia* (1963; tiled and thatched roofs) attacks those who put status and wealth above love in marriage. Ali Aziz (b. 1935), in *Hang Jebat menderhaka* (1957; Hang Jebat rebels), tried to apply techniques of Shakespearean tragedy to the duel between two blood brothers: Hang Tuah, who upholds the cardinal Malayan traditional value of unquestioning loyalty to the sultan; and Hang Jebat, who rebels for the sake of justice. Usman Awang's *Muzika Uda dan Dara* (1976; the musical play of Uda and Dara), a simple tale of unrequited love between two young villagers, has been presented as a musical play as well as a dance drama.

Since the late 1960s, dramatists like Syed Alwi (b. 1930) and Nordin Hassan (b. 1929) have experimented with techniques from the traditional drama: images reflected on a screen, as in the shadow play, have been used for special effects or to convey a character's past experiences. And drama in the round often uses the techniques of traditional dance theater like the *randai*.

In Chinese

Before the Pacific War writings in Chinese echoed those of China proper. Early Chinese writers in Malaya had migrated from China, and sentiments expressed were mainly directed at the homeland. In the 1930s, after the Japanese invaded China, nationalism dominated the writing of overseas Chinese. Chinese writing had to go underground during the Japanese occupation of Malaya (1942–45). From prison Siew Yang (dates n.a.) and Chin Chung (dates n.a.) wrote clandestine anti-Japanese works.

The early postwar years saw a revival of literary activity, but writing in Chinese again suffered a setback after the communist insurrection of 1948. Between 1948 and 1957 hardly any literary activity took place, partly because of the local situation and partly because of the break in communication with China.

The desire to produce a truly *Ma-hoa*, or Malaysian Chinese, literature was nurtured in the years following independence in 1957. Young writers who had grown up in Malaysia realized that *Ma-hoa* literature should have its own identity, but the legacy and influence of classical Chinese literature remained formidable.

The preferred genre of Chinese literature in Malaysia has been the short story. Between 1945 and 1965, works were mostly anticolonial and antifeudal. They reflected the life of the middle and lower classes. Since 1965 Malaysian settings and problems specifically related to the country have characterized Chinese writing in Malaysia.

In Tamil

Tamil writing in Malaysia began with religious poetry toward the end of the 19th c. The first Tamil novel was Venkitarattinam's (dates n.a.) *Karunacakaran; allathu, Kathalinmatchi* (1917; Karunacakaran; or, the glory of love). Short stories appeared during the 1930s, coinciding with the proliferation of Tamil newspapers. Many of the stories were moralizing. During this period those writing for local publications were in constant contact with developments in the homeland in south India. The influence of the Indian Tamil journal *Manikkodi* brought new themes into Malaysian Tamil short stories: political, economic, and social questions were raised.

Poetry has dominated Tamil literature in Malaysia. And the majority of poems until the 1940s were religious in content. Since the 1950s Tamil poetry had a variety of themes, ranging from social reform and patriotism to romantic love, nature, and the mother tongue.

Short stories became more numerous in the 1950s. The periodical *Tamil necan* regularly published stories by Suba Narayanan (b. 1938) and Bairoji Narayanan (b. 1931). Contact with the Tamil homeland still provided the literary guide for local writers. S. Vadivelu's (b. 1929) stories show an unusual ability to create a vivid setting; his stories that take place during the Japanese occupation are especially notable. Short stories now have a variety of themes: politics, education, economics, citizenship problems, family organization, human relationships, alcoholism, and national unity.

Only in 1958, a year after Malaysian independence, did the Association of Tamil Writers in Malaya come into being. By the 1960s there was a marked shift in Tamil literature toward Malaysian themes and problems. S. Vadivelu, who has continued to be a leading figure, published the collection of stories *Irunda ulagam* (1970; dark world) dealing with the problems of the Indian community in Malaysia.

In English

Literature in English can be called Malaysian after Malaysian writers began to write a distinctive literature in English. Before that there was only writing in English with a Malayan setting, written both by foreigners living in the country and by locals. Of the former, the most notable is Anthony Burgess, who served as an education officer toward the end of British rule and wrote *The Malayan Trilogy* (1956–59). Gregory de Silva (dates n.a.) with *Sulaiman Goes to London* (1938), Chin Kee Onn (b. 1908) with *Malaya Upside Down* (1946), Ooi Cheng Teck (dates n.a.) with *Red Sun over Malaya: John Man's Ordeal* (1948), and Gurchan Singh (dates n.a.) with *Singa: The Lion of Malaya* (1959) represent the latter.

The seeds of Malaysian literature in English were sown by natives who used English because it was the language of their education, and hence the only language they were proficient in. Although some of them were conscious of their dilemma—inheriting a colonial culture while the country was readying itself for independence—they still could not shake off the influence of English. The best they could do was to adopt certain Malayan elements in their writings.

Wang Gungwu (b. 1930) was one of the early writers who attempted to forge a Malayan identity while using English; the poems in his collection *Pulse* (1950) have a definite Malayan quality. There were others like Wang Gungwu, but they could not sustain their creativity, and after a year or two they would stop publishing. Of the few who continued writing consistently, the leading poets have been Ee Tiang Hong (b. 1933), Wong Phui Nam (b. 1936), and Muhammed Haji Salleh. Ee Tiang Hong is fond of writing about different places in Malaysia. In "Heeren Street, Malacca" (1968), for example, he sees the old Baba Chinese culture, a relic of a past age, coming face to face with modern times. His early poems are collected in *I of the Many Faces* (1960). His tone became more critical of society as years went by. Wong Phui Nam excels in beautiful descriptions. Muhammed Haji Salleh, who studied in England and first wrote in English, now writes in Malay.

In prose, there are almost no novels, but short stories appear regularly in both popular magazines and more serious journals, like *Tenggara* and *Lidra*. Of the novels, *Scorpion Orchid* (1976) by Lloyd Fernando (b. 1926) is the best. Innovative in form, it deals with that period when the struggle for independence was not a clear-cut issue for the English-educated elite.

BIBLIOGRAPHY: Mohd. Taib bin Osman, *An Introduction to the Development of Modern Malay Language and Literature* (1961); Kirkup, J., Introduction to Majid, A., and Rice, O., eds., *Modern Malay Verse* (1963), pp. vii–xiv; Subramaniam, M., "Growth of Modern Tamil Literature in Malaysia," *Proceedings of the First International Conference-Seminar of Tamil Studies* (1969), Vol. II, pp. 304–8; Dhandayudham, R., "The Development of the Tamil Short Story in Malaysia," *JTamS*, No. 3 (1973), 7–16; Mohd. Taib bin Osman, "Classical and Modern Malay Literature," *Handbuch der Orientalistik*, 3, 3, 1 (1976), pp. 116–86; Zainal, B., "A Guide to Malay Literature (1970–76)," *Tenggara*, 8 (1976), 70–79; Wahab Ali, A., "The Role of Literature in Transmitting National Values: Malaysia," in Bresnahan, R. J., ed., *Literature and Society: Cross-Cultural Perspectives* (1977), pp. 32–42; Bennett, B., "The Subdued Ego: Poetry from Malaysia and Singapore," *Meanjin*, 37 (1978), 240–46; Ismail, Y., "The National Language and Literature of Malaysia," in Perez, A. Q., et al., eds., *Papers from the Conference on the Standardisation of Asian Languages, Manila, Philippines, December 16–21, 1974* (1978), pp. 93–103; Hong, E. T., "Malaysian Poetry in English: Influence and Independence," *PQM*, 4 (1979), 69–73; Simms, N., "The Future of English as a Poetic Language in Singapore and

Malaysia," *CNLR*, 2, 2 (1979), 9–13; 3, 1 (1980), 10–14; and 3, 2 (1980), 8–12; Wong, S., "The Influence of China's Literary Movement on Malaysia's Vernacular Chinese Literature in the 1930's," *TkR*, 10 (1980), 517–34

MOHD. TAIB BIN OSMAN

SHAHNON Ahmad

Malaysian novelist and short-story writer (writing in Malay), b. 13 Jan. 1933, Sik

S. was born in a village in the state of Kedah. After attending secondary school in Alor Setar (1947–53), he began a career as a schoolteacher in 1954, and except for a stint as an army officer (1955–56), he continued to teach until he went to Australia in 1968 for university study. He received his B.A. in 1971. He later earned an M.A. (1975) from the University of Science in Penang, where he is currently a professor of Malay literature. Although an academician now, S., who began writing in 1956, continues to publish novels and short stories as well as essays and criticism.

Above all, S. is a fighter. His essays and literary works always contain a note of protest and defiance at the order of things. The twist of fate, irony, and pathos are the hallmarks of his short stories, but at the same time he believes that literature should have a social function. His novels in particular are realistic and deal with sensitive issues.

Although S.'s early short stories, collected in *Anjing-anjing* (1964; dogs) and *Debu merah* (1965; red dust), are superior to most Malaysian short fiction, it was not until he began publishing novels that he was acclaimed as the master of modern Malay prose. His first novel, *Rentong* (1965; burned to ashes), deals with Malaysia's unfortunate rural population. Having come from a peasant village himself, S. showed his sympathy for these people, who are ill-equipped to deal with natural disasters and social change.

Ranjau sepanjang jalan (1966; *No Harvest but a Thorn*, 1972) also concerns the extreme difficulty of the peasants' lives, detailing not only their struggle with the physical environment but their relationships with one another and their belief in the supernatural. Man's relationship with his fellow-men is also the subject of the novels *Protes* (1967; protest), *Menteri* (1967; the minister), and *Perdana* (1969; premier). *Protes* is largely an argument between the main characters about religious subjects;

Menteri is a satirical treatment of political and bureaucratic corruption; and *Perdana* deals with the political events of the period of the struggle for independence. All three novels illustrate S.'s contention that weakness is found among urban dwellers and the educated middle class as well as the peasantry.

Srengenge (1973; *Srengenge*, 1980), which won an important literary prize in Malaysia, is more symbolic than S.'s earlier fiction. The hill of the title is believed to be possessed by a powerful evil spirit. By showing how the people who live around the hill react to this spirit, S. examines man in relation to religion and the supernatural. Religious themes have been the primary focus of S.'s recent writings.

FURTHER WORKS: *Terdedah* (1965); *Sampah* (1974); *Kemelut* (1977); *Selasai sudah* (1977); *Seluang menolak Baung* (1978); *Penglibatan dalam puisi* (1978); *Gubahan novel* (1979); *Kesusasteraan dan etika Islam* (1981). FURTHER VOLUME IN ENGLISH: *The Third Notch, and Other Stories* (1980)

BIBLIOGRAPHY: Mohd. Taib bin Osman, Modern Malay Literature: A Reflection of a Changing Society and Culture," *ASPAC Quarterly,* 5, 3 (1973), 23–37; Johns, A. H., on *No Harvest but a Thorn, Hemisphere,* Sept. 1973, 40–41; Fernando, L., Introduction to *The Third Notch, and Other Stories* (1981), pp. i–xiv; Nazareth, P., on *The Third Notch, and Other Stories, WLT,* 56 (1982), 408

MOHD. TAIB BIN OSMAN

USMAN Awang

(pseud.: Tongkat Waran [policeman's truncheon]) Malaysian poet, dramatist, short-story writer, and novelist (writing in Malay), b. 12 July 1929, Kota Tinggi

U. received an elementary education and some secondary schooling in his native state of Johore. He began working while very young, during the Japanese occupation (1942–45). In 1946, after the return of the British to Malaya, he became a policeman. He went to Singapore in 1951 to work as a newspaper and magazine proofreader; he later became an editor of several of these Malay publications. In 1963 he became an editor for the Language and Literary Agency in Malaysia, a position he holds to the present day.

U. is one of the writers credited with the development of modern Malay *sajak* (free-verse) poetry in the early postwar years. Nevertheless, his early poetry, collected in *Gelombang* (1961; waves), showed the unmistakable characteristics of the older, traditional *pantun* and *syair* forms. Only in ideas and tone can U.'s early poetry be said to represent new directions. The collection *Duri dan api* (1967; thorn and fire) shows a development. The clarion call for independence, the cry of the struggling poor, the peasants, fishermen, and laborers; the difficult life in the cities, especially for the workers; and the general social and political problems of the day are his favorite early subjects. Alongside these themes, which showed U. to be an angry young man, there were others that were simply human, personal, and romantic: love, peace, godliness, and family life.

In his early poetic experiments U. was groping in both form and theme. After his horizons were broadened by reading and travel, in addition to poems on local subjects he wrote on international themes, such as "Salam benua" (1970; greetings to the continents), which criticizes leaders of powerful nations for perpetuating a divided world, and "Darah dan doa" (1972; blood and prayer), a message of peace to all mankind.

U. is also a playwright. His best-known dramatic work is *Muzika Uda dan Dara* (1976; the musical play of Uda and Dara), with music by Basil Jayatilaka. It is a powerful drama of two young lovers thwarted by the evil designs of the girl's rich suitor.

The versatile U. has written fiction as well. Twenty-one short stories are collected in *Degup jantung* (1963; the heart beats). In these the reader can trace the author's development from a romantic and idealistic youth to a more mature writer concerned with social justice. His only novel, *Tulang-tulang berserakan* (1966; the scattered skeleton), is a less successful work. More an autobiography than a novel, it is based on U.'s experiences in Malacca and tells of a policeman who must fight communist insurgents without fully understanding the situation. This straightforward narrative is redeemed by its language and style.

U.'s primary importance is as a poet. Many younger writers have been influenced both by his style and by his passionate and committed treatment of social and political themes.

FURTHER WORKS: *Dari bintang ke bintang* (1965); *Serunai malam* (1966); *Tamu di Bukit Kenny* (1968); *Di bawah matahari* (1969); *Tirai zaman* (1969); *Kaki langit* (1971)

BIBLIOGRAPHY: Kirkup, J., Introduction to Majid, A. and Rice, O., eds., *Modern Malay Verse*, 6th ed. (1971), pp. x–xii; Mohd. Taib bin Osman, "Modern Malay Literature: A Reflection of a Changing Society and Culture," *ASPAC Quarterly*, 5, 3 (1973), 23–37

MOHD. TAIB BIN OSMAN

MONGOLIAN LITERATURE

Mongolian literature begins with Chinggis Khan (Genghis Khan) in the early 1200s and the famous *Secret History of the Mongols,* an imperial chronicle of family genealogy and conflict. The later centuries of internal warfare were not conducive to writing or preserving literature. Not until the introduction of Lamaist Buddhism in the late 1500s did an upsurge occur. The next centuries saw a prodigious output of translations from Tibetan sacred scriptures, but only rarely histories or epics.

There was a widespread and popular oral literature, which encompassed: central Asian story cycles, some from Indian sources; didactic literature; stories, poems, legends; and particularly heroic epics, lengthy verse compositions about mighty heroes, their steeds, beautiful heavenly daughters, marvelous palaces, and the many-headed mangus, the monster of Mongolian folklore. In the last decades of the 19th c. collectors of folklore and epics began to transcribe many of these long works, saving them from extinction as old cultural ways yielded to incursions of the West.

At the fall of the Manchu (Ch'ing) dynasty under revolutionary pressures around 1910, the new government of the Chinese Republic was no longer able to exert effective control over its more distant provinces; Inner Mongolia, beyond the Great Wall, heavily settled with Chinese agriculturalists, remained part of the Republic, but Outer Mongolia cast off its ties to the Manchus and declared itself autonomous.

Outer Mongolian Literature

The proclaiming in 1924 of the Mongolian People's Republic, the first political satellite of the U.S.S.R., with its attendant socialization and collectivization of the economy, led to the creation of a new literature of Socialist Realism, in line with similar developments in the U.S.S.R. itself. The creation of an educational system, where none had existed before (except for training for the religious hierarchy), presented young Mongols with the possibility of becoming writers, artists, and intellectuals.

Dashdorjiin Natsagdorj (1906–1937), called the founder of modern Mongolian literature, is known for fiction, drama, poetry, and translations. His poem "Minii nutag" (1933; "My Native Land," 1967) is almost an anthem for Mongolia and is known to everyone. He wrote a libretto for an opera on native Mongolian themes, *Uchirtai gurvan tolgoi* (the three hills of sorrow), which was first produced in 1934 and is still performed regularly in Ulan Bator. Another important achievement is his short story "Tsagaan sar ba khar nulims" (1932; New Year's and bitter tears), which compares the life of a rich landlord's daughter with that of a poor servant girl.

Tsendiin Damdinsüren (b. 1908) is a noteworthy poet, translator, literary critic, and scholar. His first success was *Gologdson khüükhen* (1929; the rejected girl), the first Mongolian novel, a story of class struggle in the feudal countryside and the changes in a poor hired girl's life brought about by the revolution. It was considerably influenced by traditional folklore. His most famous poem is probably "Buural iiji minii" (1934; my gray-haired mother), a letter-dialogue whose theme is the tender affection between mother and son. He contributed to scholarship by editing an immensely important anthology, *Monggol uran jokiyal-un degeji jagun bilig* (1959; the hundred best selections of Mongolian literature), revealing hitherto unsuspected depth and richness in the literature of his country. He also published a study of the Geser epic, which appeared in Russian under the title *Istoricheskie korni Geseriady* (1957; historical bases of the Geser cycle).

Chadraavolyn Lodoidamba's (1917–1970) famous adventure novel *Altaid* (1949–51; in the Altai range) which, typically for Mongolian fiction, focuses more on exciting events than on character development, was followed by *Tungalag Tamir* (1962; the transparent Tamir River), the latter made into a successful motion picture. The dean of academics, Byamba Rinchen (1905–1977), wrote a three-volume historical novel, *Üüriin tuya* (1951–55; the ray of dawn), a detailed and historically accurate reconstruction of prerevolutionary times, treating battles, trials, social structure, shamanism, love and politics.

A number of other versatile authors have all written poetry, short stories, novels, and plays: Bökhiin Baast (b. 1921), Shanjmyatavyn Gaadamba (b. 1924), Püreviin Khorloo (b. 1917), Erdenebatyn Oyuun (b. 1913), Dashzevegiin Sengee (1916–1959). Sengiin Erdene (b. 1929) became a spokesman for his generation with his lyrical novels, whose heroes have some psychological depth.

Inner Mongolian Literature

Although in the mid- and late-19th c. there were noted writers of Inner Mongolian origin and residence, their works formed part of a general Mongolian culture. Nonetheless, such writers as Khesigbatu (1849–1916), Güleranja (1820–1851), Gelegbalsan (1846–1923), Injannashi (1837–1892), and Ishidanzanwangjil (1854–1907) were important forerunners of a 20th-c. Inner Mongolian literature.

During the period when the young Mongolian People's Republic was launching Communism, the Inner Mongolian region of China was struggling with factions of Chinese nationalism (later to result in the split between Nationalists and Communists), a struggle followed by hegemony by Japan until the end of World War II. Among young Mongolian nationalists sent to Japan for education was the essayist and poet Saichungga (later known as Na. Sainchogtu, b. 1914).

After the Chinese Communist victory in 1949, writers in Inner Mongolia, still heavily Chinese in settlement (ten to one in some areas), were permitted as a minority to publish in their native script. One figure who kept old traditions alive was the bard Pajai (1902–?), an original poet as well as a singer of epic poems.

During the Cultural Revolution in the 1960s it was difficult to secure information about literary figures and publications, a situation that holds true even today. The continued use of traditional script in Inner Mongolia now acts as a barrier to literary exchange with the Mongolian People's Republic, where a modified Cyrillic alphabet is used. And the decades-long Sino-Soviet tensions have played their roles, too. Inner Mongolian literature today is largely a vehicle for socialist thought, dominated by the Chinese (Han) educational and administrative system.

BIBLIOGRAPHY: Poppe, N., *Mongolische Volksdichtung* (1955); Gerasimovich, L. K., *History of Modern Mongolian Literature (1921–1964)* (1970); Hessig, W., *Geschichte der mongolischen Literatur,* Vol. II (1972)

JOHN R. KRUEGER

PACIFIC ISLANDS LITERATURES

The Pacific Islands consist of about eighteen large islands and number-less smaller ones spread over an ocean area of about eight million square miles. They were colonized beginning in the mid-18th c. by waves of Dutch, French, and English traders. Today the three large island-complexes—Fiji, Western Samoa, and Papua New Guinea—have political, economic, and cultural ties with England, the U.S., and Australia respectively.

Although the islands have an oral literature dating back a thousand years, they did not have a written literature until recently. In the last twenty years there has emerged a growing body of "South Pacific" literature from Fiji, Western Samoa, and Papua New Guinea that has been generated by an indigenous cultural renascence and supported by centers of learning such as the University of the South Pacific in Suva, Fiji, the Institute of Papua New Guinea Studies, and the South Pacific Creative Arts Society, which publishes *Mana,* the journal that introduced contemporary Pacific literature.

Fiji. Indo-Fijians were the first to produce written literature in the islands. Sixty thousand indentured laborers from India were brought to the sugar plantations of Fiji between 1879 and 1916. The second wave of immigrants were mainly educated middle-class people, and they drew upon India's heritage of thirty centuries of written literature to start a literature in Fiji. Totaram Sanadhya (dates n.a.), author of *Fiji dwip men mere ikkis varsh* (1919; my twenty-one years in the Fiji Islands), Pandit Amichand Sharma (dates n.a.), Kamla Prasad (dates n.a.), and Pandit Pratap Chandra Sharma (dates n.a.) wrote in Hindi and were published in India. Their writings describe and comment on their experiences; Sharma's *Pravas bhajanamjali* (1947; a foreign offering of verse) shows that an Indo-Fijian dialect had evolved; the volume is mainly a panegyric of India, however, and does not explore the meaning of the indenture or expatriate experience. Indeed, we have very few firsthand accounts of the *girmit* (distorted pronunciation of "agreement," i.e., the indenture contract) experience; *Turn North-East at the Tombstone* (1970) by Walter

Gill (dates n.a.), an Australian who worked as an overseer, is one of the few books that reconstruct the indenture period.

Through the 1950s and 1960s, English became progressively more important as the literary medium of Fiji, and the 1970s saw the emergence of accomplished writers such as Satendra Nandan (b. 1939), Raymond C. Pillai (b. 1942), and Subramani (b. 1943) among Indo-Fijians, and Pio Manoa (b. 1940) among Fijians. Vijay C. Mishra's (b. 1945) critical essays give a penetrating and cogent analysis of the ethos of Indo-Fijians.

Western Samoa. Whereas much of Indo-Fijian literature reflects the psychological interaction between the present and an idealized Indian past that Mishra calls a "sophisticated construct, false, but necessary," Western Samoan writers deal with the cultural interaction between the old and new dispensations, the ambivalence and triangular relationships between the white, native, and mixed components of the island's and islander's identity. Albert Wendt (b. 1939) put Western Samoa on the literary map in the 1960s with his short stories and poems. His first full-length publication was a novel, *Sons for the Return Home* (1973); this was followed by a short-story collection, *Flying Fox in a Freedom Tree* (1974); *Inside Us the Dead* (1976), a volume of poems; and the novels *Pouliuli* (1977) and *Leaves of the Banyan Tree* (1979); he has also edited an anthology of Pacific poetry, *Lali* (1980). *Sons for the Return Home* deals explicitly with the theme of the clash between old and new, but in having his nameless hero shake off all commitment to family and country at the end of the novel, Wendt is perhaps going beyond cultural and cross-cultural externals into a universal, personal dilemma. We see the same pattern in *Leaves of the Banyan Tree,* which has all the same tensions as *Sons for the Return Home,* but as the critic Chris Tiffin says, "overriding all these is the question of self-esteem," that is, the personal (and universal) problem of how to live with oneself.

Papua New Guinea. Although Papua New Guinea has its own growing core of fiction and poetry in English, its noteworthy feature lies in the creative use of native languages and in translations of folklore and chants. The German scholar Ulli Beier's (b. 1922) contribution in the latter field has been significant. In the last decade, Beier has edited several volumes of literary work, including *The Night Warrior, and Other Stories* (1972) and *Voices of Independence: New Black Writing from New Guinea* (1980).

The connections, and frictions, between the oral native traditions and the written Western tradition characterize both the form and content of contemporary Papua New Guinea literature. As in several other emerging nations, literature is often more preoccupied with political and sociological problems than with personal and psychological ones. Writers who were once expressing the hopes and ideologies of a nation fighting for independence are now expressing people's disillusionment with their politically independent but bureaucracy-enslaved country.

Several now-expatriate writers of Anglo-Saxon stock, including Edward Lindall (dates n.a.), Maslyn Williams (dates n.a.), and Margaret Reeson (dates n.a.), have written well about New Guinea. Among emerging native writers are the novelists Vincent Eri (b. 1936), author of *The Crocodile* (1970), and Albert Maori Kiki (b. 1931), who wrote *Ten Thousand Years in a Lifetime* (1968); and the poets Pokwari Kale (dates n.a.), John Kasaipwalova (b. 1949), who gained international recognition in 1972 with his long poem *Reluctant Flame,* and Kumalau Tawali (b. 1946). Russell Soaba (dates n.a.) is a versatile new writer who began as a poet with a Westernized voice and went on to become a short-story writer. Among his better-known stories are "A Portrait of the Odd Man Out" (1971), "A Glimpse of the Abyss" (1972), "The Victims" (1972), "The Villager's Request" (1974), and "Ijaya" (1977); in his play *Scattered by the Wind* (1972) he utilized the native oral tradition.

Some of the best contemporary works have appeared in the journals *Kovave* (1969–75), *New Guinea Writing* (1970–71), *Papua New Guinea Writing* (1970–78), and *Bikmans* (1980 ff.)

Two writers who belong to New Zealand literature but should be mentioned here because they bear a kinship to those of the other islands are the Maoris Witi Ihimaera (b. 1944) and Hone Tuwhare (b. 1922). Their work shows a degree of excellence that surpasses all others mentioned above.

BIBLIOGRAPHY: Arvidson, K. O., "The Emergence of Polynesian Literature," *WLWE,* 14 (1975), 91–115; Krauth, N., "Contemporary Literature from the South Pacific," *WLWE,* 17 (1978), 604–45; McDowell, R. E., and McDowell, J. H., eds., *Asian Pacific Literatures in English: Bibliographies* (1978); Tiffin, C., ed., *South Pacific Images* (1978); Mishra, V. C., ed., *Rama's Banishment: A Centenary Tribute to the Fiji Indians* (1979); Beier, U., ed., Introduction to *Voices of Independence:*

New Black Writing from Papua New Guinea (1980), pp. i–xvi; Subramani, ed., *The Indo-Fijian Experience* (1980); Nandan, S., "Beginnings of a Literary Culture in Fiji: The Role of Language, Commonwealth Literature and the Writer," *Chimo* (Quebec), 2 (1980), 36–50

UMA PARAMESWARAN

PHILIPPINE LITERATURE

For twenty years before the outbreak of the revolution of 1896, Filipinos who favored civil reform and freedom without independence published novels and newspapers in Spanish and directed them hopefully at liberals in Madrid and Barcelona. Among these were the essays of Marcelo H. del Pilar (1850–1896) and Graciano Lopez-Jaena (1856–1896), and the panoramic, accusatory novels of José Rizal (1861–1896), *Noli me tangere* (1887; *The Lost Eden*, 1961) and *El filibusterismo* (1891; *The Subversive*, 1962), which cast shadows of excellence far into the 20th c.

Yet, with the end of the Spanish-American War in 1898, virtually all Spanish literature as well as political influence ceased. Rear-guard critics sometimes speak of the first half of the new century as the "golden age" of Philippine literature in Spanish. However, aside from Jesús Balmori's (pseud.: Batikuling, 1886–1948) nationalistic lyric poetry—*Rimas malayas* (1904; Malayan verses) and *Mi casa de nipa* (1941; my house made of palm leaves)—and the poems of Claro Recto (1890–1960) in *Bajo los cocoteros* (1911; under the coconut trees) and his play *Solo entre las sombras* (1917; alone among the shadows), Antonio M. Abad's (dates n.a.) Commonwealth Prize-winning novel, *El campeón* (1939; the champion), and occasional speeches left by Recto and President Manuel Quezon (1878–1944), little that is comparable with the end-of-century flowering can be discovered. Less biased historians record, instead, a prolonged cultural pause before general education in English, which replaced education of the elite in Spanish, could produce its own literature and, by example, elevate literature in the vernacular as well.

The beginning of commonwealth status in 1935, with anticipation of full independence after ten years, gave special urgency to the search for a national identity among people with varied cultural and linguistic backgrounds. Although this was also the year of the founding of the Institute of National Language, which made Tagalog the core of various composite vernaculars, at least temporarily Filipinos found in English rather than native languages and literary traditions the same creative challenge that Spanish once brought.

To assert some kind of continuity between otherwise alienated generations, the works of Nick Joaquin (q.v.) have attempted to recover the moral and religious orientation, which constitute the most enduring aspect of the Spanish heritage. Aside from several imitations of late-medieval saintly legends and random essays, his concern has been less with the past re-created than with its modern vestiges. Joaquin's short story "Three Generations," in *Prose and Poems* (1952), reveals irrevocable family resemblances—a rigorous Spanish sense of kinship—even in the midst of recurrent revolt against family pieties. Other stories, such as "The Summer Solstice," also in *Prose and Poems,* find in Filipinos counterparts of Spanish ambivalences: primitivistic sensuousness and Christian asceticism. His 1952 omnibus volume also contains the play *Portrait of the Artist as Filipino,* in which descendants of the declining Don Lorenzo finally confirm his inborn integrity by their own. Despite impoverishment, they refuse to sell the masterpiece which he has painted for them and which depicts Anchises being borne like a household god from burning Troy. The faces of son and father are identical. Joaquin has depicted the Filipino's need to take the burden of history on his back. However, Aeneas was not only deliverer of the past but founder of the future: and Joaquin's novel *The Woman Who Had Two Navels* (1961) respects but does not admire without qualification the ex-revolutionary, Monson, who hides in Hong Kong exile, afraid to face the trials of postwar independence.

The Spanish past is viewed with an equally discriminating eye in *The Peninsulars* (1964), Linda Ty-Casper's (b. 1931) novel of the confusion of loyalties that made possible British occupation of Manila in the mid-18th c. Each figure of colonial authority—even those with the highest concern for the ruled—has some imperfection of motive, some overriding personal ambition that maims his magistracy. However, the *indios* too (as Spaniards called the natives) are torn between national loyalties and self-interest. Only the dying governor-general and the *indio* priest Licaros achieve a sufficient understanding of the need for mutual dependence: on one level, love; on another, the social contract. Such a novel represents an increasingly selective salvaging, by the Philippine writer, of his various usable pasts. Similarly, Ty-Casper's novel *The Three-Cornered Sun* (1979) depicts the revolution of 1896 as a series of individually motivated acts rather than as an orchestrated uprising guided by national purpose.

The epic impulse, the concern with rendering history as meaningful fable, has shaped the writings of poets such as Ricaredo Demetillo (b.

1920) and Alejandrino Hufana (b. 1926). *Barter in Panay* (1961) represents the first portion of Demetillo's verse adaptation of the Visayan folktale *Maragtas,* about ten groups led by *datus* (chiefs) who, in 1212, fled tyranny in Brunei. Its twenty-one cantos explain the peaceful arrangement between *Datu* Puti and the pygmy Negrito inhabitants of Panay island; and begin to explore the lust of Guronggurong for *Datu* Sumakwel's young wife, which was to test intimately the new rules of social order. Demetillo's verse-play sequel, *The Heart of Emptiness Is Black* (1975) suggests how only love can reconcile personal desire and impersonal social codes.

Hufana's early volume *Sickle Season* (1959) deals with this same theme of the one and the many but is less restricted historically: for it, he invented Geron Munar, timeless Malayan wanderer and culture hero, mirrored in many facsimiles throughout Philippine history, legend, and myth. In *Poro Point: An Anthology of Lives* (1961), Hufana substituted for Munar personae from the author's tribal family, all Ilocanos, who, as the most migrant of Filipinos, epitomize both their countrymen's unity and their diversity.

The Philippine dream of a national identity compatible with an open, pluralistic society, evident in such adaptations from ethnohistory, has been tested severely even by Bienvenido N. Santos (b. 1911), sometimes considered a sentimentalist. The Philippine expatriates in his story collection *You Lovely People* (1956), caught in the U.S. by World War II, long passionately to return to their kinfolk. In the aftermath of war, however, many discover their homeland changed, their loved ones not inviolable; and, disillusioned, some retreat into exile once more. Similarly, his second collection, *Brother, My Brother* (1960), and his two novels, *Villa Magdalena* (1965) and *The Volcano* (1965), continue to rely on the imagery of rejection and return. However far ambition takes his characters from the ancestral home that once seemed to deprive them of personal potential, that home remains the place of least loneliness; and no satisfactory sense of self is found outside one's native community. How that problem is exacerbated among "overseas Filipinos" is encapsulated in his collection *Scent of Apples* (1979).

Although all major Philippine writers may be said to be searching for those constants that define their identity as a people, many have avoided the historical/epic modes and have confined themselves to fundamentally agrarian aspects that are continuous in their culture. Their fiction maintains a slowness of pace and cautious simplicity appropriate to the sacred, seasonal mysteries of timeless folkways, as well as to the patient, modern search for reassurance. That pace is represented in Francisco Arcellana's (b. 1916) peasant/working-class sketches, *15 Stories* (1973), characterized by Scriptural simplicity and cyclic repetition. Manuel Arguilla (1910–1944), in the rural tales collected in *How My Brother Leon Brought Home a Wife* (1940), undercuts folk romanticism with the realism of social protest as he engages the causes of the Sakdal uprisings among tenant farmers during the 1930s. Similarly, N. V. M. Gonzalez's (q.v.) tales of the frontier country, the *kaingin* (cultivated clearing burned out of forest land) ricelands—*Seven Hills Away* (1947); *Children of the Ash-Covered Loam* (1954)—as well as the novel *A Season of Grace* (1956), reveal both the hardships and enduring self-possession of his tradition-centered pioneers. In his collection *Look, Stranger, on This Island Now* (1963) the *kainginero* enjoys a kind of consoled loneliness when compared with the peasant who has migrated to the metropolis; and his restricted life is far more meaningful than that of the sophisticated *ilustrado* (a member of the "enlightened," intellectual elite) who is the protagonist of the novel *The Bamboo Dancers* (1959), a homeless international wanderer.

The provincial's life is a trial, even in Carlos Bulosan's (1914–1956) humorous tales in *The Laughter of My Father* (1941), which were intended as a satiric indictment of sharecropping penury. At the same time, Bulosan expresses admiration for the good humor, love, and other humane virtues that survive the peasant's near-penal conditions.

This capacity to endure marks each of the four major Philippine war novels—Stevan Javellana's (b. 1918) *Without Seeing the Dawn* (1947); Juan Laya's (1911–1952) *This Barangay* (1950); and Edilberto Tiempo's (b. 1917) *Watch in the Night* (1953) and *More than Conquerors* (1964)—all of them, appropriately, stories of small-scale, rural, guerrilla action supported by a kind of primitive communal interdependence.

When this close group identity is sacrificed by the ambitious provincial migrant to the city, he suffers from the anonymity of mass living without his poverty's lessening measurably. Only occasionally is adequate human warmth rediscovered among slumdwellers, as in the stories of Estrella Alfon (b. 1917)—*Magnificence* (1960)—and Andres Cristobal Cruz (b. 1929) and Pacifico Aprieto (b. 1929)—*Tondo by Two,* 1961); or in Alberto Florentino's (b. 1931) *The World Is an Apple, and Other Prize Plays* (1959).

Far less sympathy is directed toward other urban classes. The pretensions of the nouveaux riches are constantly satirized in Gilda Cordero-Fernando's (dates n.a.) collections of stories *The Butcher, the Baker, the*

Candlestick Maker (1962) and *A Wilderness of Sweets* (1973); as well as Wilfrido Guerrero's (b. 1917) four volumes of plays (1947, 1952, 1962, 1976). Movement from a rural area to suburbia involves risking loss of character. The consequences of social mobility unaccompanied by maturing morality are more savagely exposed in the novels of Kerima Polotan-Tuvera (b. 1925)—*The Hand of the Enemy* (1962)—and of F. Sionil Jose (b. 1924)—*The Pretenders* (1962). In both instances, the mountaineer or uprooted rural peasant is corrupted by industrialism and the new self-seeking elite, just as the agrarian revolts at the turn of the century allegedly were betrayed by the *ilustrados,* first to the Spaniards and later to the Americans. This tension between classes is central in Jose's ongoing series of novels about Rosales, an imaginary northern town: *Tree* (1978) and *My Brother, My Executioner* (1979). Social discrimination finds its parallel in the oppression of women in Polotan-Tuvera's *Stories* (1968). Wilfrido Nolledo's (b. 1933) *But for the Lovers* (1970), a parable of wartime grotesques awaiting liberation, suggests a similar situation for the masses mutilated by the forces of leftist radicals and of government by martial law.

Because, like Rizal's novels before them, they constitute assessments of agrarian values during decades of challenging cultural transition, such works will always be of historical value regardless of what other Philippine literatures emerge in the vernaculars. Even José Garcia Villa's (q.v.) poetry, which, beginning with *Many Voices* (1939), has been criticized for not focusing on national concerns but rather offering disembodied Blakean encounters between God and the luminous poet, are in some ways relevant to the Philippine experience. Villa's dependence on devices of negation and rejection, the nearly solipsistic alienation of the protagonist, at least parallel the national passion for self-determination and the overcompensatory self-enlargement of a people reduced to colonial status for centuries.

For inventiveness and for dynamic selfhood in revolt, the counterpart of Villa in Pilipino (Tagalog) is A. G. Abadilla (1905–1969), whose volumes include *Piniling mga tula* (1965; selected poems). Sometimes as antagonist, sometimes as complement, his name is juxtaposed with the socialistically inclined Amado V. Hernandez (1903–1970), a labor leader and later premier writer in the vernacular. With his prize play *Muntinlupa* (1958; tight place; also the name of a national prison), his poems in *Isang dipang langit* (1961; a stretch of sky), and his novel *Mga ibong mandaragit* (1965; birds of prey), Hernandez revived the polemical tradition of the 19th c. and recapitulated the social protest evident in Lope K.

Santos's (1879–1963) earlier novel *Banaag at sikat* (1906; false dawn and sunrise). Together with Andres Cristobal Cruz (b. 1929), author of the novel *Sa Tundo, may langit din* (1961; even in Tondo the sun shines) and the contributors to the short fiction collection *Agos sa diyerta* (1965; oasis in the desert), these writers, by avoiding the sentimentality and floridity of vernacular conventions, have made Pilipino equal to English as a reputable instrument for self-discovery.

Those conventions, derived from centuries of reducing literary function to either moral indoctrination or pure emotional expressiveness, have proven more resistant in the case of other vernacular literatures. Zarzuelas, for example, introduced as a form of concealed protest under the American occupation, deteriorated before 1930 into either musical comedies or melodramas. This predisposition toward literature as either instruction or entertainment, reinforced by the dearth of book publication and reliance on serialization of magazine fiction, has kept minimal the number of vernacular models equivalent in seriousness to their English counterparts. These would include, in the Bisayan languages, the novels of Magdalena Jalandoni (1893–1980) in the 1920s and 1930s, the political sketches of Vicente Sotto (1877–1950) throughout the 1920s, Buenaventura Rodriguez's (1893–1941) plays *Ang mini* (1921; counterfeit man) and *Pahiyum* (1935; a smile), and the prewar poetic experiments of Vicente Ranudo (1883–1930), as well as the sampling of breakthrough pieces in the 1967 anthology by the Lubasan group; and in Iloko, the early-20th-c. plays of Mena Pecson Crisologo (1844–19??), especially *Natakneng a panagsalisal* (n.d.; noble rivalry), which concerns the Philippine-American War (1898–1902), Marcelino Pena Crisologo's (1866–1923) novel *Pinang* (1915; Pinang), and Constante Casabar's (dates n.a.) sociopolitical novels (published serially), *Puris iti barukong* (1956–57; thorn in the side) and *Dagiti mariing iti parbongon* (1955–57; those awakened at dawn).

Like their Pilipino compatriots, contemporary writers in Bisayan and Iloko are, typically, bilingual and thus manage to enrich their work from many sources and to choose which readers they will address.

BIBLIOGRAPHY: Bernad, M., *Bamboo and the Greenwood Tree* (1963); Del Castillo, T., and Medina, B., Jr., *Philippine Literature* (1964); Casper, L., *New Writing from the Philippines: An Anthology and a Critique* (1966); Manuud, A., ed., *Brown Heritage: Essays on Philippine Cultural Tradition and Literature* (1967); Galdon, J., ed., *Philippine Fiction*

(1972); Mojares, R., *Cebuano Literature* (1975); Galdon, J., ed., *Essays on the Philippine Novel in English* (1979)

LEONARD CASPER

GONZALEZ, N(estor) V(icente) M(adali)

Philippine novelist, short-story writer, and poet (writing in English), b. 8 Sept. 1915, Romblon

As a child, G. was taken by his father, who was a teacher, to pioneer Mindoro Island, whose farmers and fishermen have dominated his fiction ever since his autobiographical novel, *The Winds of April* (1940), won a prize in the Commonwealth Literary Contest in 1940. After a Rockefeller-funded postwar visit to U.S. writing centers, G. returned to teach creative writing at the University of the Philippines.

For his defense of traditional Philippine values, G. received the Republic Award of Merit (1954), the Republic Cultural Heritage Award (1960), and the Rizal Pro Patria Award (1961). Since 1969 G. has taught Third World literature at the University of California, Hayward, and in several essays he has offered lessons learned from other developing nations as advisories to his countrymen.

Social change, in G.'s fiction, tends to be subtle to the point of near invisibility, because his frontiersmen take their tempo from natural cycles. Yet although there is a seemingly static quality to the folk life represented in *Seven Hills Away* (1947), a pattern of slow change and movement toward new horizons emerges from these sketches. Women and children are often the narrators in his fiction. G.'s deceptively simple style not only authenticates the quiet manner of ordinary folk but makes their daily encounters with birth and death seem less staggering to the reader.

But while the poor are admired for their honesty and resilience, G. also reveals the destructiveness of their slash-and-burn method of farming, which makes hard field work still harder. Still, their family closeness protects them from the loneliness of those—in the second half of *Look, Stranger, on This Island Now* (1969)—who leave the land entirely and are corrupted in the mainland metropolis. Not only the greedy merchant but also the self-styled intellectual are criticized for the increasing separation between themselves and the peasantry. Ernie Rama, antihero of

The Bamboo Dancers (1959), is portrayed as a wandering Fisher King whose apathy is both his wound and the symptom of the modern wasteland, which is contrasted to the values of communitarian responsibility indigenous to the Philippines' traditional agrarian culture.

FURTHER WORKS: *Children of the Ash-Covered Loam* (1954); *A Season of Grace* (1956); *Selected Stories* (1964); *Mindoro and Beyond* (1979)

BIBLIOGRAPHY: Casper, L., *New Writing from the Philippines* (1966), pp. 42–55; Galdon, J., ed., *Philippine Fiction* (1972), pp. 153–59; Galdon, J., *Essays on the Philippine Novel in English* (1979), pp. 108–24

LEONARD CASPER

JOAQUIN, Nick

Philippine novelist, poet, short-story writer, dramatist, and essayist (writing in English), b. 3 May 1917, Manila

In 1947 J.'s essay on what was believed to be the miraculous defeat of a Dutch fleet by the Spaniards off the Philippines in 1646 led the Dominicans to offer him a scholarship to study in Hong Kong. But in 1950 he left Hong Kong to write for the *Philippines Free Press,* under the pseudonym "Quijano de Manila" (an anagram of his name). In 1970 he became coeditor of the *Asian-Philippines Leader,* subsequently suspended for its political views when martial law was declared in 1972.

Because of his seminarian training and his antiquarian expertise in Spanish influences on Philippine culture, J. used to be accused of pious nostalgia. More recent critics, however, impressed by J.'s decades of reportage on contemporary issues, both knowledgeable and passionate, have come to understand his sense of the interplay between all periods of history. The struggle for individuality within contesting cultural contexts not only is his recurrent theme but finds expression through the non-chronological structures of such stories as "Guardia de Honor," "May Day Eve," and "The Mass of St. Sylvestre," as well as through fusion of legend, myth, and history in "The Summer Solstice" (all four first published in *Prose and Poems,* 1952) and "The Order of Melkizedek" (first published in *Tropical Gothic,* 1972). Figures representing the voice of conscience and the pressures of the past upon the present dominate his key works: Marasigan, the offstage father in his play *Portrait of the*

Artist as Filipino (1952); the elder Monzon in the novel *The Woman Who Had Two Navels* (1961).

His sometimes gemlike style has often been imitated, but rarely with an understanding of its function in his work, which is to suggest with crystalline brilliance the various planes and prismatic angles in human affairs. J. reminds his countrymen of the uneasy coexistence of "primitive" and "civilized" dimensions in all men; the difficulty the moral intelligence has in distinguishing sinner from saint; and the special problem that Filipinos have of reconciling their mixed Asian and Western heritages, and then of shaping the best of these traditions into a continuing, compassionate national identity.

His short stories about these cultural ambiguities having already made him the most anthologized of all Philippine authors, he was declared a National Artist in 1976.

FURTHER WORKS: *Selected Stories* (1962); *A Question of Heroes: Essays in Criticism on Ten Key Figures in Philippine History* (1977); *Reportage on Crime* (1977); *Reportage on Lovers* (1977); *Nora Aunor, and Other Profiles* (1977); *Ronnie Poe, and Other Silhouettes* (1977)

BIBLIOGRAPHY: Furay, H., "The Stories of N. J.," *PSM*, 1 (1953), 144–53; Busuego-Pablo, L., "The Spanish Tradition in N. J.," *PSM*, 3 (1955), 187–207; Constantino, J., "*The Woman Who Had Two Navels*," *PSM*, 9 (1961), 639–50; Casper, L., ed., *Modern Philippine Short Stories* (1962), pp. 21–56; Casper, L., *New Writing from the Philippines* (1966), pp. 137–45; Manuud, A., ed., *Brown Heritage* (1967), pp. 765–92

LEONARD CASPER

VILLA, José Garcia

Philippine poet and short-story writer (writing in English), b. 5 Aug. 1908, Manila

Already alienated from his father, a physician, V. became an exile from his motherland as well when he was suspended by the University of the Philippines for writing controversial poems. His stories of rejection and self-reassertion, written while a student at the University of New Mexico and Columbia University, drew the attention of the renowned editor

Edward O'Brien, who dedicated his collection *Best American Short Stories of 1932* to him. By then V.'s drawing inward had turned him to poetry, three volumes of which eventually were published in the U.S., carrying Edith Sitwell's praise on their jackets. V. became a revered figure to his countrymen who aspired to acceptance abroad.

In all his poetry transfiguration of intimate sensations occurs. Instead of providing any identifiable cultural content, his poetic images are romantic and visionary, intended to be universal and to convey the sense of a liberated spirit ascending. Deliberately, it is selfhood that is celebrated—self either as benevolent lover of woman or as contending rival for the Godhead. Doveglion (Dove-eagle-lion), a pseudonym he used, indicates his self-assigned magnitude.

In addition to influences from William Blake (and less significantly from Walt Whitman and E. E. Cummings), V. has been affected by his early attachment to cubist painting. In extended notes to his *Selected Poems and New* (1958) he explains his two technical innovations, both apparently inspired by the geometry of faceted gems. His "comma poems" introduce a symbol shaped like a comma but attached without space to the words on either side, thus providing a weighted and dignified (if unvaried) pace to the moving line. "Reversed consonance" makes rhymes out of the last-sounded consonants in any line, those same consonants being then reversed by ingenious word choice at the end of the succeeding line. The effect on the ear is subliminal, at best; but the trained eye responds to the technique as to a mirror device promoting reflective thought. Both devices epitomize the poet's dense inward-turning.

Although his interests are peripheral to the community service traditional in the Philippines, V. received the Republic Cultural Heritage Award in 1962, and in 1973 he became the first Philippine writer in English to be declared a National Artist, with a lifetime pension.

FURTHER WORKS: *Footnote to Youth: Tales of the Philippines and Others* (1933); *Many Voices* (1939); *Poems by Doveglion* (1941); *Have Come, Am Here* (1941); *Volume Two* (1949); *Poems 55* (1962); *Selected Stories* (1962); *Appasionata: Poems in Praise of Love* (1979)

BIBLIOGRAPHY: Lopez, S. P., *Literature and Society* (1940), pp. 152–65; Casper, L., *New Writing from the Philippines* (1966), pp. 103–13; Tinio, R., "V.'s Values," in Manuud, A., ed., *Brown Heritage* (1967), pp. 722–38

LEONARD CASPER

SINGAPORE LITERATURE

Singapore is an island republic, independent since August 9, 1965. It is a multiracial and multilingual city-state, and its literature is written in the four official languages of the country: Chinese, Malay, Tamil (spoken by people originally from southern India), and English. Strictly speaking, only literature produced after 1965 can be regarded as Singapore literature; most works written before 1965 belong to Malaysian (Malayan) literature. Nevertheless, some pre-1965 writing may be regarded as Singapore literature by virtue of the authors' Singapore residence or subsequent citizenship.

Before 1965

Before 1965 it is difficult to isolate a specifically Singapore literature. But the period 1945–57 saw a blossoming of Singapore writing in Chinese and Malay. The main theme of Chinese works was the suffering of the poor and the struggle against the British colonial government. Miao Hsiu (b. 1920), a prolific novelist and short-story writer, depicts the love between a gangster and his prostitute-mistress in *Hsin Chia Po wu ting hsia* (1962; under the roofs of Singapore). Hsieh Ke (b. 1931), in the short-story collection *Wei le hsia yi tai* (1954; for the next generation), and Tu Hung (b. 1936), in the collection of poems *Wu Yueh* (1955; the month of May), delineate the students' and workers' agitation and struggle against the colonial government. There were, however, those who preferred to write on personal themes. One example is the poet Chao Tsan (b. 1934), author of *Hai tze te meng* (1953; a child's dream). Yao Tze, also known as Huang Huai (pseuds. of Zheng Meng Zhou, 1924–1982), a master storyteller, published many novels and short stories marked by detailed descriptions of sex, because of which his writings are regarded by some as pornographic.

The Malay writers who thronged to Singapore because of the Emergency (1948–60)—a period of communist insurrection during which the colonial government curtailed freedoms—also took as their main theme the injustices suffered by the urban poor, fishermen, and villagers. They formed an association, Asas '50 (generation of the 1950s), to fight for equality. Suratman Markasan (b. 1930), in his short stories and in the novel *Tak ada jalan keluar* (1962; *Conflict*, 1982), captured the spirit of the age.

The few Malay writers who remained in Singapore (there was an exodus to Kuala Lumpur after Malaya's declaration of independence on August 31, 1957) are not typical of the Malay writers of the period. Harun Aminurrashid (b. 1907), has published nearly twenty historical novels glorifying the heroic deeds of the Malays of generations past, the most famous being *Panglima Awang* (1958; *A Malay among the Portuguese*, 1961).

Masuri S. N. (b. 1927) has published three collections of poems, in which he philosophizes on the meaning of life, morality, and peace. Noor S. I. (pseud. of Ismail bin Haji Omar, b. 1933) is the forerunner of symbolic poetry in Malay. His poems are difficult to understand, but they have a sonorousness not often found in Malay verse. His most famous work is *Rakaman roh* (1963; the soul's records).

During this period poetry in English began to emerge. Most of the works were imitative and based on models learned at school. They do not reflect the spirit of the age, either. But among the poets writing at that time was Edwin Thumboo (b. 1933), who was to become a major poet as well as a professor of English in the 1970s.

The Tamil writers focused on the social problems of their own community. N. Palani-velu (b. 1908) attacked meaningless traditional practices in his short stories, while P. Krishnan (b. 1932) dealt with the problems of intermarriage. The most popular subjects, however, were love and passion.

After 1965

There was not much literary activity during the first few years after Singapore's independence. Gradually the tempo picked up. A Singapore identity has been manifested in nearly all postindependence writing. Writers, especially those in Chinese and Tamil, began to praise Singapore's effort at nation building, as well as the country's beauty. Malay writers tend to be nostalgic, missing the noisy coffee houses and the familiar landscape. Some express anxiety about the future of the Malay community in fast-changing Singapore. Among the works of new writers, particularly promising are Abdul Ghani Hamid's (b. 1933) landscape poems, Muhammad Latiff Muhammad's (b. 1950) social poems, and Fuad Salim's (b. 1939) short stories.

The pre-1965 Chinese writers mentioned above, with the exception of Yao Tze, continued to publish after independence. Among the many new writers, Mu Ling-Nu (b. 1943) and Wong Yoon Wah (b. 1941) have introduced Western techniques into poetry, especially symbolism—Mu in *Chu jen* (1968; the giant), Wong in *Hsiang chiao shu* (1980; rubber trees). Perhaps the greatest achievement in this period was the publication of the longest narrative poem (3254 lines) in Chinese outside China, *Wu se te hung* (1977; the colorless rainbow) by Liu Pei An (b. 1903), which describes the checkered career of an immigrant from China. Fang Hsiu's (b. 1921) and Wong Meng Voon's (b. 1937) essays have contributed greatly to an understanding of Chinese writing both in Singapore and Malaysia.

Many Tamil poets praise Singapore's success in building an independent nation, for example, K. Perumal (1921–1979) in *Singapore paadalkal* (1979; songs of Singapore). In novels and short stories Tamil writers deal with the problems of national identity, multiracialism, and marriage between Indian men and Chinese women. Prominent among these writers are S. V. Shanmugam (b. 1933), P. Krishnan, and M. A. Elangkanan (pseud. of M. Balakrishnan, b. 1938). The future of Tamil writing in Singapore, however, is not bright. Most literary works are published in India and do not sell more than three hundred copies locally.

The 1970s witnessed the flowering of writing in English. Many anthologies of short stories and individual collections were published. The best story writer in English, perhaps, is Catherine Lim (b. 1942). In *Little Ironies* (1978) she captures the fast changes in Singapore, especially the conflict between Western-educated children and their elders. Among many autobiographical novels, the most notable has been Tan Kok Seng's (b. 1936) *Son of Singapore* (3 vols., 1972–75). This trilogy tells the success story of a coolie. Goh Poh Seng (b. 1936) has written several novels. In *The Immolation* (1977), set in South Vietnam, he writes about the disillusionment of a young student, returned from Europe, with war and revolution in his country. Goh's poems—as in *Lines from Batu Feringgi* (1972) and *Eyewitness* (1976)—are records of his love for nature and his distaste for modern life.

The greatest achievements in English have been in poetry, with Edwin Thumboo the most important practitioner. In his recent collections, *Gods Can Die* (1977) and *Ulysses by the Merlion* (1979), he has gone beyond his earlier exploration of self, as in *Rib of Earth* (1956). He has tried to understand the events taking place in Singapore and to record the reaction of the various ethnic groups toward the changes. Another poet who has this preoccupation with society is Robert Yeo (b. 1940), whose collection of poems *and napalm does not help* (1977) has a strong Singapore identity. Arthur Yap (b. 1943), a painter as well as a poet, however, prefers to depict the changing landscape, and his collection of poems *Commonplace* (1977) gives a vivid picture of his sojourn in England as a postgraduate student.

Today, English is used in all schools in Singapore. In the future it is likely that English will become the dominant literary language. The publication of *Singapore Writing* (1977), edited by Chandra Nair (b. 1944)—a collection of short stories and poems in English, with some translations from the Chinese and Malay—may well herald a new phase in the development of literature.

Writers in other languages, however, are trying to maintain the status quo. In January 1982 an International Chinese Writers' Conference was held in Singapore, to which prominent writers from all over the world— Peking, Taiwan, Hong Kong, Malaysia, and United States—were invited. That year, too, saw the establishment of the Tamil Language and Literature Society. A Malay Language Month was also organized.

BIBLIOGRAPHY: Yap, A., *A Brief Critical Survey of Prose Writings in Singapore and Malaysia* (1971); Indian Language Society, University of Singapore, *Tamil Language and Literature in Singapore* (1977); Ban Kah Choon and Lee Tzu Pheng, " 'Only Connect': Quest and Response in Singapore-Malayan Poetry," in Crewe, W., ed., *The English Language in Singapore* (1977), pp. 189–208; Singh, K., "Singaporean and Malaysian Literature in English," *SoRA*, 10 (1977), 287–99; Crewe, W. J., "The Singapore Writer and the English Language," *RELC*, 9, 1 (1978), 77–86; Thumboo, E., "Singapore Writing in English: A Need for Commitment," *Westerly*, No. 2 (1978), 79–85; Singh, K. "Singapore-Malaysian Fiction in English," and Aveling, H., "Towards an Anthology of Poetry from Singapore-Malaysia," in Tiffin, C., ed., *South Pacific Images* (1978), pp. 68–80, 81–92; Gordon, J. B., "The Crisis of Poetic Utterance: The Case of Singapore," *PQM*, 4 (1979), 9–16; Wong Meng Voon, Introduction to *An Anthology of Singapore Chinese Literature* (1983), pp. ix–xvi

LIAW YOCK FANG

THAI LITERATURE

Literature in the Thai language goes back to the 13th c. Before the second half of the 19th c., when Thailand (formerly Siam) came into close contact with Western civilization, imaginative writing had appeared in three main genres: songs and lyric poems, narrative poetry, and dance drama. Prose was used chiefly for practical purposes, such as recording history and promulgating laws.

Literature in 20th-c. Thailand is usually written in the national language, but regional oral literatures can still be found in other languages: Mon, Khmer, Karen, and Chinese. During the modernization of Thailand in the Chulalongkorn period (1868–1910) new forms, techniques, subjects, ideas, and goals were introduced into literature, and several new genres emerged.

The Novel

The Thai novel has generally been aimed more at the senses than at the intellect. Nevertheless, some novelists have dealt with serious issues and have presented more diversified subjects, including a broader spectrum of Thai society.

In *Lakhon haeng chiwit* (1929; the circus of life), the first Thai autobiographical novel, Prince Akatdamkoeng Raphiphat (1905–1932) deals with alienation. The protagonist sees his homeland as in serious need of development, a country whose cultural system has deprived him of personal fulfillment. After working abroad as a journalist, he returns home, becomes a novelist, and hopes through his work to bring about a better-educated society.

The most famous humorist, P. Intharapalit (Pricha Intharapalit, 1910–1968), had a large readership, encompassing adults and schoolchildren, intellectuals and the common people. His most popular work is his series of unconnected, self-contained episodes about the "Trio"—Phon, Nikon, and Kim-ngaun—whose behavior and attitudes reflect the development of Thai society since the end of World War II.

Suwanni Sukhontha (Suwanni Sukhonthiang, 1932–1984), a painter turned novelist, became well known for her novel *Khao chu Kan* (1970; his name is Kan), whose protagonist is an idealistic physician who has left Bangkok for a job in the provinces. Confronted by many problems, social as well as personal, his efforts fail, and he dies in the end.

The life of the old upper class is portrayed by such writers as M. R. Kukrit Pramoj (q.v.), also a prominent journalist and politician. His greatest novel, *Si phaendin* (1953; *Four Reigns,* 1981), is a saga centered on an upper-class woman. Botan (pseud. of Supha Lusiri Sirising, b. 1945), of Chinese descent, was the first writer to express the pride of her ethnic group in novel form. Her *Chotmai chak muang Thai* (1969; *Letters from Thailand,* 1977), which depicts the lives of Chinese immigrants making their fortune in Thailand, won a SEATO award for the best novel of 1969, although it aroused great controversy.

Among novelists focusing on the countryside, Nimit Phumithawon (1935–1981), a schoolteacher in the northern part of the central plain, often depicted the local people. *Dae khun khru duai khom faek* (1969; to sir with a club), tells how a young schoolteacher in rural Thailand faces and overcomes severe educational and social problems. Villagers in the northeast are portrayed by Khamphun Bunthawi (b. 1928). His *Luk i-san* (1971; a son of the northeast) shows how the peasants suffer from poverty yet still manage to enjoy life.

The spiritual confusion arising from rapid social change and disintegrating morality finds expression in the works of Buddhist scholars, such as Wasin Inthasara's (b. 1934) *Phra A-non Phuttha anucha* (1965; Phra A-non, the brother of the Lord Buddha), in which he discusses aspects of Buddhism applicable to modern life, in a language that can be grasped by laymen.

Some writers use the novel as an instrument for social change, for example, Si Burapha (pseud. of Kulap Saipradit, 1906–1974) and Seni Saowaphong (pseud. of Sakchai Bamrungphong, b. 1918). These writers want the voice of the people to be heard and their needs to be felt. In the unfinished novel *Lae pai khang na* (2 parts, 1955, 1957; look forward) Si Burapha shows his admiration for the People's Party, which was successful in bringing about a constitutional monarchy in 1932, and his antipathy toward dictatorial government. Seni Saowaphong's novel *Pisat* (1944; the ghost) tells of a country youth who comes to Bangkok to study, earns a law degree, and returns to the countryside, where he feels he is more needed. Seni shows the hardships of Thai farmers, struggling against poverty and debt. Both Seni and Si Burapha point out the error of the old upper class in trying to preserve the status quo.

Concern for better social conditions also features prominently in *Raya* (1955; Raya) by Sot Kuramarohit (1908–1978), which takes place during and after World War II. Raya is a country youth determined to fight against evil. During the war he joins the Free Thai Movement and afterward battles corruption and wickedness in politics. Sot suggests that a cooperative system could solve economic problems.

The leading woman novelist has been Dokmai Sot (q.v.), whose works, mainly dealing with upper-class women, are conservative in outlook. Unlike most women novelists, who emulate Dokmai Sot in her choice of domestic subjects, Boonlua (M. L. Boonlua Debyasuvarn, 1911–1982), Dokmai Sot's sister, created in *Surat nari* (1971; women of Surat) an imaginary country in which women are in control and progressive-minded men campaign for equal rights. This satirical novel reflects many aspects of contemporary Thailand.

The Short Story

In the early part of the century most short stories were didactic, often sentimental, with love as the principal subject. Later, as with the novel, subjects and themes became more varied. Nearly all Thai novelists have tried their hands at the genre, but a few writers are noted primarily for their stories. Manat Chanyong (1907–1965) published over a thousand short stories. Although he wrote about a variety of middle- and lower-class types, his most famous works are those about country folk. The way of life Manat portrays preserves the old values, when rural people lived simply and in harmony with their surroundings. Friendship, gratitude, and integrity govern the community.

Lao Khamhom (pseud. of Khamsing Sinok, b. 1930), who also writes about country people, presents a different view. In his two small volumes—*Fa bo kan* (1958; the sky bars none), a collection of short stories, and *Kamphaeng* (1974; the wall), containing short stories and other writings—he depicts the poor and superstitious peasants of the northeast, who are virtually isolated from the modern world. Twelve of his stories were published in English translation as *The Politician, and Other Stories* (1973).

A-chin Panchaphan (b. 1927) draws his subjects from his own experiences in the tin mines in southern Thailand. His mine stories focus on an engineering student who has dropped out of the university to work in the mines.

The most unusual short-story writer has been Rong Wong-savun

(Narong Wong-savun, b. 1932), who began as a journalist and photographer. His distinctive style is characterized by word coinages, new expressions, and unusual images. His subject matter is wide-ranging, and his stories are set in a variety of places: a café in Bang Lamphu Square in the heart of old Bangkok, the Thai countryside, a clean street in Peking, an expensive nightclub in the "concrete jungle" of San Francisco.

Poetry

Although the Thais still think of themselves as a poetry-minded people, there are not many who have composed substantial works in the 20th c. Historical narratives have sometimes been used in Thai verse. A remarkable work of this kind is the posthumously published *Sam krung* (1952; the three capital cities), in which Prince Bidyalankarana (1876–1945), also a short-story writer of note, not only employed all the Thai verse forms but also invented a new one, as well as using the punctuation marks of Western grammar. The poem begins in 1767, the year the capital city of Ayutthaya was destroyed by the Burmese, and ends shortly before the close of World War II. *Sam krung* is remarkable not only for its style but for its humor and sharp wit.

Buddhist ethics pervade much of Thai poetry. Using a variety of conventional *chan* forms, Nai Chit Burathat (1896–1942), in *Samakkhi phet kham chan* (1915; unity destroyed), asserts that once unity is lost, no matter how strong a state had been, its destruction is inevitable.

A new note in poetry was sounded with the publication in 1964 of the collected poems of the revolutionary Ang-khan Kalayanaphong (b. 1926), who broke with the old conventions. His love of nature, art, and poetry itself is set against his disgust with modern society, which caused him anguish and bitterness. Ang-khan has been accused of corrupting the beauty of Thai poetic diction by using "unpoetic" and vulgar language. But this very technique enables him to express emotions and ideas strikingly. A number of his poems have been published in English translation in journals. Also a visual artist, Ang-khan sometimes uses elaborate calligraphy.

After the student-led popular uprising in October 1973, lyric poetry with overtones of Maoist theories of art and literature filled book stands in Bangkok. Some poets drew their material from the uprising, including eulogizing those who died in it. Works of this sort vanished after October 6, 1976, the chaotic day when the elected government was ousted; a number of prominent figures fled the country, and a few days later a military-supported government took power. This regime imposed strict censorship and banned leftist books.

In the past two decades graffiti has become an important form of poetry. The scribblers use the conventional forms of proverb, saying, and aphorism, but with fresh content. These often humorous writings—on walls and vehicles—reflect problems of contemporary society and also affirm the traditional Thai penchant for poetry amid the influx of foreign influences and rapid social change.

Recently another new form of expression has appeared—concrete or visual poetry. This kind of work is still in an experimental stage in Thailand and appeals more to students than to the general public.

Drama

After Crown Prince Vajiravudh (1881–1925) returned from England, where he had been educated, he introduced Western-style prose drama to Thailand. He encouraged translations and adaptations of European plays and wrote a number of original plays himself (as well as an epistolary narrative).

There were also innovations in the classical dance drama, moving it in the direction of musical drama and opera. Prince Vajiravudh, who later became king, and other princes and noblemen established their own repertory theaters. In more recent times films and television have become more popular than theater. Many novels are dramatized for these media. It is thus left to the universities to promote stage plays.

Modern Thai literature also encompasses children's literature and many forms of nonfictional prose: autobiographies, biographies, essays, diaries, letters, memoirs, travel books, and literary criticism.

Literature in this century has become increasingly public. Poetry readings, lectures, discussions about literature, and contests of impromptu poetry have become frequent. Book fairs are held from time to time, with prizes awarded to the best works. This lively activity bodes well for the future of Thai literature.

BIBLIOGRAPHY: Jumsai, M. L. M., *History of Thai Literature* (1973); Rutnin, M., ed., *The Siamese Theatre: A Collection of Reprints from the Journal of the Siam Society* (1975); Senanan, W., *The Genesis of the Novel in Thailand* (1975); Umavijani, M., *The Domain of Thai Literature* (1978); Chitakasem, M., "The Development of Political and Social

Consciousness in Thai Short Stories," in Davidson, J. H. C. S., and Cordell, H., eds., *The Short Story in South East Asia: Aspects of a Genre* (1982), pp. 63–99

WIBHA SENANAN KONGKANANDA

DOKMAI Sot

(pseud. of M. L. Buppha Kunjara Nimmanhemin) Thai novelist and short-story writer, b. 17 Feb. 1905, Bangkok; d. 17 Jan. 1963, New Delhi, India

D., one of Thailand's first important novelists was born into a noble family and educated in a French convent school in Bangkok. While a student there, she was introduced to Western literature and became particularly interested in the French woman writer M. Delly, author of didactic romantic novels for young women. They influenced her early works, *Sattru khong chaolon* (1929; her enemy) and *Nit* (1930; Nit), both of which were serialized in *Thai Khasem*, a leading magazine of the time.

D. believed it her responsibility to improve young people's conduct and morals, and a number of her novels, such as *Phu di* (1937; a well-bred person) and *Nung nai roi* (1934; one in a hundred), were written specifically for this purpose. But even the works that are not explicitly didactic reflect D.'s conservative and traditional moral and religious philosophy.

In most of D.'s works, the main characters are female, and their portrayal demonstrates the writer's genuine interest in and astute perception of women's nature. Additionally, the majority of D.'s fiction reflects the life she knew best—that of the Thai upper class from the last decades of the absolute monarchy up to World War II. Her novels are novels of manners, in which most of the characters are confined to the narrow world of their own class and interests. Nevertheless, the life style of the middle class did not escape her keen observation. "Ponlamung di" (1948; "The Good Citizen," 1958), a short story that realistically depicts that segment of Thai society, was awarded a prize by the Canberra Fellowship of Australian Writers.

D. reached the height of her fame when *Ni lae lok* (1935; this is the world) won an international award. It was a marked departure from her earlier romantic fiction, since in this novel she endows her characters with much greater complexity and psychological realism. In fact, it is only in this book and in *Ubattihet* (1934; the accident) and in the posthumously published *Wannakrum chin sud thai* (1973; the last literary work) that her characters step out of their circumscribed world to display an interest in social problems and world affairs. Nevertheless, in spite of the generally limited scope of her writing, D. is recognized in Thailand as a novelist who truthfully depicted the life of the people of her time.

FURTHER WORKS: *Di fo* (1927); *Sam chai* (1932); *Karma kao* (1935); *Khwampit khrang raek* (1935); *Chai chana khong Luang Naruban* (1936); *Phu klin* (1937); *Nanthawan* (1942); *Busababan* (1948)

BIBLIOGRAPHY: Bhanthumchinda, S., *Jane Austen and Two Modern Thai Women Novelists: A Comparative Study* (1957); Senanan, W., *The Genesis of the Novel in Thailand* (1975), pp. 91–98 and passim

SAOWANEE INDRABHAKTI

KUKRIT Pramoj
Thai novelist, philosopher, historian, and journalist, b. 20 April 1911, Sing Buri

K., the youngest son of Prince Khamop, received his early education in Thailand. At the age of fifteen he was sent to England to complete his secondary schooling; he then went to Oxford, from which he graduated in 1933. Returning to Thailand, he worked in the ministry of finance and later in banking; he also taught at two Thai universities. K. entered politics in 1946, serving as a cabinet minister for a time. His experiences as a politician, as well as his several months as a Buddhist monk, have colored his literary works. He has also been active in Thai theater, acting and directing.

K. did not reach prominence as a literary figure until the early 1950s. His major works were written between 1950, when he left active politics, and 1973, when he returned to it (he was prime minister, 1975–76). In 1950 he founded the now greatly respected newspaper *Siam Rath*, in which all of his major works were to appear first. Because of this newspaper serialization, it is almost impossible to set exact dates to his works.

Sam kok chabab nai thun (c. 1949–51; three kingdoms: a capitalist's version) was K.'s first major novel. It retells the story of the Chinese classic of the 14th through 17th cs., *Three Kingdoms*, but from the point of view of the traditional villain, Tsao Tsao, rather than that of the hero, Liu Pei, to prove that the concept of heroism or villainy depends on the narrator's political point of view.

K.'s greatest novel, *Si phaendin* (1953; *Four Reigns*, 1981), tells the life story of a Thai upper-class woman, Ploy, from 1892, when she goes to live in the Grand Palace as a servant of a royal princess at the age of ten, until her death in 1946 as a married woman outside the palace, with children and grandchildren. But the story of Ploy is a pretext for analyzing and commenting on the times and ever-shifting fashions. The book is, indeed, a detailed social record.

Another novel, *Phai daeng* (1953; *Red Bamboo*, 1961), tells of a Buddhist monk's conflicts with a local communist agitator in a fictitious town in central Thailand.

Huang maharnob (early 1950s; the deep ocean) is K.'s most important nonfiction work. In it he shows the truth of Buddhist doctrine as proved by biology, and vice versa. The book has been criticized because K. assumes the truth of Buddhist teachings *a priori*. This is one of the strangest books of philosophy in Thai, and a puzzling work to many readers.

K.'s writings are always didactic, but his style is so fluent and humorous that he has an enormous readership in Thailand.

FURTHER WORKS: *Thok khmer* (early 1950s); *Lai chivit* (1950s); *Phuen non* (3 vols., 1950s–60s); *Tsu hsi t'ai hao* (1950s); *Lok suan tua khong phom* (c. 1961–62); *Yiu* (1968); *Khrong kraduk nai tu* (1971); *Tueng khong khon rak ma* (1978); *K. pho krua hua pa* (1979); *Tob panha hua jai* (1980)

BIBLIOGRAPHY: Wyatt, D. K., "K. P. and *Red Bamboo*," *Solidarity*, 5, 6 (1970), 68–73

AYUMONGOL SONAKUL

TIBETAN LITERATURE

Tibetan literature in the 20th c. reflects adaptation—for the most part deliberate and restrained—to life without the ancient Tibetan cultural traditions. This is particularly true of the period from 1959 to the present, following the Chinese invasion. A discussion of contemporary works must be limited to those of the refugees who have lived in India since the Chinese takeover; literary production inside Tibet since 1959 is little known and inaccessible to most outsiders.

Tibetan literature—a body rivaling that of the Arabs or Chinese in size—is overwhelmingly religious and thus neither "fiction" nor "nonfiction" as commonly defined. On a more popular level are the oral tales about A-khu Ston-pa, an often obscene Falstaffian figure, and about Gesar, Tibet's favorite heroic personage. These tales are secular in origin, with much narrative description of peasant or nomad life. An interesting example of a recent creation is Don-brgyud-ñi-ma's (dates n.a.) *Dzam-gliṅ Ge-sar* (1961; Gesar conquers Germany), inspired by recent military history. Transcribed oral versions of the Gesar epic are important literary documents; as opposed to written literature, some of these works have escaped tampering by monastic censors, who controlled the printeries and thus, to a great degree, what emerged from them.

Perhaps the most important literary figure in the first half of this century was Dge-'dun-chos-'phel (1895–1951), an artist, poet, and literary critic. Unfortunately, his revolutionary views on the art of creative writing seem not to be available, if they have survived. Today many Tibetans see him as a prophet in the realm of literary innovation. He wrote of sex and physical love in a personal manner that shocked Lhasa authorities, who referred to him as a madman. His views on the limits and forms of Tibetan literature are no doubt a key to understanding the foment among Tibetan intellectuals caused by British and other foreign influences in this century.

Contemporary refugee literature remains predominantly religious—for example, exegeses on Buddhist texts. Little fiction has been produced, but Tshe-dbaṅ-don-ldan (dates n.a.) wrote a novel, *Mig gi gra mag* (c. 1978; drama of the eyes), set in Ladakh, in the Himalayas. It is consciously based on Hindi texts and Western fiction. Emotional situations are played out through a series of dialogues, with character development and psychological analysis less important than the events themselves. The fact that the author, as a Ladakhi, is probably not a refugee may be significant in his acceptance of outside influences.

External forces are destined to become more important in Tibetan refugee literature as well, while older authors publish collections or separate works written before their exile. Mkhas-btsun-bzan-po's (dates n.a.) *Gtam dpe sna tshogs dan gźas tshigs kha śas* (1974; some songs and stories) is a collection of great beauty and interest, containing everything from drinking songs and acrostics to reverential works. Several are similar in form to the famous love poems of the sixth Dalai Lama, Tshans-dbyans-rgya-mtsho (1683–1706), *Mgul glu* (*Love Songs of the Sixth Dalai Lama*, 1930), often cited as early examples of purely romantic poetry.

BIBLIOGRAPHY: Richardson, H., *Tibet: Past and Present* (1967); Snellgrove, D. L., and Richardson, H., *A Cultural History of Tibet* (1968; rev. ed., 1980); Stein, R. A., *Tibetan Civilization* (1972)

MICHAEL L. WALTER

VIETNAMESE LITERATURE

Nourished by centuries of patriotic protest against Chinese rule, yet with a poetic tradition patterned after Chinese models, modern Vietnamese literature has flourished, first under some eighty years of French colonial administration, then during the war against the French (1945–54), and more recently during the period of partition and war (1954–75) and subsequent reunification. The importance of sociopolitical changes in the 20th c. cannot be overstated. But the single most important factor in the development of modern Vietnamese literature was the introduction by Catholic missionaries of the roman script, whose use began in the early 20th c., accompanied by a vigorous literacy campaign, and which gradually displaced both Chinese characters and the demotic Vietnamese characters.

After the establishment of French colonial authority in Indochina in 1862, many works in both verse and prose appeared, with the latter predominating. Although poetry, written in both Chinese and Vietnamese according to the constraints of traditional Chinese Tang prosody, had held sway in previous centuries, Western prose genres began to be cultivated, including journalism, literary criticism, the essay, drama for the formal theaters (as opposed to the traditional folk play), and the realistic novel.

The main trends at the turn of the century were romanticism and patriotism. At the same time masterpieces of French and Chinese literature became known through translations using the new alphabet, thanks to the efforts of the lexicographer Paulus Huỳnh Tỉnh Của (1834–1907) and of the polyglot scholar Petrus Trương Vĩnh Ký (1837–1898), who themselves wrote delightful short stories.

Chinese and French writing influenced the movement known as the Đông-kinh (Eastern Capital, i.e., Hanoi) School of the Just Cause, founded in 1906 by such patriotic scholar-writers as Phan Bội Châu (1867–1940) and Phan Châu Trinh (1872–1926). With the decline of classical poetry, the prose writings serialized in the reviews *Đông-dương tạp-chí* and *Nam-phong,* edited respectively by Nguyễn Văn Vĩnh (1882–1936) and Phạm Quỳnh (1892–1945), were avidly read by the urban petite bourgeoisie during the period 1913–30. Romantic and lyrical poetry was, however, published by such writers as Tản-Đà Nguyễn Khắc Hiếu (1889–1939), Đông-hồ Lâm Tấn Phát (1906–1969), and Á-nam Trần Tuấn Khải (1894–1983).

Young intellectuals of the time admired both the moralistic stories of Nguyễn Bá Học (1857–1921) and the humorous stories with vivid dialogue by Phạm Duy Tốn (1883–1924). *Tố-tâm* (1925; Tố-tâm), a psychological novel by Hoàng Ngọc Phách (1896–1973) about an unfortunate love affair, was hugely successful and spawned many works of romantic individualism. Inspired by a traditional folktale, the novelette *Quả dưa đỏ* (1927; the watermelon) by Nguyễn Trọng Thuật (1883–1940) won an important literary prize. Notable plays of the period were *Chén thuốc độc* (1921; the cup of poison), a comedy by Vũ Đình Long (1901–1960), about a wastrel who is talked out of committing suicide, and three plays by Vi Huyền Đắc (b. 1899): *Uyên-ương* (1927; lovers), a tragedy about true love; *Kim-tiền* (1937; money), a drama about a businessman; and *Ông Ký Cóp* (1938; Mr. Clerk Cop).

Besides the development of journalism, the 1930s saw the birth—and triumph—of the so-called new poetry among both the adherents and the opponents of the Self-Reliance literary group. Members of this group rejected the style patterned after Chinese writing and advocated a clearer and more naturally Vietnamese style. They also favored the emancipation of women and the rights of the individual. One member, Thế Lữ (b. 1907), saw himself as a dreamer and nature lover caught in the web of competitive urban life, with all its cruelty, loneliness, and deprivation. Compared with those of the previous generation, "our deepest feelings are more complex," he asserted. "When we burst with joy, that joy also embraces strange colors and shades." The lyrical poetry of Xuân Diệu (b. 1917), another Self-Reliance writer, expressed his craving for love as well as his appreciation for scenic beauty and sweet music. A third member, the poet Hàn Mặc Tử (1913–1940), wrote powerful poems evincing his obsession with death. The new verse still had familiar themes, such as autumn impressions, homesickness, nostalgia, bereavement, and moon gazing. But it utilized nontraditional tones, rhymes, and rhythms, and it also affirmed the importance of the individual, the presence of the "self."

Amid political turmoil and economic crisis, the review *Phong-hoá*, launched in 1932 and renamed *Ngày nay* in 1935, contributed to the "defense and illustration" of the Vietnamese language, now fully groomed for the new genres—a language that had gained in simplicity, clarity, and elegance through the efforts of social reformers, led by Nhất-

Linh (q.v.) and Khái Hưng (1896–1947). Nhất-Linh wrote editorials, novels, and short stories; Khái Hưng was a novelist and short-story writer. Hoàng Đạo (1907–1948) was the theoretician of the group, Thạch Lam (1909–1943) specialized in short stories and vignettes, and Tú Mỡ (1900–1976) wrote satirical poems.

As the Self-Reliance group declined in prestige and the literary output of its members waned, several other groups came into being, and the realistic novel made a tentative appearance, followed by revolutionary writing with Marxist tendencies in the late 1930s. *Bước đường cùng* (1938; *Impasse,* 1963), a poignant tale of misery and despondency among the oppressed peasantry, was the work of the most outstanding and prolific of the realist authors, Nguyễn Công Hoan (q.v.). Ngô Tất Tố (1894–1954), in *Tắt đèn* (1939; *When the Light Is Out,* 1960), depicted the misery of the wife of a poor peasant who is coerced into selling their eldest daughter and their dog and puppies in order to pay the couple's taxes. Two other works of note are *Chí Phèo* (1956; Chi the outcast) by Nam Cao (1917–1951), and *Bỉ vỏ* (1938; thieves and pickpockets) by Nguyên Hồng (1918–1982), both of which deal with social injustices as they describe the dregs of society. The commentary both works evoked indirectly helped bring about literary criticism as a new genre.

While works of Socialist Realism began to appear during the early days of the Democratic Republic of Vietnam, before 1954 there had been a socialist tendency among writers of the anti-French resistance and a "wait-and-see" attitude among noncommunist writers, most of whom chose to move south when the armistice with the French was signed.

Poetry in North Vietnam was essentially political: works by Tố Hữu (b. 1920), Chế Lan Viên (b. 1920), and Nguyễn Đình Thi (b. 1924), for instance, were preoccupied with the longing for territorial reunification and characterized by exalted expressions of revolutionary zeal and of concern for the masses. Prose writing, too, reflected new aspects of life: the most popular topics were land reform, rent reduction, activities of cooperatives, the collectivization of the countryside, and attacks on American involvement in the war.

Meanwhile, in South Vietnam a multitude of private publishing houses and a plethora of magazines and reviews offered outlets for poets and prose writers, many of them refugees from the north. Love, family relations, army life, and city life were some of the favorite themes of writers associated with the Saigon P.E.N. Club. Lãng Nhân (b. 1907) and Trọng Lang (b. 1906), two older writers, continued to produce essays and chronicles, while Vũ Khắc Khoan (b. 1917) and Vi Huyền

Đắc concentrated on playwriting. In addition to Nhất-Linh—who committed suicide in 1963—and such "old guard" writers as Tam Lang (pseud. of Vũ Đình Chí, 1901–1986) and Vũ Bằng (1913–1984), both journalists, essayists, and novelists, there were many prolific, perceptive, social-minded young novelists in South Vietnam, with either a strong anticommunist stance or an apolitical attitude bordering on pessimism and fatalism. Alongside such established poets as Vũ Hoàng Chương (1916–1976) and Đông-hồ Lâm Tấn Phát, younger poets appeared, in some of whose works the influence of French writers like Jean-Paul Sartre and Saint-John Perse can be detected. After the communists took over the south, scores of writers were jailed and their works seized as "specimens of a depraved culture."

In 1979 a collection of "prison songs" written between 1954 and 1978 was smuggled out of Vietnam. The author was later revealed to be Nguyễn Chì Thiện (b. 1933). Circulated under various titles, the collection was first published as *Tiếng vọng từ đáy vực* (1980; voices from the abyss) and *Bản chúc-thư của một nguời Viêt-nam* (1980; testament of a Vietnamese), although the intended title was later revealed to be *Hoa địa-ngục* (flowers of hell), after Baudelaire's *Les fleurs du mal*. Twenty of the poems were set to music, and this version was published as *Ngục-ca/Prison Songs/Chants de prison* (1982, trilingual). These poems, over 150 of which appear in the bilingual *Flowers from Hell* (1984), remind one of the Nhân-văn affair, a short-lived protest movement in 1956–57 of a number of writers and artists who advocated art for art's sake and expressed their weariness of war themes.

Writers in exile since 1975 have maintained a limited literary output. Inside unified Vietnam one can expect a growth in literary production in the socialist vein and under the government-decreed motto "literature and arts about the new life and the new man." How many of these writings will emerge as works of enduring artistic value remains to be seen.

BIBLIOGRAPHY: Hoàng Ngọc Thành, *The Social and Political Development of Vietnam as Seen through the Modern Novel* (1969); Bàng Bá Lân, "Some Remarks on Contemporary Vietnamese Poetry," *Viet-Nam Bulletin*, 5, 13 (1971), 2–13; Nguyễn Khắc Viện, et al., eds., Introduction to *Anthologie de la littérature vietnamienne, Tome III: Deuxième moitié du XIXe siècle–1945* (1975), pp. 7–68; Nguyễn Khắc Kham, "Vietnamese National Language and Modern Vietnamese Literature," *SEACS*, 15, 1–4 (1976), 177–94; Nguyễn Khắc Viện, et al., eds.,

Introduction to *Anthologie de la littérature vietnamienne, Tome IV: De 1945 à nos jours* (1977), pp. 7–72; Nguyễn Đình-Hoà, "Vietnamese Language and Literature," in Nguyễn Thị Mỹ-Hường, P., ed., *Language in Vietnamese Society* (1980), pp. 9–26; Davidson, J. H. C. S., "To Aid the Revolution: The Short Story as Pro-liberation Literature in South Viet-Nam," in Davidson, J. H. C. S., and Cordell, H., eds., *The Short Story in South East Asia: Aspects of a Genre* (1982), pp. 203–26; Durand, M. M., and Nguyễn-Trần Huân, *An Introduction to Vietnamese Literature* (1985)

DINH-HOA NGUYEN

NGUYỄN Công Hoan

Vietnamese novelist and short-story writer, b. 6 March 1903, Bắc-ninh; d. 6 June 1977, Hanoi

Scenes N. witnessed in French Indochina—first as a boy aware of the plight of peasants pitilessly exploited by village bullies and greedy, corrupt mandarins; later as a teacher assigned to different areas of the country—he incorporated into some twenty novels and over three hundred short stories. N., who began writing in the 1920s, became one of the most accomplished representatives of social realism in modern Vietnamese literature.

N.'s finest works, which offer insight into Vietnam's outmoded customs and the life of the peasantry and the urban middle class, appeared before the 1945 revolution. His most important novel, *Bước đường cùng* (1938; *Impasse*, 1963), portrays the miserable existence of a poor, debt-ridden peasant whose life is constantly threatened by natural disasters. The protagonist dares to rise up against his enemies: the landlords, the usurers, the petty local officials. This book was banned by the colonial administration.

N. is at his best when, using clear and witty language, he lashes out against injustices and corruption condoned by the French administration and against injustice and oppression in his feudal and colonial society. He treats bribery, for example, in about ten stories.

In N.'s novels plot is secondary to theme and style. For example, family conflicts, occasioned by the influence of Confucian ethics, are analyzed through skillfully constructed dialogue, as in *Cô giáo Minh* (1936; teacher Minh). Whether he portrays an audience unwittingly forcing an actor to prolong his jokes at the very time when his father is about to die, or a rickshaw boy getting stuck on New Year's Eve with a penniless prostitute as his passenger, or a mother leaving her child home to go out with her lover, N. exposes the meanness, wickedness, and deceit of people around him.

After 1954, when the French were defeated and a Communist government was established in North Vietnam, N.'s central themes became nationalism and socialist construction. In 1957 he was elected president of the Vietnam Writers' Association in Hanoi.

FURTHER WORKS: *Kiếp hồng nhan* (1923); *Nhũ'ng cảnh khốn nan* (1932); *Ông chu* (1934); *Bà chu* (1935); *Kép Tư Bền* (1935); *Tấm lòng vàng* (1937); *Tờ vương* (1938); *Lá ngọc cành vàng* (1938); *Tay trắng, trắng tay* (1940); *Chiếc nhẫn vàng* (1940); *Nợ nần* (1940); *Lệ Dung* (1944); *Đồng-chí Tư* (1946); *Xổng cũi* (1947); *Tranh tối tranh sáng* (1956); *Hỗn canh hỗn cư* (1961); *Đống rác cũ* (1963)

BIBLIOGRAPHY: Hoàng Ngọc Thành, *The Social and Political Development of Vietnam as Seen through the Modern Novel* (1969), pp. 222–30; Bùi Xuân-Bào, *Le roman vietnamien contemporain* (1972), pp. 218–28; Trương Đình Hùng, "N. C. H. (1903–1977): A Realist Writer," *Viet Nam Courier,* Oct. 1977, 26–29; Durand, M. M., and Nguyễn-Trần Huân, *An Introduction to Vietnamese Literature* (1985), pp. 146–47

DINH-HOA NGUYEN

NHẤT-LINH

(pseud. of Nguyễn Tường-Tam) Vietnamese novelist and short-story writer, b. 25 July 1906, Hai-duong; d. 7 July 1963, Saigon

N.-L. was one of the founders, in 1933, of the "Self-Reliant" group, which rejected traditional Vietnamese literature. He was also a social reformer and a political leader. He served as foreign minister in the Vietminh-dominated government of the Democratic Republic of Vietnam, took part in the negotiations with the French, and at the time of partition chose to live in South Vietnam. He committed suicide while a political prisoner of the Ngo Dinh Diem regime.

N.-L. began writing early: the short stories "Nho phong" (1926; the scholars' tradition) and "Ngư ờ'i quay tơ" (1927; the spinner) appeared before his three-year stay in Paris (1927–30) as a student. These romantic and traditional stories contrast with his later works, which are realistic, patriotic, and revolutionary.

N.-L.'s most famous novel, *Đoan tuyệt* (1934; break-off), is a sophisticated and resolute work championing individual freedom and the pursuit of happiness. The heroine, Loan, is ill-treated by a superstitious, cruel, and greedy mother-in-law; Loan, who kills her husband by accident, is acquitted because she is seen as a victim of the conflict between traditions and the new concept of women's rights. The title of the book pinpoints the movement away from the oppressive paternalistic kinship system.

The novels N.-L. wrote between 1935 and 1942 all depict the weaknesses of Vietnamese family and social structures. His characters, struggling for changes in their own lives and in society, rebel against age-old traditions. *Lạnh lùng* (1937; loneliness) tells the story of a young widow in love with her son's tutor. The happiness she feels in the tutor's arms cannot last, since she is afraid of social ostracism. In *Đôi bạn* (1938; two friends), a sequel to *Đoạn tuyệt*, N.-L.'s revolutionary ideals are evident. Patriotic zeal and anticolonialism are equated with dreams of individual freedom and a youthful thirst for heroic action.

In collaboration with Khái-Hưng (pseud. of Trần Khánh-Giư, 1896–1947), N.-L. wrote two excellent novels: *Gánh hàng hoa* (1934; the florist's load), about the innocent love of a young florist, and *Đời mưa gió* (1936; a stormy life), which depicts the life of a girl who, emancipated from the shackles of traditional clan life, has to become a prostitute to earn her rights as an individual.

N.-L.'s style is alternately poetic and precise. In a work like *Lạnh lùng* it is a model of clarity, precision, and balance.

FURTHER WORKS: *Anh phải sống* (1933, with Khái-Hưng); *Tối tăm* (1936); *Hai buổi chiều vàng* (1937); *Bướm trắng* (1941); *Nắng thu* (1948); *Xóm Cầu mới* (1958); *Dòng sông Thanh-thuỷ* (1961); *Mối tình "Chân"* (1961); *Thương chồng* (1961); *Viết vàđọc tiểu-thuyết* (1961)

BIBLIOGRAPHY: O'Harrow, S., "Some Background Notes on N.-L. (Nguyễn Tường Tam, 1906–1963)," *France-Asie*, 22 (1968), 205–20; Hoàng Ngọc-Thành, *The Social and Political Development of Vietnam as Seen through the Modern Novel* (1969), pp. 182–204; Bùi Xuân-Bào, *Le roman vietnamien contemporain* (1972), pp. 164–83, 364–72; Durand, M. M., and Nguyễn-Trần Huân, *An Introduction to Vietnamese Literature* (1985), pp. 161, 164, 180–82

DINH-HOA NGUYEN

Index to Author Articles